"As a researcher of serial murder, I am all too
and other media offer no citations of sou
and claims about those who commit these heinous crimes. In the book *Killer Data: Modern Perspectives on Serial Murder*, prolific researcher and gifted author Enzo Yaksic brings us on a fascinating empirical exploration of this phenomenon. While acknowledging that we are just beginning to understand some of the factors that motivate predatorial perpetrators of serial homicide, Yaksic takes us on a scientifically informed journey through killer facts and theories. He introduces us to the scientific study of serial homicide, reviews and compares historical and contemporary research, and provides new, fascinating data about modern incarnations of these murderers. This book is a must-have foundational guide for any researcher or student of serial homicide, and it will appeal to members of the public interested in these criminals and crimes that fascinate us and fuel our nightmares."

—**Marissa A. Harrison**, Penn State Harrisburg, Research Psychologist and Author of *Just as Deadly: The Psychology of Female Serial Killers* (forthcoming, Cambridge University Press)

"*Killer Data* provides a contemporary exploration and insight into serial murder. A must-read contribution to the field!"

—**Clare Allely**, University of Salford, England, Reader in Forensic Psychology and Author of *The Psychology of Extreme Violence: A Case Study Approach to Serial Homicide, Mass Shooting, School Shooting and Lone-actor Terrorism*

"Enzo Yaksic has been immersed in serial murder research for nearly two decades, amassing information about deviants and psychopaths to better understand them. The culmination of that effort is *Killer Data*, a definitive state-of-the-union report on serial killers in the 21st century. Through his research and insights into the continually changing and evolving phenomenon of serial homicide, Yaksic ushers students, scholars, police officials, and the news media into a new unprecedented understanding of serial killers today and potentially in the near future."

—**Peter Vronksy**, Ryerson University, lecturer and Author of *Sons of Cain: A History of Serial Killers From the Stone Age to the Present (2018)*, and *American Serial Killers: The Epidemic Years 1950–2000*

KILLER DATA

Killer Data examines the phenomenon of serial murder using data collected from a variety of sources to review offender patterning with a focus on contemporary cases. This type of attention will allow for a broader understanding of modern-day serial murderers and will help to dispel some of the myths that surround offenders.

The current serial murder classification scheme incorrectly types serial murderers as supremely intelligent killing machines while discounting their socialization, experiences, and choices. This book exposes serial murderers as run-of-the-mill hometown losers, who brutalize women, and are lucky to escape apprehension. Like other atypical homicide offenders, modern-day serial murderers are propelled forward by a deep sense of entitlement, easy access to firearms, and a nonchalant attitude toward using murder to attain their goals. Readers should come away with a deeper understanding not of the ultra-rare or "deadliest" serial murderers but of the more common offenders who pose a consistent threat to day-to-day life. The book utilizes the Consolidated Serial Homicide Offender Database, one of the largest and most robust open access databases of multiple murders available, presenting new thinking on areas such as:

- myths and stereotypes
- the impact of entertainment on the perception of serial murder
- inaccurate prevalence estimates
- spree/serial hybrid offenders
- the classification of two and three victim serial murderers
- how serial murderers pursue longevity
- the characteristics of aspiring serial murderers
- whether hit men and gang members are serial murderers
- if and why serial murder is in a state of decline

- how many serial murderers are responsible for the homicides that sent innocent people to prison
- luck as a factor of "success" for serial murderers.

These findings are illustrated with 210 narrative vignettes of serial murder series that occurred between 2011 and 2021, such as Itzcoatl Ocampo, Charles Severance, Nikko Jenkins, and Pamela Hupp, offenders who may be unfamiliar to many but represent the next iteration of the serial murderer.

Correcting decades of flawed assumptions about serial murderers, and written in an accessible and concise style, *Killer Data* is essential reading for students and scholars of criminal justice and criminology, law enforcement professionals, and the interested general reader.

Enzo Yaksic has studied serial murder for 20 years and is the director of the Atypical Homicide Research Group (AHRG), a think tank that strives to understand the modern-day multiple homicide offender through the systematic collection and analysis of data. The AHRG organizes and maintains the Consolidated Serial Homicide Offender Database, the largest open repository for information on atypical homicide offenders. As the author of 15 manuscripts on serial homicide, Enzo is at the forefront of serial murder research. Enzo's current work with the Murder Accountability Project aims to educate Americans on the importance of accurately accounting for unresolved homicides within the USA by using the Supplementary Homicide Report to help uncover suspicious clusters of potential serial homicide activity. Enzo has been quoted in the *Los Angeles Times*, *The Washington Post*, *The New Yorker*, and *USA Today*. Enzo was profiled in a *Boston Magazine* article titled "Enzo Yaksic: Profiler 2".

ROUTLEDGE STUDIES IN CRIMINAL BEHAVIOUR

Domestic Homicide
Patterns and Dynamics
Marieke Liem and Frans Koenraadt

Intergenerational Continuity of Criminal and Antisocial Behaviour
An International Overview of Studies
Edited by Veroni I. Eichelsheim and Steve G. A. van de Weijer

Evidence-Based Offender Profiling
Edited by Bryanna H. Fox, David P. Farrington, Andreas Kapardis and Olivia C. Hambly

Empathy versus Offending, Aggression and Bullying
Advancing Knowledge using the Basic Empathy Scale
Darrick Jolliffe and David P. Farrington

The Life Course of Serious and Violent Youth Grown Up
A Twenty-year Longitudinal Study
Evan C. McCuish, Patrick Lussier, Raymond Corrado

Killer Data
Modern Perspectives on Serial Murder
Enzo Yaksic

For more information about this series, please visit: www.routledge.com/Routledge-Studies-in-Criminal-Behaviour/book-series/RSCB

KILLER DATA

Modern Perspectives on Serial Murder

Enzo Yaksic

LONDON AND NEW YORK

Cover image: Khurram Designs

First published 2022
by Routledge
4 Park Square, Milton Park, Abingdon, Oxon OX14 4RN

and by Routledge
605 Third Avenue, New York, NY 10158

Routledge is an imprint of the Taylor & Francis Group, an informa business

British Library Cataloguing-in-Publication Data
A catalogue record for this book is available from the British Library

Library of Congress Cataloging-in-Publication Data
Names: Yaksic, Enzo, author.
Title: Killer data: modern perspectives on serial murder/Enzo Yaksic.
Description: Abingdon, Oxon ; New York, NY: Routledge, 2022. |
Series: Routledge studies in criminal behaviour | Includes bibliographical references.
Identifiers: LCCN 2021051427 (print) | LCCN 2021051428 (ebook) |
ISBN 9780367672690 (hardback) | ISBN 9780367672706 (paperback) |
ISBN 9781003130567 (ebook)
Subjects: LCSH: Serial murders. | Criminal psychology. |
Criminal behavior, Prediction of. | Criminal statistics.
Classification: LCC HV6515 .Y35 2022 (print) |
LCC HV6515 (ebook) | DDC 364.152/3–dc23/eng/20220105
LC record available at https://lccn.loc.gov/2021051427
LC ebook record available at https://lccn.loc.gov/2021051428

ISBN: 978-0-367-67269-0 (hbk)
ISBN: 978-0-367-67270-6 (pbk)
ISBN: 978-1-003-13056-7 (ebk)

DOI: 10.4324/9781003130567

Typeset in Bembo
by Newgen Publishing UK

Dedication

I have to say I'm honored to be able to write a few words about my longtime friend and mentor, Steven A. Egger. The world of the study of serial murder is a lesser place without him; the world in general is as well. I met Egger in the Spring of 1992, when I took his serial murder class. This wasn't quite the common occurrence as it is today, but I'd heard so much about the opportunity to study under an international expert on a fascinating topic. It was challenging, addicting, even. One night after class, I asked Egger if he would be interested in a copy of the interview of an offender whose name had recently become a household name, Jeffrey Dahmer. I had a contact who obtained a copy for me along with crime scene photos. Most of this is easily found on the Internet today, but in 1992 it was gold. Steve said, "where did you get this?" I said, "I dunno." He grinned and it was clear we spoke the same language after that. As a teacher, Steve pushed you to accomplish all you could. He always encouraged me to explore my interest in abnormal psychology within serial murder, as he felt it was underdeveloped at the time. He was right. As my Thesis Advisor, he would often make a comment I'd learn to expect from him: "Ummm, that's a good start." In the years following, we exchanged ideas on book content, research, consulting and potential travel to do interviews. We also continued to be friends and respected colleagues. After making presentations in his class, I ended up taking over his Serial Murder class when he had a personal illness, and I continue to teach it to this day. This class is his legacy. Egger proudly served in the U.S. Army and was a Police Officer, a homicide investigator, consultant and law enforcement academy director. He earned a master's degree at Michigan State University, and a Ph.D. at Sam Houston State where he completed the first dissertation on serial murder in the world. Steve taught at the University of Illinois Springfield and at the University of Houston for over 25 years. He lectured internationally in England, Germany, Spain, Canada, the Netherlands and France, as well as at the landmark FBI serial murder symposium. He was project director of the Homicide Assessment and Lead Tracking System (HALT) for the state of New York. HALT, which was the first statewide computerized system to track and identify serial murderers, has been a blueprint for future systems since. I could go on about his amazing career, his groundbreaking books in the study of serial murder, his developments of a serial murderer database and more, but I think he'd need his own book. Steve Egger was a giant in his field. A pioneer and a legend. He was also a fine human being and I'm proud to have counted him as a mentor and a friend.

By Stephen J. Giannangelo

CONTENTS

FIGURES

TABLES

FOREWORD

I first began multiple homicide investigation and research in 1981 as the Atlanta Child Murders drew national attention. There were a handful of professionals such as Robert Ressler (FBI), Elliott Leyton, Ph.D., Steve Egger, Ph.D., Ronald Holmes, Ph.D., and Kim Rossmo, Ph.D., who also were intrigued by persons capable of orchestrating mass and/or serial murder. At the same time, forensic psychology, a new field of science that was forming, along with the introduction of DNA and advanced criminalistics, and the technology explosion that gave birth to mass and social media, brought increased scrutiny to homicides and other crimes of violence. Like the American gold rush of 1849, academics, professional practitioners, and law enforcement turned their attention to this "emerging social phenomena" of mass and serial murder.

One of these very astute and dedicated individuals was Enzo Yaksic. I met him several years ago via email. He had been assisting a well-established researcher but expressed interest in my work. Enzo offered his assistance in supporting my ongoing research. As we emailed and talked by phone, I found him to be intelligent and genuinely interested in discovering truths about serial murder, a topic smothered in mythology, popular opinion, and error. Of course, intellectual curiosity, like any scientific tool, requires constant examination and questioning. Enzo understood that the questions to be asked were far more important than simply finding answers. Enzo, as it turned out, was not only a data-miner but also sought to develop understanding of the dark world of serial murder.

Over the past several years, Enzo has participated in and been invited to many professional events related to serial murder investigations and research. He has helped organize online professional forums, assisted some of the most well-known and respected researchers in the field, and collaborated and published scholarly articles on serial murder. His penchant for accuracy and detail is impressive. He has earned respect among those of us in the scientific community of serial murder research. His new book, *Killer Data: Modern Perspectives on Serial Murder*, is the culmination of many years of data collection and analysis. Like most social science research, his work is foundational, not definitive. He has parsed serial murder data and has come to some conclusions that will, no doubt, spur other researchers to investigate. This is, indeed, the nature of scientific inquiry and discovery.

In this timely work, Enzo reviews the origins of the serial murder phenomenon and where we are now in serial murder research. This is followed by expanding our perceptions of serial murder and projecting future research. In his section on Case-Specific Factors, Enzo examines the use of technology in tracking and examining serial murderers. He notes that some offenders refuse to age out and includes insights on certain violent parolees who murder fellow inmates. He broaches the issues in warehousing the remains of serial murderer's victims and includes an important discussion of military service victims. Each of these topics offers insights and ideas for additional research, data collection, analysis, and publication. To that end, we owe Enzo a debt of gratitude for his collaborative spirit, integrity, and loyalty. May his ongoing data-mining quests for those scholarly gold nuggets benefit us all.

Onward Enzo!

Eric W. Hickey, Ph.D.
Author of Serial Murderers and Their Victims

PREFACE

Killer Data arrives 20 years after my first exposure to serial homicide, which occurred in the summer of 2001 when Gary Lee Sampson murdered retiree Philip McCloskey in Marshfield, Massachusetts, college student Jonathan Rizzo in Abington, Massachusetts, and Robert Whitney in Meredith, New Hampshire, over a 3-day period. I was mystified as to how someone could victimize others in that manner, especially those offering aid. Perhaps my proximity to the homicides bolstered my interest. My sheltered life certainly contributed to my astounded sense of confusion. These homicides shattered my belief in a quick and judicious justice system as Sampson could have been apprehended before the murders if not for his call to surrender being disconnected by the FBI. Sampson's actions also fervently shook away any remnants of a belief that the world was a safe and welcoming place. After his capture, it was revealed that Sampson had apparently suffered some adverse childhood experiences, and I grew curious what exactly separated his experiences from my own.

I was a psychology student at Northeastern University but was inspired by these events to transfer to their world-renowned criminal justice program. Through my coursework, I learned just how little was known about people like Sampson. Definitional discordance made it difficult to determine even basic facts such as his standing as either a spree killer or a serial murderer. No one knew if there was one factor or many circumstances that transformed Sampson into a killer. There simply was not a large and reliable base of data from which inferences about multiple murderers could be drawn. What was understood about these types of offenders was derived from anecdotal evidence and came from individual case studies conducted by disparate scholars, psychiatrists, true crime authors, and the FBI, each with their own agendas. The FBI's Criminal Personality Research Project was similar to other efforts of the time in that the small number of subjects and the limited racial makeup of the offender cohort made the generalization of findings controversial.

Knowing this, and after repeatedly encountering the same offender profiles, I decided to learn from the source. I applied for and obtained an internship at the FBI's training facility at Quantico, Virginia. It was here that I discovered through an independent data collection effort that half of serial murderers since 1995 had been African American, a finding that directly contested established beliefs. After returning to Northeastern, I continued to develop this spreadsheet of offender data as part of a directed study. Initially a rudimentary effort, this project quickly grew to thousands of names and attracted the attention of others amassing their own information. We soon began to pool our spreadsheets and built a team of like-minded scholars invested in breaking down the barriers to the open exchange of serial homicide data. This network of committed researchers, practitioners, and police personnel faced several obstacles, many of which originated as one-sided motivations on a personal and institutional level. But we carried forth and formed the Atypical Homicide Research Group and succeeded in creating the Consolidated Serial Homicide Offender Database, the first open serial murder database in the world. These resources will prove critical as we begin the arduous process of identifying the next generation of researchers who will carry forward the foundational work of the pioneers who are beginning to retire or pass away.

Although the research and investigation of serial murder has improved since the early days, the entertainment realm – with output such as *Mindhunter*, *A Killer by Design: Murderers, Mindhunters, and My Quest to Decipher the Criminal Mind*, *The Killer Next Door*, *Clarice*, and *The Little Things* – clamors to reset our progress by intentionally transporting viewers and readers back to the 1970s, 1980s and 1990s, the peak of serial murder in the United States. In so doing, we are made to think that these offenders continue to present an unmanageable threat. Without accurate prevalence estimates, some researchers and police officials have taken advantage of a wider societal fear of the serial murderer to scare the public and create a continual need for expert services. *Killer Data* is an opportunity to quiet the noise surrounding the topic of serial murder, focus attention on modern perspectives of the phenomenon, reignite academic interest, and highlight recent research in the area. As someone taken in by the attractive presentation of federal agents in *Manhunter* and *The X-Files* as possessors of omniscience, I wrote *Killer Data* to stand as both a warning to students yearning to become 'profilers' and a call to resist the romanticization surrounding serial murderers and the stylized image of those who hunt them. Readers of *Killer Data* may be frustrated to find that more questions are raised than are answered. Some might think that there are too many numbers while others may demand even more. But until we determine how serial murderers have adapted to the modern world and agree on who has the expertise necessary to properly interrogate the phenomenon, there will always be confusion surrounding what it will look like and what our collective response should be in the coming years.

There is much more work to be done so let us get to it.

ACKNOWLEDGMENTS

Like many things in life, *Killer Data* would not have come to fruition without the guidance and mentorship of several individuals. To get to this stage of my career as a serial homicide researcher and stay the course, I have relied on a great deal of patience, perseverance, luck, and good timing when facing a variety of odds. Please allow me to thank those that helped me get to where I am today.

Academic giant Jack Levin was an eccentric and defining figure in my life during my time at Northeastern University. As an early pioneer of serial murder research, Jack normalized academic interest in what can be viewed by outsiders as a strange area of study. Without Jack, I may have dedicated my efforts elsewhere. It was through Jack that I was able to help resolve the homicide series of Felix Vail and I am grateful for that experience.

Around this time, I met investigator Todd Davis during an internship at the Public Protection Bureau of the Massachusetts Attorney General's Office. Todd showed me the basics of how to conduct interviews, the processes and procedures of background checks, and the manner in which to track down the most minute detail, all of which helped to hone my research skills.

Retired FBI Special Agent Vickie Woosley's support of my early aspirations in serial homicide research, coupled with her institutional contacts, allowed me to make inroads with leading scholars and set me up for long-term success. The lessons in decency, patience, and fortitude that Vickie taught me have never left me and have proven useful every day since. I have been able to approach many adverse situations due to the lessons I learned while under Vickie's mentorship. Knowing Vickie changed my life in countless ways, and I cannot be more grateful.

Eric Hickey's contributions to the field of serial murder research and investigation are legion. As one of the first to statistically analyze serial murder, Eric set the precedent for the rest of us. Eric displayed immense courage and fortitude to stay the course professionally as others sought fame and fortune on the backs of victims during the heyday of serial murder. By not following the crowd, Eric was able to gain insight into the criminal workings of serial murderers that others overlooked. Eric's support of the next generation of researchers makes him the most forward-thinking person in the field today. I looked to Eric when thinking about how best to navigate the obstacles in the way of a long-standing career. Without Eric elevating my work, I may have grown weary and petered out long ago. I cannot hope to repay Eric for the valuable life lessons and the innumerable hours he has dedicated to our work. I can only hope to have a tenth of the impact on serial homicide research that Eric has had.

The foresight shown by retired journalist Thomas Hargrove in the formation of the Murder Accountability Project and his leadership since its founding have been inspirational. Tom's dedication to the victims of homicide has been infectious. Many thanks to Tom for those early foundational conversations all those years ago. It is important work. While we do not always agree on the prevalence of the phenomenon, I respect the search for answers. What a journey it has been.

The late Leonard Morgenbesser was among the first to see the merit of forming the Atypical Homicide Research Group (AHRG) and gave an early iteration of this think tank a chance by providing institutional support. Thank you for your foresight, Leonard. Rest in peace, old friend. Thanks go to the late Robert Keppel for being the first to reject my invitation. You made me work harder to refine our mission statement and purpose. Rest in peace, Bob.

To all the members of the AHRG and the early contributors to the Consolidated Serial Homicide Offender Database (Eric Hickey, Ronald Hinch, Brigadier Gérard Labuschagne, Janet McClellan, Bryan Nelson, Michael Newton, Kenna Quinet, Cloyd Steiger, and John White): history will look favorably on you for your belief in open access to information. Rivalries and turf wars have no place among scholars. Your support of these networked activities should be widely commended. It is critical that we remember that siloed thinking led to the creation and subsistence of serial murder myths and stereotypes for decades.

Many thanks to Evelin Csabai for your research assistance. This work is better off for your involvement. To my buddy, Clare Allely, thank you for keeping me on track and talking me off the ledge during this process. I dare say I would not have finished this book if not for your support. Thank you to Routledge editor Lydia de Cruz who had the foresight to see that the field needed a new perspective on serial murder and approached me to provide it. Lydia was a strong ally who was patient and kind when I needed it throughout the publishing process. Thank you to Senior Production Editor Emma Harder-Collins without whom this book would not have come together. Emma allowed for many late game changes and ensured that all the i's were dotted and t's were crossed. Emma was expertly thorough in locating and correcting errors and was quite responsive in doing so, for which I am very grateful. Thanks to my family for providing the resources and support necessary to begin my foray into higher learning.

Lastly, I would like to thank my wife, Rose, for never judging or condemning my pursuit of answers in this area of research no matter how much time it has taken away from our lives. Your insight on how to navigate the various personalities associated with this area of research has been heeded on more occasions than I wish were necessary, but it has always been on point. Thank you for your encouragement and for being my travel buddy when in-person conferences were the norm. I could not have done it without you, Rose!

1

SERIAL MURDER

Then and Now

Introduction

Killer Data arrives at a time when empirical interest in serial homicide has waned in light of the rising impact of intimate femicides, human trafficking, sovereign citizens, incels, mass shootings, the dark web, domestic terrorism, racial injustice, and police brutality. The study of serial murder exists on the fringe of more serious inquiries into what are perceived to be more prominent and prevalent criminal threats. The quest to discern the intricacies of serial murder has been outpaced by facetious coverage of these offenders by the entertainment industry and others who profit from what amounts to a cursory inspection of a complex topic. As victimization rates continue to plummet, some are satisfied with the established decades-old research findings. Others are willing to retire a subject viewed to have oversaturated the discourse of atypical homicide. But the study of serial murder is in its infancy with more unanswered questions than satisfying explanations. Such is the landscape where those that study and investigate this topic find themselves today.

Because several authors (Allely, 2020; Hickey & Harris, 2013; Homant & Kennedy, 2014; Sarteschi, 2016) have thoroughly and expertly documented certain aspects of the phenomenon (e.g., typologies, profiling, paraphilias, signatures, and psychopathy), doing so here would amount to a perfunctory retread. As such, those works should be consulted alongside this review. *Killer Data* aims to provide a succinct overview of serial murder using contemporary data from 2011–2021 while making its study compelling and relevant to the next generation of researchers. The goal of *Killer Data* is to remove the mysticism that has enhanced the stature of serial murderers as superior offenders and mechanistic killing machines. In reality, serial murderers are often run-of-the-mill hometown losers, who brutalize women, and are lucky to escape apprehension. They are propelled forward by a deep sense of entitlement, fragile masculinity, easy access to firearms, and a nonchalant attitude

DOI: 10.4324/9781003130567-1

toward using murder to attain their goals. One recent example saw a team of father and son target their friends after their relationships went awry, shoot them to death, and escape capture after a neighbor of 20 years failed to recognize their faces in a sketch (Ormseth, 2021). As a critical review, *Killer Data* is needed to spotlight modern-day serial murders, their often-mundane methods and motives, how the attitudes of academics and the police have evolved, and the sometimes-muted response from people who know these offenders. It is critical that serial murder is rigorously interrogated as its offenders learn how to adapt to life in the 21st century.

A New Criminal Type ... or All Concerted Hype?

At the 1990 American Academy of Forensic Sciences meeting, a Special Agent of the Federal Bureau of Investigation's (FBI) burgeoning Behavioral Science Unit (BSU)[1] proclaimed that mid-1940s multiple murderer William Heirens was the nation's first such offender who helped the United States become the "most murderous country in the world" (Crime Control Digest, 1990, p. 7). Determined to establish serial murder as a modern-day, unmanageable problem, the FBI pronounced that the increase in stranger-to-stranger violent crime by "traveling predators killing women and children for no apparent motive" (Depue, 1986, p. 4) had to be addressed. As the idyllic 1950s gave way to the turbulent 1960s, the tumultuous 1970s, and the hedonistic 1980s, the homicides of multiple African American boys and one serial murderer's grandiose claim of responsibility for hundreds of deaths caused a panic (Lester, 1995, p. 45) that a "new criminal type" had "emerged from the underground" (Hickey, 2013, p. 2). From all outward signs, it certainly did seem like the so-called stranger homicides were a new plague on the horizon (Vronsky, 2018).

The New York Police Department then warned that there "...has been an increase in sexually sadistic homicides" (Michaud, 1986, p. 42), later supported by an FBI report stating that such killings had become "more commonplace in society" (Federal Bureau of Investigation, 1992, p. 1). Serial murder was soon declared the "crime of the 1990s" (Holmes & Holmes, 2001, p. 15). But multiple murderers have been an ever-present facet of human culture since the formation of societies. Because social scientists, police, journalists, and the media began their inquiries into the phenomenon only recently, facts about serial murder had been derived from anecdotes and other unfounded sources. Historians, who began to study the confusion surrounding the frequency and nature of serial murder as it became more widely recognized, found that its true prevalence was obscured for several reasons: serial murder was not a criminal act in past ages (Schechter, 1996), no press existed to broadcast such deeds, many crimes were not recorded, and offenders were killed without judicial procedure prior to the 1450s (Vronsky, 2018). Given the lack of available case-specific information, vague definitional boundaries, and opinions based on conjecture that began to surround serial murder, early scholars and police came to think of its offenders as compulsive, irrational, lustful, and egregiously violent evil monsters, aberrations supposedly beyond understanding (Jenkins, 2002).

Myths and Stereotypes

Knowledge about serial murder quickly became rooted in a sensationalist and simplified stereotype of the evil, psychopathic killer (Hodgkinson, Prins, & Stuart-Bennett, 2017). According to serial homicide scholar Eric Hickey (2013), some use the term "evil" to label those who kill for enjoyment or the catch-all term "psychopath" to characterize callous and remorseless killers because recreational murder is not well understood. It is easier to label someone than to try to comprehend their actions, but these strategies do not offer an answer to those asking why (Egger, 2002). Serial murders "embody a host of gnawing anxieties" about unending sexual violence and the corruption of society (Schechter, 1996, p. 2) and generate fear due to its "apparent randomness" (Egger, 2002, p. 4). The late criminologist Steven Egger (2002) notes that this causes information to be hyped and contain a number of inaccuracies.

According to several authors (Culhane, Walker, & Hildebrand, 2019; Egger, 2002; Hickey, 2013; Morton & Hilts, 2008; Sarteschi, 2016; Yaksic, 2019), it is a myth that *all* serial murderers have or are:

- experienced child abuse
- preyed on all who cross their path
- graduated from killing animals to human beings
- increased their violence as the series progresses
- engaged with the police to learn about the progress of their investigation
- traveled and operate interstate
- used hands-on methods to kill dozens of victims
- followed a predetermined model for their behavior
- targeted victims based solely on their physical appearance
- spurred forward by pornography, drugs, or alcohol
- left either organized or disorganized crime scenes
- wanted to get caught
- begun to unravel toward the conclusion of their series
- an uncanny ability to elude the police for long periods of time
- an unusual relationship with their mother
- intensely psychopathic
- constantly evolving toward the perfect murder
- grossly disfigured, dysfunctional loners who do not resemble the average person
- insane, evil geniuses
- incapable of maintaining long-term relationships
- only motivated by sex
- Caucasian males
- compelled to continue killing
- no interactions with the criminal justice system.

Many of these myths and stereotypes encompass much of the knowledge generated during the early days of the study of serial murder. The "striking level of repetition across the discourse of serial murder" (Warwick, 2006, p. 556) not only gave rise to these myths and stereotypes but continues to sustain them when combined with a lack of innovation called "the stagnancy error" (DeLisi, 2015, pp. 221). There are several examples of these phenomena worth mentioning:

- To study animal cruelty (Wright & Hensley, 2003), identity management (Henson & Olson, 2010), and "cooling-off periods" (Dilly, 2021), scholars selected several infamous serial murderers.[2] These offenders began killing in the late 1950s, 20 years before the start of an era known as the "Golden Age" of serial murder (Ehrlich, 2021) that would last through the early 1990s.
- In *Using Murder*, Jenkins (1994, p. 7) notes that notorious serial murderers provide an opportunity for rhetorical development, to persuade the public into believing in an "enormously amplified" threat.
- The television show *Invisible Monsters: Serial Killers in America* grouped several notorious serial murderers – referred to as "The Five"[3] – to give the impression that the country was overrun by them. Another show, City of Angels | City of Death, followed a similar format. One expert stated that "These individuals provided the base to start studying [serial murderers]" (TMZ Live, 2021), a process that began almost 50 years ago. Experts dissect the lives and crimes of "The Five" for information to be applied to the study and capture of today's criminals.
- In an online video series, another expert referenced three notorious serial murderers[4] and claimed that they provide "…an amazing volume of institutional knowledge, and it tells us how they killed, and why they killed, and it helps us to hunt them down" (Wired Tradecraft, 2019).
- Scholars are entrenched in the most extreme and popular cases (Berger, 2021; Woollaston, 2015), design studies to conform to these archetypes (Yaksic, 2018), and use mythical language to describe serial murderers (Ruzsonyi, 2017), at the detriment of knowledge regarding more common murderers (Booth, 2021; James, 2019).
- Even when a modern serial murderer is discovered, experts compare them with this same handful of notorious offenders (Seewer & Welsh-Huggins, 2009).

The overuse of infamous serial murderers to inform on the phenomenon raises an interesting question: how can these offenders' behaviors still be relevant and of use to the academic and police communities today, half a century later? It is dangerous to rely on behavior patterns from decades-old cases to inform on modern-day crimes as doing so introduces selection bias, a problem that hampers the generalizability of the characteristics of these serial murderers to the wider population at large. To understand how pervasive the repeated use of notorious serial murderers has become, a content analysis conducted for this review (see Table 1.1) revealed that just 16 infamous serial murderers, active between 1954 and 1991, receive the majority of attention among published works. As such, the scholarly serial murder profile overlooks 30 years of data.

TABLE 1.1 Repetitive case studies across 15 serial homicide publications, 1986–2020

Offender	*Mentions*	*Active Years*
Theodore Bundy	10	1974–1978
Aileen Wuornos	8	1989–1990
Edmund Kemper	8	1964–1973
Jeffrey Dahmer	8	1978–1991
Albert DeSalvo	7	1962–1964
John Gacy	7	1972–1978
Kenneth Bianchi	7	1977–1979
Henry Lucas	5	1960–1983
Andrei Chikatilo	5	1978–1990
Edward Gein	5	1954–1957
Dennis Nilsen	5	1978–1983
Dennis Rader	5	1974–1991
Gerald Gallego	5	1978–1980
Jerry Brudos	5	1968–1969
Joseph Kallinger	5	1974–1975
Richard Ramirez	5	1984–1985

Myths and stereotypes benefit serial murderers as they transform a banal crime into a mysterious one while transfiguring lowlifes into celebrities. Serial murderers have enjoyed an unearned stature enhancement by being called the "cream of the crop" among killers (Cable News Network, 2002), advanced predators with exceptional abilities and expertise (Wiest, 2016). Some regard serial murderers as icons of "ultimate freedom" (Dietrich & Hall, 2010, p. 11). Others portray serial murderers as "impelled by impulse, or instinctual compulsion" (Shanafelt & Pino, 2013, p. 263) who lack internality and human qualities (Warwick, 2006). Taken as a whole, myths and stereotypes suggest that serial murderers not only act in disturbing ways apart from their criminal acts but also display abhorrent behavior that is detectable by those around them. But, as Shanafelt and Pino (2013) point out, serial murderers try to separate themselves into a "nice-guy self" and a "murdering self" as part of the killing process. Those who are not adept at doing so sometimes isolate themselves by avoiding strong friendships to better hide their real identity (Pino, 2005).

There are certain words that have become part of the lexicon when speaking about serial murder – beastly, crazy, creepy, depraved, devilish, fiendish, gruesome, heinous, and vile – to name only a few. But these designations do little to explain serial murder. Today, police, prosecutors, and even judges have taken to publicly labeling serial murderers with descriptors such as "crazy," "evil," and "monster." A prosecutor recently argued that a defendant could not be impaired because he was "not some nut job serial killer" (Li, 2021). Harry Little was called demonic, while Harold Haulman,[5] Leeroy Rogers, Jeffrey Willis, and James Bradley were labeled as evil, and Mark Beebout was termed a psychopath by officials. Freddie Grant, James Harris, and Reta Mays were deemed monsters, one for helping search for his victim, the next for the sexual assault of a tenant where he was the maintenance man, and another for victimizing patients at a Veterans hospital. The news media handles these cases similarly. A recent story spoke about the "shocking" details victims endured to "bring the monsters to justice" (Banfield, 2021).

Around the late 1970s, Jenkins (1994) spoke on serial murderers who became the personification of wickedness as public interest in the offenders coincided with a political trend of blaming deviancy on personal sin and evil rather than social dysfunction. But myths and stereotypes that keep these descriptions in the public's consciousness discount the aspect of the serial murderer's complex psychology where they create rationalizations that aid them in killing (Shanafelt & Pino, 2013), which makes them more difficult to identify. For instance, the ex-wife of serial murderer Gregory Green, the daughter of a pastor who lobbied for Green's release, killed her children, and she then regarded him as "a devil in disguise … now exposed" (Phillips, 2017). Rather than seething creatures roaming the countryside, this review exposes serial murderers as banal individuals who are encountered in public and not given another look. Some believe that serial murderers reject social norms and violate the social contract (Warf & Waddell, 2002), but these offenders "drift" toward serial murder only after a practiced use of neutralizations aids them in constructing an identity, and putting forth a "normal self," to allow them to balance their deviant and criminal lifestyle with conventional societal commitments and mainstream values (such as marriage, family, and church) (James & Gossett, 2018). While serial murderers are human, the lore surrounding them can create an environment that allows them to hide in plain sight (Branson, 2013). Even though potential victims are more alert today, they are apt to ignore warning signs if someone does not immediately conform to the preconceived notion of what a serial murderer looks like. Serial murderer Patrick Watkins, for example, was a generous neighbor who gave drum lessons to children, lifted heavy furniture for those who could not, and handed out food and fruit. Serial murderers often know that they are psychologically and emotionally damaged, but they use biological ailments as excuses, see themselves as victims of society and circumstances, and struggle with their alternate identities due to their inability to experience life normally because of personality or psychological problems (Henson & Olson, 2010).

Although the term *serial killer* has become synonymous with any strange or odd behavior, it can be misleading to view people exhibiting such characteristics as deranged enough to kill. After all, these attributes are typically basic idiosyncrasies.[6] Reliance on such hallmarks to signal serial murder activity has become another dangerous myth. Before buying into the fervent hype surrounding serial murder, we must remember how little is currently understood about it: there is no consensus on what constitutes overkill (Trojan, Salfati, & Schanz, 2019), necrophilia is understudied (Pettigrew, 2019a), and totem-taking has been studied only in the context of sexual murders (Warren, Dietz, & Hazelwood, 2013). Because the presence of these behaviors among one-off homicides is undercounted, and both dismemberment and posing are used by one-off murderers to delay apprehension by way of evidence disposal (Adams, Rainwater, Yim, & Alesbury, 2019) and the misdirection of investigations, respectively (Ferguson, 2021), their association with serial homicide is overblown. Additionally, serial murderers who dismember their victims do so for the same practical reasons (Petreca, Burgess, Stone, & Brucato, 2020) as one-off murderers.

Few serial murders feature overkill (13%), torture (9%), mutilation (8%), dismemberment (4%), totem-taking (4%), necrophilia (2%), posing (2%), cannibalism (1%), or vampirism (.3%).[7] Among the 16 infamous serial murderers repeatedly featured in scholarly works (see Table 1.1), overkill, torture, mutilation, dismemberment, totem-taking, and necrophilia appear half of the time in their histories, which explains why serial murder has become synonymous with these behaviors. But only one offender (Dahmer) engaged in each of these behaviors throughout their series. Society's obsession with Dahmer and his "creepy" aesthetic partly explains how serial homicide became known for these abhorrent behaviors given that he was the poster boy of serial murder in the 1990s and is still being written about today (Chan, 2019). Britain's Dahmer, Dennis Nilsen, has also been the focus of several recent academic studies (Pettigrew, 2019a; 2019b; 2019c; 2020a; 2020b). The danger of giving credence to this particular myth is twofold: police treat the presence of any one of these behaviors as a reliable signal of serial murder activity, and potential serial murderers have begun to emulate these behaviors given that they believe this is how real serial murderers behave.

In summary, the presentation of the serial murderer as an otherworldly aberration is a byproduct of the rudimentary ways in which they were thought of and written about throughout history as well as our collective penchant to draw definitive distinctions between them and us.

Pursuing Fame Through Serial Murder

Little agreement exists on most facets of serial murder due to its commodification and influence by "the sensationalism of those competing for the public's interest" (Egger, 2002, pp. 12–13). As recognition of the crime grew, questions regarding its etiology attracted viewpoints and theories from individuals with varying degrees of exposure to the offenders. Scholars, police, journalists, and the media launched independent inquests into serial murder with vast differences in their commitment to seeking fulfilling answers. Each had a vested interest in portraying serial murder in ways that would enhance their stature and increase the likelihood that people would need their insight. A symbiosis formed between serial murderers and those involved in their study (Greep, 2020), transforming both into what social scientist Julie Wiest calls "perverse icons" (Wiest, 2011, p. 91).

Serial murder has deep roots in American culture given the headlines, exploitive books (Kaminsky, 2020; Kissel, Zebrowski, & Parks, 2020; Rosewood, 2019), merchandise (Selna, 2021), and entertainment (Osifo, 2021a) generated at its expense (Wiest, 2011). If serial murder spawned as a deviant means to gain culturally valued feelings of power, control, dominance, competition, success, satisfaction, pleasure, recognition, and fame (Wiest, 2011), our fascination with serial murder is an extension of a desire to "terrorize women and to empower and inspire men" (Wiest, 2011, p. 86). Serial murderers are kept "on the cultural surface" as they fulfill the need for unusual and shocking content (Wiest, 2011) and result in revenue as they sell newspapers due to their bizarre and extraordinary crimes (Hickey, 2013). A recent article asks, "Is Netflix making stars out of serial killers?" (Bindel, 2021), which highlights the problem of emphasizing the contextual features of American society that support serial murderers such as "dehumanization, individualism and competition, privilege associated with whiteness and maleness, thrill seeking, the normalization of violence, and the depravity in urban life" (Wiest, 2011, p. 108). Serial murderers, and those who study and pursue them, have sustained interest in this area as a gateway to fame, masculinity, power, dominance, and a pathway to immortality (Wiest, 2011) and many – including you and I – are complicit in this process (Yaksic, 2019).

Although serial murder has existed since the beginning of recorded history, it became something to do, to be, and to study only recently (Seltzer, 1998). According to historian Peter Vronsky (2018), premodern society was concerned with survival and had little time for killing serially. But when the phenomenon was more fully conceptualized in the late 1970s, offenders – and those who studied and arrested them – were given attention, elevating individuals who may not have attained fame otherwise, culminating in the erection of a museum in their honor (The Forensic Examiner, 2010). To achieve infamy, serial murderers sought higher body counts and used ever more shocking methods to top one another (Wiest, 2011). Both scholars and police profited from stories heralding themselves as heroes for interviewing, pursuing, and capturing serial murderers. Desperate for answers, researchers ignored the danger of relying on retrospective self-reports and biased sampling procedures (Muller, 2000) in favor of the notoriety that came from being called pioneers. In a paradoxical concomitance, the value of the serial murderers' stories matched their own need to tell them.

The FBI characterized serial murders as "unusual, bizarre, vicious, repetitive … baffling violent crimes" (Depue, 1986, p. 5) and placed themselves at the forefront of their investigation because few others, they claimed, were equipped to deal with such offenders. Due to the self-reports and the media's portrayal of serial murderers, offenders came to be seen as they described themselves: intelligent, wily, and masculine – qualities consistent with the power structures in America (Wiest, 2011). These stereotypes were repeated by researchers and operationalized by police (Hickey, 2013) who were, by proxy, as brilliant as serial murderers given that they were able to capture and study them (Wiest, 2011). The FBI used serial murder to enhance their image and expand their jurisdictional reach and warned that as criminals became more sophisticated, investigative tools such as the psychological assessment of crime, (an "art form" called profiling) (Ault & Reese, 1980) must also do so. In a promotional article titled *The Real Silence of the Lambs*, FBI agents compared themselves with the fictional Sherlock Holmes and stated that they blend academic knowledge and practical investigative experience to "develop a comprehensive analysis of the offense and the individual" (Van Zandt & Ether, 1994, p. 48).

But, as Egger reports, the FBI had merely been collecting data from newspaper wire services (Egger, 2002).

The Inflated Prevalence of Serial Murder

To fit the emerging narrative, some referred to serial murderers as having suddenly appeared in American society with a "rash of cases" beginning in 1960 and were on a "meteoric rise" (Egger, 2002, p. 69). Others characterized this supposed emergence as a growing menace and pitched this sensationalistic view on the talk show circuit. These individuals played into the political reasons that serial murderers were described with hyperbolic language like "super" (Hickey, 2013, p. 42), "mega" (Vronsky, 2018, p. 249), "extreme" (Leyton, 2001, p. 58), "world-class" (Schechter, 1996, p. 160), and "superstar" (Norris, 1989, p. 4), and supported their portrayal as "uniquely dangerous predatory villains" who violate state boundaries (Jenkins, 2002, p. 1). The media gave serial murderers nicknames like "ripper," "slasher," "butcher," and "monster," and prosecutors began to describe them as evil and savage (Wiest, 2011, pp. 93, 139). The truth about serial murder has been obscured by simplistic explanations while the occurrence of the phenomenon was purposely inflated to ensure that resources would be dedicated to its study and investigation.

Even though psychiatrist Park Dietz (1986, pp. 486) proclaimed that there was "no empirical evidence" that serial murder was increasing, researchers, police, and the media exaggerated the threat posed by stranger murderers. Soon, articles detailing the exploits of serial murderers and their growing death tolls began to appear (John Jay College of Criminal Justice/CUNY, 2002). Some are willing to blame serial murderers for any and all unresolved homicides no matter how implausible the linkages became (McDonell-Parry, 2018).[8] Even with evidence of a decline in serial murder (Yaksic, Allely, De Silva, Smith-Inglis, Konikoff, Ryan, Gordon, Denisov, & Keatley, 2019) (see Figures 1.1 and 1.2), with the past decade's tally at almost half what it was at the height of the 1980s, and statistics demonstrating that only one in 210 million people become serial murderers (Cullen, 2020), some still seek to create a panic by claiming that thousands of offenders exist in the United States (Wilkinson, 2017) with searches for them reaching all social classes (Kutner, 2017; Lancaster, 2021; Tiffany, 2016). A small handful of researchers have called these data sources inadequate and warned that enlarging

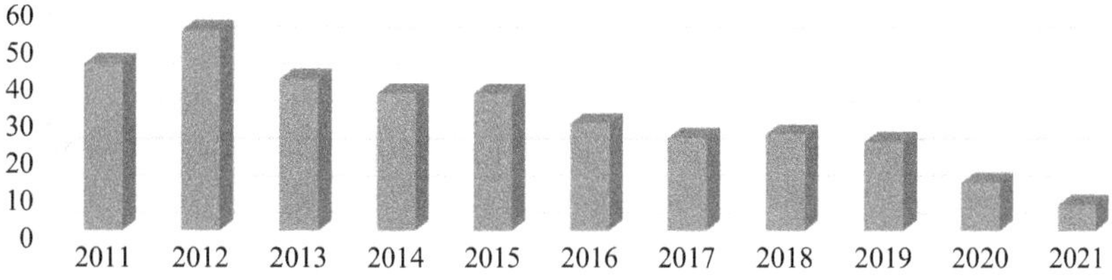

FIGURE 1.1 Frequency of serial murder types combined, 2011–2021

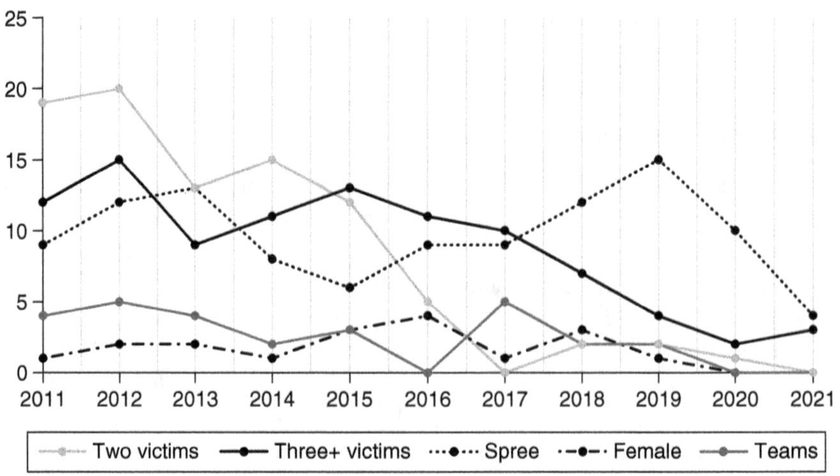

FIGURE 1.2 Frequency of serial murder by individual types, 2011–2021

the magnitude of serial murder based on conjecture will create a social problem (Jenkins, 2002; Kiger, 1990). Others noted that an inconsistent use of definitions led to the underreporting of serial murder. When researchers set out to uncover additional cases, it is thought that they artificially increased the offender's footprint (Hickey, 2013). There may be several things that are responsible for the appearance of an influx of serial murderers at certain times in history (Vronsky, 2018), but the perceived surge in serial murder may be explained by increased awareness and better record keeping (Wiest, 2011).

Some of the unanswered questions surrounding serial murder are the result of the topic not attaining the level of serious academic inquiry dedicated to other crimes. While the number of scholarly articles on serial murder saw a 1,600% increase between the 1980s and 1990s, that percentage fell to 20 between the 2000s and the 2010s. If serial murder is a "protest made by alienated persons against the society [that] they believe excluded them" (Leyton, 2001, p. 1) then the phenomenon has been eclipsed by protests of another sort – righteous movements against police brutality and racially motivated violence. The focus on seemingly grander societal issues has contributed to the view that the study of serial murder may be a waste of resources.

Obstacles to Establishing Serial Murder Research as a Legitimate Endeavor

Several obstacles have prevented serial murder research from being established as a legitimate endeavor. Many hold the opinion that serious scholars should focus on forms of crime that are more common and addressable by policy. Others believe that the phenomenon of serial murder was socially constructed (Jenkins, 1994; DeLisi, 2015). Some rely on anecdotes to inform on serial murder after having reserved that all that can be known has been discovered. So called "Ripperologists" have diminished the credibility of scholars by purporting to come to know the identity of Jack the Ripper through criminal profiling (Saunders, 2020) or forensic evidence (Yancey-Bragg, 2019) all while offering a litany of different suspects and passionately defending their territory (Cain, 2019). Resultantly, police have viewed research as operationally useless, which makes implementation of learnings difficult (Kaplan, 2017; Rosario, 2017).[9] The drive to appear knowledgeable in an area that both fascinates and confuses the public sometimes overrides adherence to facts as there is little accountability for providing uninformed statements. Hickey (2014, p. 12) succinctly summarizes the plight endured by those delving into serial murder research "...being a researcher in this area has required getting past misinformation and sensationalism, finding others who share similar research interests, and dredging up reliable data." In reviewing the challenges and limitations of utilizing data to study serial murder and the drawbacks of insular thinking, Yaksic (2015) found that information silos, definitional discordance, and a lack of access to open data inhibited the growth of serial murder research.

But above all other barriers, the intertwining of serial murder with entertainment has been disastrous for those involved in an intellectual pursuit of answers. Comingling serial murder and entertainment was a strategy engineered in the late 1970s as the FBI wittingly allowed author Thomas Harris access to their classrooms and case files before he penned *Red Dragon* of 1981 and *The Silence of the Lambs* of 1988. No other film, television program, or book has done more to "promote the mythology of serial murder" (Egger, 2002, p. 13). These books and subsequent movies not only presented serial murderers as enigmatic Caucasian men but also portrayed FBI agents as "superagents" (Wiest, 2011, p. 16) possessing almost otherworldly powers of perception and insight. FBI agents leaned into their portrayal as men who "walk the edge between good and evil, sanity and insanity," triumphing over chaos by journeying into darkness (Jenkins, 2002, p. 13). Because of this myth, the public erroneously thought that police understood serial murder and felt safer than warranted.

Interest in serial murder has steadily increased over the past 25 years (Lester, 1995), but the phenomenon has since gone mainstream. Popular television programs *The Office, American Auto*, and *Superstore* each had recurring storylines that involved serial murderers who existed merely to break up the monotony of the character's daily lives. A megastar basketball player admitted to relying on a fictional serial murderer to get him into the mindset of becoming a "stone-cold killer" on the court (Thomas, 2021). Another athlete proclaimed that his fascination with serial murder helps him become a better villain for wrestling fans (McGeorge, 2021). Serial murder has become so engrained in American culture that a US Senator has been blamed for committing the unresolved Zodiac murders, an in-joke that he fully participates in (Rodrigo, 2018), and so ubiquitous that those as young as 4 years old look up to serial murderers and proclaim their affection for them (Dawson, 2021). Actors are happy to portray serial murderers as they can be nominated for awards (Brown, 2021; Goyal, 2021) or help them shed a "good boy" image (Kohn, 2017). A book titled *My Sister, the Serial Killer* was longlisted for the prestigious Booker

Prize in 2019. The top prize at the 2021 Cannes Film Festival was won by *Titane*, a film about a serial murderer. The television program *Criminal Minds*, which features a new serial murderer each week, was the most streamed show of 2021.

Serial murderers have even begun to be used as a commercial tool. For example, to advertise the sheer size of their vehicle's interior, a major car brand showed a man – dubbed a "creep" – surrounded by trash bags with rope in his hand and had him ask whether or not he could fit these items into the car (Honda Fit TV Commercial, 2015). For no reason other than cater to true crime fans and garner "clicks," articles are written that merely list the crimes of serial murderers (Osifo, 2021b). Criminologists have fed into the hype behind serial murderers by writing about offenders who became movie stars (Berry-Dee, 2021) and even reviewing their behaviors as if they were real killers (Wilson, 2021). A satirical article correctly assessed the zeitgeist in stating that an algorithm created "exactly what our subscribers want to see" when offering a Jeffrey Dahmer stand-up comedy special (The Onion, 2021). One could even book a stay at the house of fictional serial murderer "Buffalo Bill," visit his "Workshop of Horrors," and don a kimono to live out their "fantasies" of emulating a mythical killer (Kreps, 2021). As Woody Harrelson's serial murderer character correctly states in the recent movie *Venom: Let There Be Carnage*, "People love serial killers" (Leishman, 2021).

As our curiosity morphed into a cultural obsession, a myriad of entertainment options manifested to satiate the masses. But there are serious ethical considerations with monetizing the stories of victims, profiting off of their misery, and showcasing the crimes of notorious serial murderers (Foreman, 2021), especially when these popular television programs, documentaries, books, and films[10] only pretend to present a meaningful examination of serial murder. Most efforts provide a stylized, sensationalistic, oversimplified, and inaccurate portrait of these offenders and the criminal justice system's response to them. Many offerings, for example, continue to focus on the same notorious serial murderers, prompting some to ask if another portrayal of Bundy as "charming" and "hot" is necessary (Diaz, 2021).

This trend shows no indication of slowing as a litany of media dedicated to serial murder was announced over just a few weeks in 2021:

- **Podcasts**: *Killer's Vault, Killer Psyche, The Doodler, Unraveled: Long Island Serial Killer, Algorithm, Defense Diaries, To Catch a Serial Killer, Suspect Zero, Profiling Evil, Death Island, Where the Bodies are Buried,* and *Life After Happy Face*
- **Nonfiction books**: *A Killer by Design: Murderers, Mindhunters, and My Quest to Decipher the Criminal Mind, The Flat Tire Murders: Unsolved Crimes of a South Florida Serial Killer, Defending a Serial Killer: The Right to Counsel, Church Bells at Midnight, Murder Capital of the World: The Santa Cruz Community Looks Back at the Frazier, Mullin, and Kemper Murder Sprees of the Early 1970s, Monster: The True Story of the Jeffrey Dahmer Murders, Behold the Monster, The Babysitter, The Last Call, Missing from the Village, Bait: To Catch a Killer, Our Top Story: How Ted Bundy Changed Us Forever, A Dramaturgical Approach to Understanding the Serial Homicides of Ted Bundy, The New Millennium Serial Killer, America's Femme Fatale: The Story of Serial Killer Belle Gunness, Serial Killers: 101 Questions True Crime Fans Ask,*

Saved: How One Woman's Faith Stopped the Man Who Preyed on Elderly Women, History of a Drowning Boy, The Case of the Murderous Dr. Cream: The Hunt for a Victorian Era Serial Killer, From Son of Sam to Son of Hope: The Amazing Story of David Berkowitz, Terror Town USA: The Untold Story of Joliet's Serial Killer, Random Recreational Violence, The Devil's Work: Australia's Jack the Ripper and the Serial Murders That Shocked the World, The Murders That Made Us: How Vigilantes, Hoodlums, Mob Bosses, Serial Killers, and Cult Leaders Built the San Francisco Bay Area, and *The Science of Serial Killers: The Truth Behind Ted Bundy, Lizzie Borden, Jack the Ripper, and Other Notorious Murderers of Cinematic Legend*

- **Fictional books**: *Dog Rose Dirt, The Serial Killer's Wife, Survive the Night, The 22 Murders of Madison May, The Nothing Man, The Impostor, The Bride Collector, Gone for Good, Unknown Vengeance, The Machine Murders, Unknown Male, The Twelve Murders of Christmas, Chasing the Boogeyman, In the Garden of Spite*, and *The North Face of the Heart*
- **Films**: *American Boogeywoman* (Aileen Wuornos), *The Good Nurse* (Charles Cullen), *Rodney & Sheryl* (Rodney Alcala), *Believe Me: The Abduction of Lisa McVey* (Bobby Joe Long), *American Boogeyman* and *No Man of God* (Theodore Bundy), *The Untold Story of a Serial Killer: Javed Iqbal, The Woman in the Window, The Chestnut Man, The Batman, Midnight in the Switchgrass, Muti, Vicious Fun, Love and Death, Mouse, Danger Zone, Svalta, Hinterland, Eye Without a Face, White Knuckle, Netrikann, My Girlfriend the Serial Killer, Fear Street, The Last Matinee, Midnight, When the Screaming Starts, Malignant, The Girl Who Got Away, There's Someone Inside Your House, Operation Hyacinth, Johnny & Clyde, The Execution, Boston Strangler, I Live Alone, Slumber Party Massacre, The Man in the White Van, Brazen*, and *Miranda Veil*
- **Documentaries**: *The Hunt for the Chicago Strangler, BTK: Confession of a Serial Killer, City of Angels | City of Death, Dig Deeper: The Disappearance of Birgit Meier, John Wayne Gacy: Devil in Disguise, Ed Gein: The Real Psycho, Sons of Sam: A Decent into Darkness, Ted Bundy: A Faking It Special, Ivan Milat: The Backpack Murderer, The Women and the Murderer, The Night Stalker: The Hunt for a Serial Killer, Memories of a Murderer: The Nilsen Tapes, Sasquatch*[11], *The Phantom*[12], *Invisible Monsters: Serial Killers in America, The Highway Murders, The Chameleon Killer, The Toolbox Killer, Escaping Captivity: The Kara Robinson Story, The Raincoat Killer: Chasing a Predator in Korea, The Co-Ed Killer: Mind of a Monster, Tracking the Devil: Inside the Mind of William Reece*, and *I Survived a Serial Killer*
- **Film adaptations of books**: *The Monster of Florence* and *Killers of the Flower Moon*
- **Television shows**: *Catching Killers, The Patient, The Co-Ed Killer: Mind of a Monster, Crime Scene: The Times Square Killer, Happy Face, Killer Next Door, Fatal Frontier: Evil in Alaska, Grim Sleeper: The Friends Speak, CSI: Vegas, Monster: The Jeffrey Dahmer Story, Dr. Death, In the Footsteps of Killers, Redrum, Ragdoll, The Final Girl Support Group, American Horror Stories, Why Women Kill, The Thing About Pam, I Know What You Did Last Summer, Mark of a Serial Killer, Only Murders in the Building, Stay Close* and *Mare of Easttown*
- A comic book *Killer Bad* where a group of superheroes is stalked by a "super-slasher" and another comic titled *The Ripper Gene*

- An "Extreme Violence" modification to the video game *The Sims* where players can slit each other's throats, shoot each other, and disembowel one another with chainsaws
- The video games *Nothing to Remember*, and *Bloodwash*
- A graphic novel *Did you hear what Eddie Gein done?*
- A woman who adorned her body with $2,000 dollars of Bundy and Dahmer tattoos
- A musical *Ghoul of Grays Harbor* and The Graveface Museum dedicated to serial killers
- A story about a beauty pageant queen who is obsessed with Theodore Bundy
- A story in Vulture about a former FBI profiler's entertainment production company
- A story about an *It's Always Sunny in Philadelphia* character's murderous tendencies
- A social media hashtag #HannibalDeservesMore dedicated to the television show
- Advertisements for Oxygen's *Serial Killer Week* and A+E's *True Crime Week*
- Lectures on the *Psychology of Serial Killers*, and *Inside the Mind of Serial Killers*
- Music by Trunky Juno titled *Serial Killer Vibes* and by Slipknot titled *The Chapeltown Rag*
- A revival of *Dexter*
- A revival of the *Halloween, Scream, Chucky*, *Candyman*, and *Saw* movie franchises
- References to Theodore Bundy and Dexter on *America's Most Wanted Overtime*
- The YouTube channel *Murder, Mystery, and Makeup* where the host chats about true crime while applying makeup
- A *Saturday Night Live* skit called *Murder Show* lampooning true crime

It is not just visual media that has seen an explosion in interest. As of this writing, the popular e-commerce website Etsy contains 14,546 items for purchase under the "serial killer" search term.[13] Several auction sites specialize in the sale of artifacts dedicated to murder, known as "murderabilia," with available objects ranging from the serial murderer's hair and nail clippings, soil from their gravesite, to their personal paintings (Bond, 2016). From other products dedicated to serial murder, such as escape rooms (House of Horrors & Haunted Catacombs, 2021), games (Ryan, 2020), calendars (Serial Killer Calendar, 2021), shot glasses (Sword and Scale, 2019), swag (Brand, 2021), and clothing (Serial Killer Shop, 2021; Western Evil, 2021), to the festivals that attract true crime personalities (Robb, 2019; Sarachan, 2019), notorious offenders are more than celebrated, they are revered. Serial murderers can be depicted as human monsters to be abhorred, but they are frequently presented as antiheros to cheer on (Wiest, 2011).

There are obvious drawbacks to elevating a serial murderer to a position of prominence. When we root for their "unique cleverness," and their actions reflect our hidden impulses (Lester, 1995, p. 43), we may be bolstering the serial murderer's feelings of self-righteousness as they remove groups like sex workers and the homeless from the streets (Egger, 2002). Marginalizing sex workers and other undesirable individuals creates a "blindness to perpetrators" where offenders may be overlooked and victims ignored or blamed for their victimization (Wiest, 2011, pp. 153–158).[14] Adorning serial murderers with fame also inspires a generation of "wannabes" – those harboring a propensity to kill and who have attempted at least one homicide but have yet to be successful. These potential serial murderers consume violent imagery to fuel fantasies and homicidal ideation while self-identifying as future killers (Yaksic, Harrison, Konikoff, Mooney, Allely, De Silva, Matykiewicz, Inglis, Giannangelo, Daniels, & Sarteschi, 2021). So called "one-off" killers can also turn to the methods and motives of serial murderers in attempts to replicate their strategies and tactics (Thompson, 2021).

Author Skip Hollandsworth, who wrote *The Midnight Assassin: Panic, Scandal, and the Hunt for America's First Serial Killer*, supposes that our fascination with serial murder is rooted in our lack of understanding of the "alien" motives of the offenders. Hollandsworth surmises that most of us have fleeting feelings of wanting to kill a spouse, our parents, or those close to us, but it is the serial murderer's "eccentric techniques," the drama built into their chronological narrative, and their selection of victims who look like us that is compelling to many who yearn to consume all media related to serial murder (Lavin, 2016). Others believe that interest in serial murder originates with a desire to experience death without becoming a victim in an effort to control the process. Serial murder historian Harold Schechter refers to tales of serial murder as "fairytales for grownups … about being pursued by monsters" (Bond, 2016).

Marketers have seized upon these facets to better sell serial murder merchandise. For example, book covers are adeptly designed to capture a reader's interest. To understand how serial murder is marketed, a content analysis of 15 book covers was performed as part of this review. In six works, the inner turmoil experienced by serial murderers is depicted as manifesting in physical form through: (1) a shadow painting a picture of a man with half of his face overtaken by disfigurement; (2) a blurred version of an artist's rendition of Henry Lee Lucas, calling attention to a deformity to the eye and a gaping, open mouth; (3) an image called "dehumanization" that shows a person being slowly consumed by their shadow self; (4) a downtrodden man about to be eclipsed by a large shadow figure that is looming over him; (5) a cowering, blacked out figure hugging themselves as they are being ignored by everyone among the crowd; and (6) a courtroom photo of "Dating Game Killer" Rodney Alcala's face melded with Dr. Frankenstein's monster. Three covers convey the author's belief in the dangers of looking into serial murder through: (1) placement of the reader in the first-person perspective as they look down from a lit hallway into a dark stairwell, which elicits a sense of dread as we stare into the unknown; (2) a focus on the eyes of various serial murderers which vary between wild and dead; and (3) an assortment of photos with faces scratched out, meant to draw upon the feeling that these are the offender's victims. Three covers altered the title's lettering to illustrate dramatic effect through: (1) blurred out photos of murderers and victims with the words "Serial Killer" in scratched lettering; (2) the word "killers" written in blood; and (3) a hodgepodge of images such as a man transformed into a wolf, Vlad Tepes the Impaler, a fan dressed in a Dracula costume, H. H. Holmes, text from a Jack the Ripper letter, and the faces of David Berkowitz and Jeffrey Dahmer. Two covers were nondescript with one using a stock cover image of a blue background and the other a firearm placed upon the American flag with a chalk outline overlay. The final cover depicts an x-ray of a skull, implying that the book will provide penetrating insights into the criminal mind.

As Schechter stated 25 years ago, "serial murderers exert a dark attraction" (Schechter, 1996, pp. 2–3). The state of affairs has grown far more bleak since then, as summarized by Clark and Palattella (2017, pp. 17): "No matter how insightful the findings of criminologists, their research can be secondary to a source that has perhaps most influenced Americans' views of serial killers: the movies." But while the public has allowed serial murderers to invade their homes through their television screens, board games, and other merchandise, researchers and police continue to search for a more complete understanding of the methods and motives of offenders – behaviors that have consistently eluded them.

Notes

1 Although the BSU has since been renamed as the Behavioral Analysis Unit (BAU), it will be referred to as the BSU throughout this review for the purpose of historical consistency.
2 David Berkowitz, Kenneth Bianchi, Theodore Bundy, Jeffrey Dahmer, John Wayne Gacy, Edmund Kemper, Henry Lee Lucas, Richard Ramirez, Dennis Rader, and Gary Ridgway.
3 Bundy, Dahmer, Gacy, Rader, and Ridgway.
4 Bundy, Kemper, and Berkowitz.
5 The judge in this case called Haulman "a different kind of evil." Haulman is also relevant here given his research of the movie *The Silence of the Lambs* and the fictional serial murderer Hannibal Lector (Kernan, 2021).
6 Several "TikTokers" have made inferences about the residents of homes that contain odd items (Charles, 2021). One woman was criticized for the manner in which she cut her sandwich, with the method being called the "mark of a serial killer" (Daily Star, 2021). Another woman was mocked and labeled a serial killer merely for dancing (Dickson, 2021). A participant in a reality show was even likened to a serial killer due to his awkward behaviors (O'Brien, 2021).
7 Per a computation of all US-based serial homicides from the Consolidated Serial Homicide Offender Database.
8 One author believes that one offender is not only the Zodiac Killer but also the Atlanta Child Murderer and responsible for some of the most well-known unresolved homicides in the United States: JonBenet Ramsey, Adam Walsh, Chandra Levy, Jimmy Hoffa, Martha Moxley, and Elizabeth Short.
9 In at least two instances, police rejected assistance from researchers on ongoing serial homicide investigations.
10 *You, Barry, Killing Eve, Mindhunter, Dexter, The ABC Murders, Hannibal, Criminal Minds, The Most Dangerous Animal of All, Clarice, Big Sky, Prodigal Son, The Pembrokeshire Murders, Smiley Face Killers, My Friend Dahmer, The Serpent, Luther, Extremely Wicked, Shockingly Evil and Vile, Des, Fatma, The House That Jack Built, You Were Never Really Here, Spiral, The Little Things, In With the Devil, The Ripper, I'll Be Gone in the Dark, The Confession Killer,* and *Confronting a Serial Killer.*
11 Which asks if "Bigfoot" is a serial murderer of marijuana farmers.
12 Which aims to prove a serial murderer got away with murder.

13 One particularly egregious item is a tee shirt adorned with the phrase, "Choke me like Bundy, eat me like Dahmer."

14 Samuel Little, who is African American, was able to hide behind the FBI's white-centric serial murder profile and capitalized on the fact that police did not rigorously pursue investigations when victims came from lower social status.

References

Adams, B., Rainwater, C., Yim, A., & Alesbury, H. (2019). A retrospective study of intentional body dismemberment in New York City: 1996–2017. *Journal of Forensic Sciences*. 64(4):1012–1016.

Allely, C. (2020). The Psychology of Extreme Violence: A Case Study Approach to Serial Homicide, Mass Shooting, School Shooting and Lone-Actor Terrorism. Routledge.

Ault, R., & Reese, J. (1980). A psychological assessment of crime: profiling. *FBI Law Enforcement Bulletin*. 49(3):22–25.

Banfield, A. (2021). Banfield: "I survived a serial killer". NewsNation. Retrieved from www.newsnationnow.com/banfield/full-episodes/banfield-i-survived-a-serial-killer/

Berger, R. (2021). Sadipaths: A look at the public's familiarity with some of the most nefarious serial killers. *Studies in Social Science Research*. 2(3):31–40.

Berry-Dee, C. (2021). Serial Killers at the Movies: My Intimate Talks with Mass Murderers Who Became Stars of the Big Screen. Ad Lib Publishers.

Bindel, J. (2021). Why feminists should watch serial killer dramas. The Spectator. Retrieved from www.spectator.co.uk/article/is-netflix-making-stars-out-of-serial-killers-

Bond, M. (2016). Why are we eternally fascinated by serial killers? BBC Future. Retrieved from www.bbc.com/future/article/20160331-why-are-we-eternally-fascinated-by-serial-killers

Booth, H. (2021). A Criminological Analysis of Notorious Serial Killers in the United States. Unpublished Thesis.

Brand, L. (2021). Siren of San Quentin shop. Personal website. Retrieved from https://sirenofsanquentin.threadless.com/

Branson, A. (2013). African American serial killers: Over-represented yet under acknowledged. *The Howard Journal of Criminal Justice*. 52(1):1-18.

Brown, B. (2021). David Tennant nominated for an International Emmy Award. BBC America. Retrieved from www.bbcamerica.com/blogs/david-tennant-nominated-for-an-international-emmy-award--62988

Cable News Network. (2002). Sniper keeps D.C. area on alert. CNN. Retrieved from http://transcripts.cnn.com/TRANSCRIPTS/0210/08/i_ins.01.html

Cain, S. (2019). Hallie Rubenhold: "Jack the Ripper's victims have just become corpses. Can't we do better?" The Guardian. Retrieved from www.theguardian.com/books/2019/mar/01/hallie-rubenhold-jack-the-ripper-victims

Chan, H. (2019). Case 10—The Milwaukee cannibal-murderer: The case of Jeffrey Dahmer (1978–1991; USA). In A Global Casebook of Sexual Homicide (pp. 161–180). Springer. Retrieved from https://link.springer.com/chapter/10.1007/978-981-13-8859-0_11

Charles, D. (2021). TikToker discovers home for sale that comes with its own private prison in the basement. Brobible. Retrieved from https://brobible.com/culture/article/tiktok-home-for-sale-prison-basement/

Clark, J., & Palattella, E. (2017). Mania and Marjorie Diehl-Armstrong: Inside the Mind of a Female Serial Killer. Rowman & Littlefield.

Crime Control Digest. (1990). FBI developing standards to help police detect potential serial killers. *Crime Control Digest*. 24(8):6–7.

Culhane, S., Walker, S., & Hildebrand, M. (2019). Serial homicide perpetrators' self-reported psychopathy and criminal thinking. *Journal of Police and Criminal Psychology*. 34:1–13. Retrieved from https://link.springer.com/article/10.1007/s11896-017-9245-x

Cullen, E. (2020). American Evil: The Psychology of Serial Killers. Waterside Press.

Daily Star. (2021). Woman branded a "serial killer" after cutting sandwich in "chaotic" way. Retrieved from www.dailystar.co.uk/real-life/woman-branded-serial-killer-after-25026410# comments-wrapper

Dawson, L. (2021). Fearless 4-year-old girl runs into the arms of Michael Myers in viral video. Today. Retrieved from www.today.com/popculture/fearless-4-year-old-girl-runs-arms-michael-myers-viral-t232260

DeLisi, M. (2015). Mayhem by occupation: On the relevance of criminal careers to sexual homicide offenders. In A. Blokland and Patrick Lussier (Eds.), Sex Offenders: A Criminal Career Approach (pp. 219–229). Wiley Blackwell. Retrieved from https://books.google.com/books?hl=en&lr=&id=87lJCgAAQBAJ&oi=fnd&pg=PA219&dq=DeLisi,+M.+(2015).+Mayhem+by+occupation&ots=8gQyDj3AvP&sig=JYyURcuaC2LMZs_jRhEDOFlpxR0#v=onepage&q=DeLisi%2C%20M.%20(2015).%20Mayhem%20by%20occupation&f=false; https://scholar.google.com/scholar?hl=en&as_sdt=0%2C47&q=DeLisi%2C+M.+%282015%29.+Mayhem+by+occupation&btnG=

Depue, R. (1986). An American response to an era of violence. *FBI Law Enforcement Bulletin*. 55:2–5.

Diaz, A. (2021). Chad Michael Murray cast as yet another "hot" Ted Bundy. New York Post. Retrieved from https://nypost.com/2021/05/26/internet-slams-casting-of-yet-another-hot-ted-bundy/

Dickson, E.J. (2021). All She Wanted Was to Dance. Then TikTok Spun a Conspiracy Theory That She's a Serial Killer. Rolling Stone. Retrieved from https://www.rollingstone.com/culture/culture-features/tiktok-true-crime-conspiracy-theory-fake-1264687/

Dietrich, E., & Hall, T. (2010). The allure of the serial killer. In S. Waller (Ed.), *Serial Killers and Philosophy*. Wiley-Blackwell. Retrieved from https://philpapers.org/archive/DIETAO-3

Dietz, P. (1986). Mass, serial and sensational homicides. *Bulletin of the New York Academy of Medicine*. 62(5):477–491.

Dilly, H. (2021). Theoretical Analysis of the Biological Basis for Serial Killers' Cooling-Off Periods. Unpublished Thesis.

Egger, S. (2002). The Killers Among Us: An Examination of Serial Murder and Its Investigation. Prentice Hall.

Ehrlich, B. (2021). Why were there so many serial killers between 1970 and 2000 – and where did they go? Rolling Stone. Retrieved from www.rollingstone.com/culture/culture-features/serial-killers-1970s-2000s-murders-1121705/

Federal Bureau of Investigation. (1992). Ted Bundy multiagency investigative team report. Retrieved from www.santarosahitchhikermurders.com/docs/Bundy_Multiagency_Team_Report.pdf

Ferguson, C. (2021). Detection Avoidance in Homicide: Debates, Explanations and Responses. Routledge.

Foreman, A. (2021). Untangling true crime. Mashable. Retrieved from https://mashable.com/feature/ethics-of-true-crime

Goyal, S. (2021). "LSD" Actor Anshuman Jha wins Best Actor-Critics Award for playing a serial killer in "Midnight Delhi". Outlook. Retrieved from www.outlookindia.com/website/story/entertainment-news-lsd-actor-anshuman-jha-wins-best-actor-critics-award-for-playing-a-serial-killer-in-midnight-delhi/395918

Greep, M. (2020). Criminologist reveals how serial killer Dennis Nilsen would "toy" with him because he "fancied him" – and says "narcissistic" murderer would have "loved" that David Tennant is playing him in ITV drama. Daily Mail.com. Retrieved from www.dailymail.co.uk/femail/article-8730631/Criminologist-reveals-serial-killer-Dennis-Nilsen-toy-fancied-him.html

Henson, J., & Olson, L. (2010). The monster within: How male serial killers discursively manage their stigmatized identities. *Communication Quarterly*. 58(3):341–364.

Hickey, E. (2013). Serial Murderers and Their Victims. Cengage Learning.

Hickey, E., & Harris, B. (2013). Serial killing. In J. A. Siegel, P. J. Saukko, and M. M. Houck (Eds.), Encyclopedia of Forensic Sciences (pp. 197–201). Academic Press Waltham.

Hickey, E. (2014). The evolution of serial murder as a social phenomenon in American society: An update. *Academy of Criminal Justice Sciences*. XXXVIIII(3):12–16. Retrieved from https://cdn.ymaws.com/www.acjs.org/resource/resmgr/ACJSToday/ACJSToday May2014.pdf

Hodgkinson, S., Prins, H., & Stuart-Bennett, J. (2017). Monsters, madmen … and myths: A critical review of the serial killing literature. *Aggression and Violent Behavior*. 34:282–289.

Holmes, R., & Holmes, S. (2001). Murder in America. Sage.

Homant, R., & Kennedy, D. (2014). Understanding serial sexual murder: a biopsychosocial approach. In W. Petherick (Ed.), Profiling and Serial Crime (3rd ed., pp. 341–372). Anderson.

Honda Fit TV Commercial. (2015). Clocks, wrestlers, creeps and centaurs. iSpot.tv. Retrieved from www.ispot.tv/ad/7MBb/2015-honda-fit-clocks-wrestlers-creeps-and-centaurs

House of Horrors & Haunted Catacombs. (2021). Escape the serial killer. Locked-Up Escape Games. Website. Retrieved from www.locked-upescapegames.com/escape-a-serial-killer.html

James, V., & Gossett, J. (2018). Of monsters and men: Exploring serial murderers' discourses of neutralization. *Deviant Behavior*. 39(9):1120–1139.

James, V. (2019). Denying the darkness: Exploring the discourses of neutralization of Bundy, Gacy, and Dahmer. *Societies*. 9(2):46.

Jenkins, P. (1994). Using Murder: The Social Construction of Serial Homicide. Routledge.

Jenkins, P. (2002). Catch me before I kill more: Seriality as modern monstrosity. *Cultural Analysis*. 3(2):1–17.

John Jay College of Criminal Justice/CUNY. (2002). Once again, a year for serial killers. *Law Enforcement News*. XXVIII:589–590.

Kaminsky, M. (2020). Serial Killer Trivia. Ulysses Press.

Kaplan, E. (2017). Is "serial offender" killing homeless men? *Albuquerque Journal*. Retrieved from www.abqjournal.com/1104656/is-serial-offender-killing-homeless-man.html

Kernan, P. (2021). "You are evil," judge tells admitted serial killer. Times Leader. Retrieved fromwww.timesleader.com/news/1511023/you-are-evil-judge-tells-admitted-serial-killer/amp

Kiger, K. (1990). The darker figure of crime: The serial murder enigma. In S. Egger (Ed.), Serial Murder: An Elusive Phenomenon (pp. 35–52). Praeger.

Kissel, B., Zebrowski, H., & Parks, M. (2020). The Last Book on the Left: Stories of Murder and Mayhem from History's Most Notorious Serial Killers. Houghton Mifflin Harcourt.

Kohn, E. (2017). How Disney Star Ross Lynch landed the role of serial killer Jeffrey Dahmer. IndieWire.Retrievedfromwww.indiewire.com/2017/11/ross-lynch-my-friend-dahmer-jeffrey-dahmer-disney-1201894652/

Kreps, D. (2021). Buffalo Bill's house from "Silence of the Lambs" opens for overnight guests. Rolling Stone. Retrieved from www.rollingstone.com/movies/movie-news/buffalo-bills-house-silence-of-the-lambs-opens-guest-lodging-1219816/

Kutner, M. (2017). Seth rich update: DNC staffer murdered by serial killer, not in botched robbery, report claims. Newsweek. Retrieved from www.newsweek.com/seth-rich-murder-report-profiling-project-627634

Lancaster, K. (2021). The saga continues: Here's what's new in the ongoing Armie Hammer scandal. Grazia. Retrieved from https://graziamagazine.com/articles/armie-hammer-story/

Lavin, T. (2016). A true-crime veteran on our fascination with serial killers. The New Yorker. Retrieved from www.newyorker.com/books/page-turner/a-true-crime-veteran-on-our-fascination-with-serial-killers

Leishman, R. (2021). Venom isn't thrilled about dealing with "a red one" in new venom: Let there be carnage trailer. The Mary Sue. Retrieved from www.themarysue.com/new-venom-let-there-be-carnage-trailer/

Lester, D. (1995). Serial Killers: The Insatiable Passion. Philadelphia: Charles Press.

Leyton, E. (2001). Hunting Humans: The Rise of the Modern Multiple Murderer. McClelland & Stewart.

Li, D. (2021). Robert Durst found guilty of murdering close friend Susan Berman in 2000. NBC News. Retrieved from www.cnbc.com/2021/09/17/robert-durst-found-guilty-of-murdering-close-friend-susan-berman-in-2000.html

McDonell-Parry, A. (2018). Inside one man's serial-killer unification theory. Rolling Stone. Retrieved from www.rollingstone.com/culture/culture-features/inside-one-mans-serial-killer-unification-theory-630621/

McGeorge, A. (2021). Happy Corbin on human skulls, FBI dream job and how serial killer fascination helps WWE career. Metro. Retrieved from https://metro.co.uk/2021/09/22/wwe-happy-corbin-on-human-skulls-fbi-dream-and-serial-killer-artwork-15301036/

Michaud, S. (1986). The F.B.I.'S new psyche squad. The New York Times Magazine. Retrieved from www.nytimes.com/1986/10/26/magazine/the-fbi-s-new-psyche-squad.html

Morton, R., & Hilts, M. (2008). Serial Murder: Multi-disciplinary Perspectives for Investigators. National Center for the Analysis of Violent Crime.

Muller, D. (2000). Criminal profiling: Real science or just wishful thinking? *Homicide Studies*. 4(3):234–264.

Norris, J. (1989). Serial Killers. Anchor.

O'Brien, J. (2021). Steven's odd habits leave 90 Day Fiance fans feeling weird. Monsters & Critics. Retrieved from www.monstersandcritics.com/tv/reality-tv/stevens-odd-habits-leave-90-day-fiance-fans-feeling-weird/

Ormseth, M. (2021). Father and son arrested in connection with 3 shooting deaths in East Los Angeles. Los Angeles Times. Retrieved from www.latimes.com/california/story/2021-09-23/father-son-arrested-in-connection-with-3-east-l-a-killings

Osifo, E. (2021a). 18 serial killer facts that are equally interesting and haunting. Buzzfeed. Retrieved from www.buzzfeed.com/ehisosifo1/interesting-horrifying-serial-killer-facts

Osifo, E. (2021b). Here are 21 awful couples who committed atrocious crimes against humanity. Buzzfeed. Retrieved from www.buzzfeed.com/ehisosifo1/serial-killer-couples

Petreca, V., Burgess, A., Stone, M., & Brucato, G. (2020). Dismemberment and mutilation: A data-driven exploration of patterns, motives, and styles. *Journal of Forensic Sciences*. 65(3):888-896.

Pettigrew, M. (2019a). Serial killing and homosexual necrophilia, an exploration. *The Journal of Forensic Psychiatry & Psychology*. 30(3):409–418.

Pettigrew, M. (2019b). Corpse dismemberment and a necrofetishist. *Journal of Forensic Sciences*. 64(3):934–937.

Pettigrew, M. (2019c). Fantasy, opportunity, homicide: Testing classifications of necrophilic behaviour. *Journal of Police and Criminal Psychology*. 34(1):14–22.

Pettigrew, M. (2020a). The sexually sadistic properties of necrophilia, in the context of serial killing, a case study. *Journal of Police and Criminal Psychology*. 35(4):472–479.
Pettigrew, M. (2020b). Confessions of a serial killer: A neutralisation analysis. *Homicide Studies*. 24(1):69–84.
Phillips, K. (2017). A woman married a paroled murderer. Years later, he killed all her children. The Washington Post. Retrieved from www.washingtonpost.com/news/true-crime/wp/2017/03/08/a-woman-married-a-paroled-murderer-years-later-he-killed-all-her-children/
Pino, N. (2005). Serial offending and the criminal events perspective. *Homicide Studies*. 9(2):109–148.
Robb, A. (2019). The women transfixed by violent crime. NewStatesman. Retrieved from www.newstatesman.com/savage-appetites-four-true-stories-women-crime-cbsession-rachel-monroe-review
Rodrigo, C. M. (2018). Ted Cruz wishes happy Halloween with Zodiac Killer letter. The Hill. Retrieved from https://thehill.com/blogs/in-the-know/in-the-know/414120-ted-cruz-wishes-happy-halloween-with-zodiac-killer-letter
Rosario, S. (2017). Dugan to amateur detectives: Stop spreading Seminole Heights rumors. WTSP. Retrieved from https://twitter.com/10TampaBay/status/931727441999093761
Rosewood, J. (2019). The Serial Killer Coloring Book. Independently Published.
Ruzsonyi, P. (2017). Serial killers on the other side of the bars: Bestial humans—human beasts. *Academic and Applied Research in Military and Public Management Science*. 16(3):5–34.
Ryan, K. (2020). This business made a killing by mailing murder mysteries. Inc. com. Retrieved from www.inc.com/magazine/202009/kevin-j-ryan/hunt-killer-murder-mystery-subscription-box-game-2020-inc5000.html
Sarachan, R. (2019). Death becomes us True Crime Festival comes To New York City this March. Forbes. Retrieved from www.forbes.com/sites/risasarachan/2019/02/28/death-becomes-us-true-crime-festival-comes-to-new-york-city-this-march/?sh=61fb15e51857
Sarteschi, C. (2016). Mass and Serial Murder in America. Springer.
Saunders, J. (2020). Jack the Ripper unmasked: Note could finally expose serial killer's identity. Express. Retrieved from www.express.co.uk/news/uk/1323900/jack-the-ripper-news-serial-killer-crime-london-real-murderer-note-history-tv-theory-spt
Schechter, H. (1996). The A to Z Encyclopedia of Serial Killers. Simon and Schuster.
Seewer, J., & Welsh-Huggins, A. (2009). Alleged Ohio Serial Killer Rare among Mass Killers. The Associated Press. Retrieved from www.courant.com/sdut-alleged-ohio-serial-killer-rare-among-mass-killers-2009nov07-story.html
Selna, E. (2021). Treat your true crime friend to a Valentine's Day card fit for a serial killer. Fansided. Retrieved from https://1428elm.com/2021/02/04/true-crime-serial-killer-valentines-day-card/
Seltzer, M. (1998). Serial Killers: Death and Life in America's Wound Culture. Psychology Press.
Serial Killer Calendar. (2021). Serial killer calendar. Website. Retrieved from www.serialkillercalendar.com/
Serial Killer Shop. (2021). Serial killer shop. Website. Retrieved from www.serialkillershop.com
Shanafelt, R., & Pino, N. (2013). Evil and the common life: Towards a wider perspective on serial killing and atrocities. In R. Atkinson and S. Winlow (Eds.), New Directions in Crime and Deviancy (pp. 252–273). Routledge.

Sword and Scale. (2019). Our new serial killer shot glasses will be shipping soon. Facebook. Retrieved from www.facebook.com/swordandscale/posts/our-new-serial-killer-shot-glasses-will-be-shipping-soon-this-four-part-set-fill/2339520116283179/

The Forensic Examiner. (2010). The FBI behavioral science unit's evil minds. *Research Museum*. 19(3):18–19. Retrieved from https://issuu.com/acfei.media/docs/fall2010

The Onion. (2021). Self-learning Netflix algorithm produces Jeffrey Dahmer stand-up special. The Onion. Retrieved from www.theonion.com/self-learning-netflix-algorithm-produces-jeffrey-dahmer-1847519550

Thomas, M. (2021). Kobe Bryant admitted he seemed "psychotic" when he confessed a fictional serial killer played a role in his pregame ritual. Sportscasting. Retrieved from www.sportscasting.com/kobe-bryant-admitted-seemed-psychotic-confessed-fictional-serial-killer-played-role-pregame-ritual/

Thompson, J. (2021). Former Ole Miss student Brandon Theesfeld pleads guilty to killing Kostial, sentenced to life. The Oxford Eagle. Retrieved from www.oxfordeagle.com/2021/08/27/former-ole-miss-student-pleads-guilty-to-killing-ally-kostial-sentenced-to-life-in-prison/

Tiffany, K. (2016). Who called Ted Cruz the Zodiac killer, why, and is he? The Verge. Retrieved from www.theverge.com/2016/2/26/11120000/ted-cruz-zodiac-killer-why-evidence-theory

TMZ Live. [@TMZLive]. (2021, August 12). Ever wonder how some of America's most notorious serial killers evaded capture for as long as they did? Retired FBI profiler Mark Safarik came on TMZ Live to talk about his new A&E docuseries "Invisible Monsters: Serial Killers in America." [Tweet]. Twitter. Retrieved from https://twitter.com/TMZLive/status/1425816334072303627

Trojan, C., Salfati, C. G., & Schanz, K. (2019). Overkill, we know it when we see it: examining definitions of excessive injury in homicide research. *Journal of Criminal Psychology*. 9(2):61–74.

Van Zandt, C., & Ether, S. (1994). The real silence of the lambs. *Police Chief*. 61(4):45–52.

Vronsky, P. (2018). Sons of Cain: A History of Serial Killers from the Stone Age to the Present. Penguin.

Warf, B., & Waddell, C. (2002). Heinous spaces, perfidious places: The sinister landscapes of serial killers. *Social & Cultural Geography*. 3(3):323–345.

Warren, J., Dietz, P., & Hazelwood, R. (2013). The collectors: Serial sexual offenders who preserve evidence of their crimes. *Aggression and Violent Behavior*. 18(6):666–672.

Warwick, A. (2006). The scene of the crime: Inventing the serial killer. *Social & Legal Studies*. 15(4):552–569.

Western Evil. (2021). Serial killer mugshot dress. Westernevil.com. Retrieved from https://westernevil.com/products/serial-killer-mugshot-dress

Wiest, J. (2011). Creating Cultural Monsters: Serial Murder in America. CRC Press.

Wiest, J. (2016). Casting cultural monsters: Representations of serial killers in US and UK news media. *Howard Journal of Communications*. 27(4):327–346.

Wilkinson, A. (2017). The serial killer detector. The New Yorker. Retrieved from www.newyorker.com/magazine/2017/11/27/the-serial-killer-detector

Wilson, D. (2021). Criminologist reviews serial killers from movies & TV. Vanity Fair. Retrieved from www.vanityfair.com/video/watch/reviews-criminologist-reviews-serial-killers-from-movies-and-tv

Wired Tradecraft. (2019). Former FBI agent explains criminal profiling. Wired. Retrieved from www.wired.com/video/watch/wired-tradecraft-former-fbi-analyst-explains-criminal-profiling?c=series

Woollaston, V. (2015). How to spot a serial killer: Criminologists reveal five key traits the most notorious murderers have in common. MailOnline. Retrieved from www.dailymail.co.uk/sciencetech/article-3169359/How-spot-serial-killer-Criminologists-reveal-five-key-traits-common-notorious-murderers.html

Wright, J., & Hensley, C. (2003). From animal cruelty to serial murder: Applying the graduation hypothesis. *International Journal of Offender Therapy and Comparative Criminology*. 47(1):71–88.

Yaksic, E. (2015). Addressing the challenges and limitations of utilizing data to study serial homicide. *Crime Psychology Review*. 1(1):108–134.

Yaksic, E. (2018). The folly of counting bodies: Using regression to transgress the state of serial murder classification systems. *Aggression and Violent Behavior*. 43:26–32.

Yaksic, E. (2019). Who is culpable in the promulgation of serial killer myths and stereotypes? The role of researchers, practitioners, law enforcement officers and the media in sustaining the serial murder entertainment complex. Medium. Retrieved from https://medium.com/@EnzoAYaksic/who-is-culpable-in-the-promulgation-of-serial-killer-myths-and-stereotypes-22170079abad

Yaksic, E., Allely, C., De Silva, R., Smith-Inglis, M., Konikoff, D., Ryan, K., Gordon, D., Denisov, E., & Keatley, D. (2019). Detecting a decline in serial homicide: Have we banished the devil from the details? *Cogent Social Sciences*. 5(1):1–23.

Yaksic, E., Harrison, M., Konikoff, D., Mooney, R., Allely, C., De Silva, R., Matykiewicz, B., Inglis, M., Giannangelo, S., Daniels, S., & Sarteschi, C. (2021). A heuristic study of the similarities and differences in offender characteristics across potential and successful serial sexual homicide offenders. *Behavioral Sciences & the Law*. 39(4):428–449.

Yancey-Bragg, N. (2019). Jack the Ripper identified by DNA evidence, forensic scientists claim. USA Today. Retrieved from www.usatoday.com/story/news/nation/2019/03/18/dna-evidence-reveals-identity-jack-ripper-scientists-claim/3206856002/

2

WHAT DO WE KNOW ABOUT SERIAL MURDER AND HOW DO WE KNOW IT?

Explanations for Serial Murder

The quest to understand repeat murderers began before the concept was termed and its offenders categorized. Although serial murder has occurred throughout history (Felton, 2021) – from the deaths attributed to werewolves, vampires, and witches, to those of tyrants, aristocrats, bandits, pirates, cannibal clans, and gunslingers (Vronsky, 2018) – for reasons such as physiological needs, sex, attention, and respect (Lester, 1995), a newly interconnected and industrialized world provided more opportunities for dejected and mobile men to victimize others. Mutilated bodies dumped on the sides of roadways signaled the emergence of a supposedly new type of killer, one whose crimes would be cataloged as extreme, "motiveless" violence.

Researchers grew curious of the etiology of serial murder and wondered what type of environment would spawn individuals with no regard for societal boundaries who existed only to bring about chaos and destruction. A litany of theories explained the phenomenon as a mixture of forces that arose out of biology, individual agency, and social construction: histories of abuse, depersonalization, alienation, valuation of vengeance-seeking, and sexual conquest (Shanafelt & Pino, 2014). Could the loss of values and hope for the future that occurs in radical cultural transitions have created the serial murderer (Vronsky, 2004)? Did a crumbling civilization, shrinking families, growing anonymous cities, failing marriages, and unavailable parents (Leyton, 2001) birth them? As people grew farther apart, they could develop secret lives dedicated to killing for enjoyment, sexual gratification, or retaliation (Pino, 2005). A generation of emotionally unavailable men who were economically ruined and war ravaged in the 1930s and 40s may have gestated disconnected outcasts inspired by pulp magazines, pornography, and the Bible who would reject social norms and become serial murderers (Vronsky, 2018). Others

DOI: 10.4324/9781003130567-2

believe that serial murder is a "syndrome" of symptoms of aggressive behavior (Norris, 1989, p. 37) with its own logic (Seltzer, 1998).

Untangling fact from fiction has proven difficult. Among ever-shortening attention spans and heavy competition for an audience today, information on dense topics is distilled to make it more palatable and quicker to consume. People unknowingly come to favor stereotypes and myths as a shortcut to knowledge. But breakthroughs in thought are often found in the crevices of contrasting narratives. From the first use of the term *serial murder* in the 1930s (Harbort & Mokros, 2001), to statements about the demographics of modern-day offenders, questionable data have been used to inform on serial murder. For that reason, sources often include cases that are well known, exceptional, or have an abundance of available information (Wiest, 2011). Online streaming services continue the trend began by books in oversaturating society with the analysis of the same offenders (Lester, 1995)[1] as their offerings rehash cases from the bygone era known as the "Golden Age of Serial Murder." Viewers are introduced not only to offenders who behaved differently from their modern-day counterparts but also to scientists whose theories – such as the notion that all serial murderers have dissociative identity disorder (DID) (Gleiberman, 2020) – are outmoded.

This outmoded science promotes a false sense of security and the belief that potential victims will be safe if they avoid people with certain traits. But even though serial murder is examined from the perspectives of psychologists, anthropologists, criminologists, geneticists, sociologists, biologists, and phenomenologists (Hickey, 2013) across sociology, psychology, culture, and biology, offenders do not fit within one framework. Many theories "combine more than one discipline" (Egger, 2002, pp. 15–16) as the cause of serial murder can be found in an offender's behavior, environment, genetics, psychology, and biochemistry (Vronsky, 2018, p. 63). The underpinnings of what could be influencing serial murderers seem to be clinical (antisocial personality, psychopathic traits, dissociation, doubling, narcissism, posttraumatic stress, depression), biological (physical abnormalities, neurological impairment, brain injuries, genetics), and environmental (esteem development, sense of self, issues with control, compulsions and rituals) (Giannangelo, 1996). When considering etiology, a likely cluster of proximate variables (e.g., developmental milieu, economic stress, personality, hormones, neurological functioning) must be considered (Harrison, Hughes, & Gott, 2019).

In spite of most literature published since the 1980s lacking empirical basis (Egger, 2002), researchers were able to deduce that: (1) the source of serial murder seems to be psychogenic (i.e., the offender's norms, values, and beliefs); (2) their motives have an intrinsic focus (i.e., the homicide results from the offender's desire); and (3) their behavior is oriented toward psychological gain. Sociogenic factors can enhance the likelihood of serial murder (Egger, 2002) due to learned behavior and exposure to cultural violence, but many serial murderers possess characteristics that are "favorable to socially approved behavior" (Holmes & Holmes, 2001, p. 32). Serial murderers are a combination of traits and experiences that are so varied that if any one of them is altered, the person may not have become a serial murderer

(Shanafelt & Pino, 2014). These offenders may each be on a different trajectory from one another, but they all end up walking the same pathway toward serial murder.

Biological predisposition can also interact with familial and sociocultural factors to support an environment in which serial murderers are created (Mitchell, 1997) where trauma and biology interact to produce stress, the relief from which is associated with gratification. Biologists attribute serial murder to brain abnormalities, genetic traits, or abnormalities caused by trauma (Egger, 2002). Genetic structures and biological subsystems do not determine behavior as they are dependent on the social environment and work in interaction with it (Shanafelt & Pino, 2013). Some suggest that serial murderers have mood disorders, but serial murderers have not been found to have violent patterns of uncontrollable behavior in the absence of provocation. The idea that autism causes serial murder gained momentum in recent years, but researchers note that if autism does play a role it is in conjunction with a complex combination of neurodevelopmental and environmental factors (Allely, Wilson, Minnis, Thompson, Yaksic, & Gillberg, 2017). Neurology cannot fully explain why people kill, since biological influences do not control behavior or predetermine outcomes (Egger, 2002). The theory that serial murderers have multiple personalities holds little merit as there "do not appear to be any well-documented cases of DID in serial killing" (Hickey, 2013, p. 79). Chemical imbalances or pathological disorders cannot explain serial murder with any certainty since offenders are made through their habits, ideas, and experiences, rationalize their violence through self-talk, and actively turn off empathy signals (Shanafelt & Pino, 2014). Williams (2021) points out that serial murderers who kill for enjoyment or pleasure must first rationalize and justify their desires by talking themselves into doing so. Biogenic explanations cannot yield answers as serial murder cannot be explained by "blows to the head received in childhood, or defective genes" or by psychogenic causes since most serial murderers are neither insane nor psychotic (Holmes & Holmes, 2001).

One popular theory posits that three maladaptive behaviors emerge in childhood – animal torture, enuresis, and fire-setting – and are meaningful, with one media personality identifying them as the "serial killer trifecta" (O'Neill, 2021). Forensic psychiatrist Michael Stone (2009) claims that one in 20 serial murderers engage in these maladaptive behaviors, but these are not good predictors of later adult violence (Hickey, 2013) as the majority of children with these symptoms do not commit murders as adults (Leary, Southard, Hill, & Ashman, 2017). Others proclaim that serial murderers inevitably graduate from animal cruelty to violence toward humans, but research also disputes this assumption (Arluke, Levin, Luke, & Ascione, 1999). Stone (2009) further supposes that serial murder is the result of a combination of nature, nurture, and unpredictable situations such as genetic risk for psychopathy, adoption, head injuries, substance abuse, parental brutality, father absence, maternal neglect, sexual molestation, low socioeconomic status, and mental illness. Stone believes that many serial murderers have attention-deficit disorder. Stone also postulates that serial murderers kill because they hate their mothers (a myth that began with highly dramatized accounts of a few select instances) (Hickey, 2013) and that many infamous serial murderers committed "serial matricide," symbolically killing their mothers.[2] The positing of several theories by one individual suggests that serial murder has a multifaceted etiology but that it is currently unknown.

In his analysis of modern serial murderers, Haggerty (2009, p. 170) points out that cultural and institutional factors shape the dynamics of this form of killing and argues that modernity provides the "institutional frameworks, motivations and structure of opportunities for serial killing" through the media, anonymity, mean/ends rationality, denigration, accessible victims, and utopian aspirations. Wiest (2011) concurs, stating that "biological and psychological explanations do not account for cultural differences in the incidence of serial murder" (p. 86) as the biographies of serial murderers ignore the historical cultural context (Hickey, 2013). Wilson, Yardley, and Lynes, (2015, p. 25) demonstrate that scholars write about serial murderers using the "medico-psychological" tradition (which refers to the biological, genetic, and psychological roots of murder) and generally overlook a "structural approach" that deals with culture, values, and how serial murderers "exploit fractured communities." That there are discernable differences between the offending patterns of male and female serial murderers that revolve around their historical hunter/gatherer roles supports this assertion (Harrison, Hughes, & Gott, 2019). From this anthropological standpoint, serial murder is an equalizer that dismantles what impedes the serial murderer's lives; these crimes are revenge for a failure to realize ambition, an overreaction to the disappointments that most everyone deals with (Leyton, 2001). Serial murder could also be a way to deal with pressures of daily life, a "solution to deprivation [which] is the provocation for frustration" (Egger, 2002, p. 37). Given that serial murders are committed by those with predetermined factors who are then subjected to specific life experiences (such as the absence of infant bonding, loneliness, isolation from peers, overbearing parents, rejection, traumatic abuse, and family instability) (Vronsky, 2004), and that this lack of emotional bonding and trauma continues into adulthood (Shanafelt & Pino, 2014), serial murderers lack self-esteem, are isolated, are maladjusted, and have poor coping skills, which makes their lives difficult (Vronsky, 2004). These difficulties lead to struggles with an internal social crisis when they become aware that their dreams are out of reach (Leyton, 2001).

These theories go beyond the idea that lack of self-control and an unwillingness to delay gratification lead to serial murder (Egger, 2002). In fact, Hall and Wilson (2014, p. 645) are confident that serial murderers are on a quest for "special liberty" and that their actions result from an engrained belief that they should be allowed to act out the drives of envy, prejudice, hatred, sadism, and hedonistic pleasure. This feeling of entitlement derives from inadequacies in other aspects of the serial murderer's personality. As Hickey (2013, pp. 99, 103, 137) states:

> The underlying pathology of serial murderers is frustration, anger, hostility, feelings of inadequacy, and low self-esteem. People who feel good about themselves do not kill others. The better a person's self-concept, the less need

> he or she has to control and dominate others. A common characteristic of most, if not all, serial offenders is feelings of self-doubt and worthlessness.

The psychopathological profile of the serial murderer culminates in problematic behaviors (e.g., social isolation, chronic lying) that lead to relational issues (familial and marital disputes) and anxiety (James & Proulx, 2016). Dysfunctionality in socialization manifests as social alienation and maladjustment (a deficiency in maintaining bonds to others, faulty conflict competency, lack of responsibility, egotistic tendencies, low frustration tolerance, reduced impulse control, and a hostile emotional state), which are the precursors to serial murder (Harbort & Mokros, 2001). These behaviors and conditions contribute to the offender's underlying antagonistic attitude, cantankerous personality, and overall ill-tempered makeup. Serial murderer James Childers, for example, was quoted in his 21-page confession as citing depression for making someone "become a serial killer … a monster" (Smith, 2010, p. 18). The various circumstances that Childers confronted over his lifespan contributed to his negative outlook. While not "true psychopaths," serial murderers kill as a result of a "general proneness to deviancy that pervades their lives as a whole" (Hickey, Walters, Drislane, Palumbo, & Patrick, 2018, pp. 575–576). When combined with lengthy arrest records, the offender's peers and police begin to notice something "off" about the individual. Although some deception is necessary to allay suspicion (as operating in the context of others means someone is usually monitoring actions) (Shanafelt & Pino, 2013), few are willing to acknowledge that such reputations could translate into a series of murders. But the likelihood of an offender receiving consistent oversight of their activities narrows when acquaintances become apathetic to individuals, like serial murderers, who embrace meanness. Without normal social connectedness, serial murderers become hypersensitive to humiliation, rejection, and insults, are callously exploitive when seeking to attain their goals (Reavis, 2011; Wolf & Lavezzi, 2007), and respond with reactive aggression (Leach & Meloy, 1999; Ostrosky-Solís, Vélez-García, Santana-Vargas, Pérez, & Ardila, 2008). One can understand how male serial murderers are deemed to have "low mate value" (Harrison, Hughes, & Gott, 2019, p. 305) and must sometimes acquire what they desire through nefarious means.

Serial murderers select killing from an array of available paths (Wiest, 2011) as they are aware of cultural values but fail to attain them through legitimate means. Serial murder may be an expression of masculinity as men who feel powerless due to their tenuous position in the social structure and may feel entitled to subordinate women to overcome their embarrassments and attain power (Wiest, 2011). Many serial murderers hold violence in high regard, as they admire other serial murderers, violent films, and violent fantasies, and use it as a means of control. Serial murder provides a sense of accomplishment, power, fame, and enjoyment, and engenders feelings of invincibility and superiority given that offenders believe that there has to be a high level of knowledge and skill necessary to kill successfully. Serial murder also increases the offender's level of connectedness to their senses through thrill-seeking and risk-taking behaviors. Serial murderers of lower social status target victims who are of even lower status as they are viewed as controllable while success in dominating others helps boost their confidence (Wiest, 2011). Wiest (2011, p. 87) calls for an examination of "cultural values transmitted through socialization to understand how culture fosters the creation of serial murderers." The United States, for example, created a culture where boundaries are adjustable; violence is acceptable; extreme offending is rewarded; risks and thrills are emphasized; power and control are accentuated; and the onus of success is placed directly on the individual. It is here, among these variables, where the serial murderer can be successful (Wiest, 2011).

Dietz provides one possible explanation for how serial murderers are created:

> Start with an abusive, criminal father and a hysterical, alcoholic mother; torture the boy as erotically as possible; have the naked mother spank him and sleep with him until age 12; let the mother appear promiscuous while condemning prostitutes; leave detective magazines around the house for him to find and fantasize over; and encourage him to watch slasher films and violence against glamourous women.
>
> *Egger, 2002, p. 31*

Although barely any serial murderers experience the scenario exactly as described above, offenders with a life history of abuse, antisocial and/or criminal behavior, and sexual deviance can come to live in a dream world after experiencing a "lost sense of self, an inadequacy of identity, and a feeling of no control" (Giannangelo, 1996, pp. 19, 48, 53). Serial murderers make a role for this fantasy world alongside fragmented identity formation, addictive patterns, the need for power and excitement, ritual, and fetishism (Shanafelt & Pino, 2014). Once the serial murderer finds solace by retreating into their imagination, they connect with a desire for omnipotence and become dependent on this fantasy world to feed the sense of self (Malizia, 2017). The literature mentions a serial murderer who "only became vibrant when he was on the prowl and when he was activating his killing fantasy" (Shanafelt & Pino, 2014, p. 101). These processes all lead the offender to internalize and condition themselves to become a serial murderer through fantastical thinking, allowing "an addictive cycle of ritualistic violence to deepen and continue unabated" (Shanafelt & Pino, 2014, p. 106). This is instrumental in serial murderers who create their own killing selves because it can familiarize them with the idea of violence and make it more ordinary by normalizing aggression (Shanafelt & Pino, 2014).

In a cross-case analysis, Egger (2002, pp. 85, 231) found that each subject experienced childhood trauma, but he cautions that "it is impossible to know if victimization in childhood is a contributing factor" in the creation of a serial murderer. Some researchers found that different types of abuse affect later typologies and murder behaviors (Marono, Reid, Yaksic, & Keatley, 2020). Other researchers believe that abuse may be overemphasized given that many offenders experienced little or no abuse or stressors during early development (Allely, 2020). Hickey (2013, p. 137) asserts that many serial murderers experience rejection in the form of an unstable, abusive home, but other factors are involved that combine to create a "synergistic response" since instability in the home is not sufficient to trigger homicidal behavior. Although the cyclical experience of serial offenders reviewed in the Trauma-Control Model begins with fantasies facilitated by pornography and alcohol, it is reinforced by traumatization, and ends in stalking and violence: serial murderers are not born to kill any more than they are to develop homicidal ideation from pornography or violent television programs, or to kill due to insanity (Hickey, 2013). To complicate matters, there are serial murderers like William Gibson who claim that experiences in childhood have no bearing on a murderer's decision to kill:

> Everybody thinks when you do the type of stuff I did, cutting people up, the egregious stuff—people automatically think it's because you had a bad childhood. They think you were molested or ask you if you started fires. I didn't do any of that. I had a perfectly normal childhood.
>
> *Ozimek, 2018*

In summary, serial murder is the result of a process involving socialization, experience, fantasy, and random opportunity (Shanafelt & Pino, 2013). There is no "perfect storm" of factors that reliably gestate a serial murderer because serial murder is primarily an exercise of choice (Egger, 2002, p. 31; Morton & Hilts, 2008). There is little validity to the concept of predeterminism as life circumstances and relationships alter and refine offending (DeLisi, Bunga, Heirigs, Erickson, & Hochstetler, 2019). Different choices, even small changes in background experiences, have tremendous effects on serial murderers (Shanafelt & Pino, 2013). Although exposure to violent subcultural elements may facilitate the transformation of violent urges into behavior (DeFronzo, Ditta, Hannon, & Prochnow, 2007), criminal events occur within a social context and are not merely the byproduct of an offender's motivation (Pino, 2005). For instance, Williams (2021) reports on serial murderers who desired to kill more frequently but had to curtail their efforts due to family, work, and community obligations, structural and interpersonal constraints that restricted their choices and required time to plan and prepare around. Contextual factors such as dehumanization, rationalization, blaming the victim, and displacement of responsibility are important to consider given that the use of fantasy, combined with rationalization and gradual drift into deviance, may be enough for a moderately unhealthy personality to become a full-fledged serial murderer (Homant & Kennedy, 2014). Conditions that lead to serial murder are created by a concatenation of events that are contingent on happenstance, and the probability of recurring patterns (Shanafelt & Pino, 2014). Some authors have found that there are no "predetermined recipes" for the making of a serial murderer but rather stressors that put them on a path toward their first homicide (Deepak & Ramdoss, 2021). It may be that serial murderers accumulate too many life-altering deficits over their lifetime for them to ever function normally. Serial murder may be idiopathic as there is no common serial murder profile as all offenders do not share the same characteristics (Egger, 2002). Hickey (2013, pp. 86, 134) notes that each serial murderer "has evolved through different life events and has responded to those experiences differently" and therefore drawing conclusions about etiology is speculative and dangerous.

The Behavioral Science Unit

At the beginning of an apparent epidemic of crimes committed by "crazed sex maniacs" (Yaksic, 2019), small case studies informed on the phenomenon. These historical sources complicated research (Egger, 2002) because they were "written quickly and focus on the more lurid aspects" (Vronsky, 2004, p. 76). Serial murderers have been described using "othering language" such as "evil," which inhibits our understanding by presenting them as being automatons, driven by compulsions, and killing outside the social context (Shanafelt & Pino, 2014). The first studies on serial murder were hampered by "anecdotal and armchair speculation" as the pioneers studied only sexually motivated serial murderers, disregarded chronic felons, omitted statistics to support typologies, restricted subject selection to those fitting the popular image, and failed to acquire knowledge of theories before writing up a case (Lester, 1995, pp. 48, 67, 84, 86, 93, 187). The methods used to address serial murder led only to more questions.

Although researcher Colin Wilson (2007, p. 2) claims credit for having spotted the "emerging pattern" of an epidemic in serial sexual murders in the late 1950s, offenders whose desires "run out of control," and criminologist Grierson Dickson's *Murder by Numbers* appeared in 1958 and focused on what would later be known as serial murders (Leyton, 2001), results from the first major effort to analyze these offenders was published by psychiatrist Donald Lunde in *Murder and Madness* in 1975. Lunde's work inspired agents from the BSU who, 4 years later, began interviewing 25 sexual serial murderers as part of the Criminal Personality Research Project. The anecdotal evidence gathered from these meetings, which ascertained what combinations of variables led these men to kill, was published in *The Men Who Murdered* (Beasley, 2004) and popularized in Netflix's *Mindhunter*. But merely 2 years after their initial work began, an article was published claiming that the BSU had been able to supply police with details such as the height, weight, body type, age, general occupation, and family environment of a suspect and that similar profiles "have been extremely helpful to law enforcement in solving bizarre and seemingly motiveless killings" (Geberth, 1981, pp. 48, 50). The work laid the groundwork for Criminal Investigative Analysis, the most well-known aspect of which is profiling. BSU agents operationalized this program but were criticized for involving "surmises, hypotheses, or preconceived theories assumed to be infallible" (Turvey, 2000, p. 4). By the time the consequences of relying on the admissions of sexual offenders to guide research efforts – those that ignored African American (Branson, 2013) and female serial murderers – were apparent, the BSU agents had retired and written books that depicted them as fighting monsters (Ressler & Shachtman, 1993), journeying into darkness (Douglas & Olshaker, 1997), hunting evil (Depue

& Schindehette, 2005), and slaying dragons (Academy Group Inc., 2004). Profiling had been described as an accurate weapon in the FBI's arsenal (Porter, 1983), but it was easy to get lost in hype and difficult to distinguish fact from fiction (Muller, 2000) because FBI agents influenced mass media's portrayal of serial murder as much as they were influenced by it.[3]

But conflicts began to form as the BSU sought to monopolize the study of serial murder. In the process, Lunde's work was minimized (Calhoun, 2017) while the BSU's reliance on "subjective qualities" excluded many viewpoints (Muller, 2000, p. 250). While these tactics kept the BSU's work at the forefront of the field for a time, the tactics disconnected it from researchers and created competing interests that determined who was allowed inside research circles, what type of data were collected, and who it was disseminated to. Most in the social science world remained unconvinced of the FBI's invention of the serial murderer as a "super predator" devoid of any social or cultural context (Branson, 2013). While researchers had just begun to interview serial murderers, the FBI was already applying their preliminary learnings in the real world (Vronsky, 2018). Police heard about the BSU's unproven "organized/disorganized" typology and profiles that focused on Caucasian males, all without empirical evidence. Subsequent writings invariably cited the BSU's work, repeating that serial murder was committed by Caucasian men for sexual reasons against female strangers – one racial subset of one gender, for one reason, against one group of people.

The growing disconnects between the BSU and researchers led to reports of large annual numbers of serial murders and a Centers for Disease Control ruling that these crimes were a rising cause of death. Congress convened committees in the early 1980s to investigate the prevalence of serial murder and heard figures of 5,000 serial homicides a year, derived from an erroneous combination of "unknown" and "stranger" murders from the FBI's Uniform Crime Report (Gill, 2000). The ensuing panic convinced most people of the supposedly growing menace of serial murder. Victim advocacy groups, anticrime lobbies, and the government used these numbers to bolster the need for the National Center for the Analysis of Violent Crime (NCAVC), a strategy that solidified the BSU's agents as the "founding fathers" of serial murder investigation. But scholars soon reasoned that the figures were constructed to intentionally raise concern and give a platform to BSU agents claiming that serial murder was an epidemic (Lester, 1995), further deepening newly forming rifts.

The BSU agent's priority then shifted to depicting themselves as heroic Hollywood characters and building their own legend. A picture in a New York Times Magazine article titled *The FBI's New Psyche Squad* shows BSU agents posing like rock stars who describe their goal for the NCAVC to be the "world's clearinghouse for the pursuit and capture of irrational, abnormal offenders, the most difficult of all criminals to apprehend" (Michaud, 1986, p. 40). But in the same year that the NCAVC was founded, BSU agents wrote to a detective managing the Green River Killer case proclaiming that none of the messages they received were authored by the killer, an error that contributed to a yearlong delay in the murderer's apprehension (Wilson, 2003). By vaulting themselves toward the mainstream to become household names, and blurring the boundaries between truth and fiction, BSU agents were distracted and inadvertently helped ensure that serial murderers would be an ever-present part of our culture.

Organizing the Study of Serial Murder

Parallel to the FBI's efforts, an interdisciplinary group of individuals – composed of anthropologists, criminologists, and historians – arose to study serial murder. These pioneers generated much of the knowledge still being studied and debated. Six years after Lunde studied 40 mass and serial murderers, Holmes and DeBurger (1985) presented a brief description of serial murder characteristics. The following year, Leyton took an in-depth look at six serial murderers. Two years later, Jenkins examined 24 cases while Joel Norris researched 260. A year later, Egger and Doney (1990) critically examined the past, present, and future of serial murder. The following year, Donald Sears reported that serial murderers were largely raised in homes with family instability, were not nurtured properly, had an inadequate sense of self-worth, fantasized heavily, failed to construct lasting relationships, pretended to be normal, were mediocre students, and had both criminal records and substance abuse problems (Lester, 1995). A decade later, Muller (2000) observed that politics and ideology influence the study of serial murder, particularly the conservative views of police and researchers. Palermo (2002, p. 384) discovered that these types of "prejudicial attitudes" led many to believe that serial murderers come exclusively from broken homes.

These pioneers encountered several other obstacles in studying serial murder:

- Prisons restricted access to offenders.
- Police refused to release case files.
- Competitive attitudes led to insular teams and siloed thinking.
- Poor research skills were used to generate descriptive statistics and explain findings.
- Researchers experienced burnout after continually viewing violent material.

As Wiest (2011) mentioned, variations of record keeping, and their quality, make it difficult to compile accurate data from previous decades. To work around the dearth of information, some researchers sought out serial murderer's diaries, confessions, psychiatric interviews, statements to the press, videotapes, and photographs (Leyton, 2001). But as researchers became compelled to provide commentary to media outlets to solidify their foothold as experts, news coverage began to rely on unfounded opinions, which altered the perception of serial murderers and their victims. This self-serving outreach, and the subsequent jealousy it produced, inhibited progress as some researchers began to amass attention and institutional support while others faded into obscurity. Often, the loudest proponents of their work saw their findings repeated for years, which fostered an attitude favoring data hoarding. Narrow interpretations of serial murderers resulted from this fracturing that occurred at such a foundational yet inopportune moment.

Egos hampered efforts to define serial murder (Newton, 2006) as many clamored for credit for creating the term. Because researchers used different definitions to segment the offender population by geography, victimology, and the offender-victim relationship (Giannangelo, 1996), these information silos prevented standardization. One definition, for example, stipulates that the victim must be a stranger to the offender whose motive should fulfill a desire for power rather than material gain. The FBI defined serial murder as "three or more separate events in three or more separate locations with an emotional 'cooling off' period between homicides" almost a decade after their initial study (Douglas, Burgess, Burgess, & Ressler, 2013, p. 115). A variable approach leads to overly inclusive definitions that find a higher incidence of certain offenders while exclusive definitions find lower incidences (Wiest, 2011). Over the years, every recorded definition has been contested in one instance or another.

Most serial murder definitions exclude subtypes such as hospital employees that kill their patients (given that they kill all of their victims at one location) and two-victim serial murderers (who fail on their intention to kill a third). Many definitions ignore murders committed by a person acting on behest of someone else, such as political terrorism, organized crime, gangs, and murder for hire (Wiest, 2011) but some offenders who have long been part of the record would be excluded under these definitions (Lester, 1995). Some believe that modern definitions are too broad and nonspecific, which allow for variation (Allely, 2020). Others state that any offenders who kill over time and display intent (Adjorlolo & Chan, 2014; Yaksic, 2015) should be included as restrictions are derived "more from speculation than verifiable evidence" (Hickey, 2013, pp. 32–33). A few researchers think that definitions are arbitrary as the drive to act out is unrelated to the offender's victim tally; in other words, if a serial murderer had been captured after their first murder, they would maintain the same desire to kill (Allely, 2020; Yaksic, Harrison, Konikoff, Mooney, Allely, De Silva, Matykiewicz, Inglis, Giannangelo, Daniels, & Sarteschi, 2021). A recent "real-world" example of the confusion surrounding the serial murder definition saw police avoid the term when describing the actions of an offender who killed over four separate years (1992, 2008, 2010, and 2021) mainly because one homicide was due to an argument and the offender's mother was the victim in another attack (7News Staff, 2021).

Another aspect of the serial murder definition that confounds researchers is the supposed "emotional cooling off" period. Not only can researchers not agree on a standard length but the offender's levels of arousal, cognition, premeditation, and the timing of the crimes are used (to varying degrees) to identify if and when the period had begun (Stefanska & Tehan, 2021). Many continue to utilize a temporal element to make distinctions between potentially similar serial offenders even though it is impossible to discern the degree to which serial murderers detach themselves from trolling for victims or if they remain entrenched in their killing lifestyle. Scholars have little comprehension of the behaviors that serial murderers partake in during interruptions in their series (Yaksic, 2015). While it may appear that serial murderers are living a "normal life" (i.e., taking care of their children or going to the store) during time intervals, they may actually be managing the impression made on others, dedicating mental effort to planning future crimes, or ruminating about past ones. While an offender's dormant period is believed to be psychologically beneficial, it connotes engagement in violence as part of a stress-relief regimen to resolve a buildup of internal conflict. This viewpoint insinuates that serial murder is driven only by aggression and that offenders work themselves into a frenzy or "heat up" before each kill. Describing this period as "emotional" conflicts with the perspective that serial murder is a predatory crime whose offenders are well-controlled, cold, and calculating. It is more likely that crime and violence are part of the context of everyday life for serial murderers and their homicides are more than incidents that punctuate periods of immense stress.

Although some police officials view definitions as semantic exercises with no real-world value, researchers believe that classifying offenders is the only way to yield a greater understanding of the serial murderer's methods, motives, and weaknesses. But without a standard definition, or an official, government-funded database, it would be more difficult to discern the similarities and differences between serial murderers. Researchers have since begun concurrent efforts to assemble datasets, each utilizing different media coverage, newspaper accounts, offender interviews, Internet archives, court records, and scholarly books. According to Quinet (2011), these efforts began when Steven Egger gathered data on 21 serial murderers and 198 victims; Kim Rossmo used FBI files and LexisNexis searches to compile information on 225 serial murderers and 1,983 victims; and Maurice Godwin scoured the Washington State Homicide Investigation Tracking System for data on 107 serial murderers and 728 victims. Other independent efforts were launched to collect serial homicide data: Gretchen Kraemer constructed a working database of 157 offenders from FBI files (Kraemer, Lord, & Heilbrun, 2004); Enzo Yaksic (2006) built a dataset of 105 serial murderers[4]; Elizabeth Gurian (2021) created a database of 994 serial murderers; and Eric Hickey (2013) built a dataset on 367 serial murderers and 2,760 victims. Hickey (2013, p. 2) was one of the first to use statistical analysis because "much of what we claim to know about serial murder is based on misinformation and myth."

These pioneering works occurred alongside the growing popularity of the Internet, making it easier to locate records and confirm their validity. This elevated the study of serial murder beyond a reliance on anecdotal evidence and allowed researchers to find that serial murderers were not a homogenous group. But not all were satisfied by this new wave of data collection and analysis given that it might challenge institutional knowledge. A former FBI Unit Chief's statement that "we have not identified any radical new ideas over the past few years"[5] discounts the great strides made in the study of serial murder. One researcher interrogated the FBI's role in investigating the serial murderer and found that since 1994 there have been no documents in the congressional record regarding their progress (Osowski, 2018). This is likely due to the FBI's belief that their contributions from the 1980s were sufficient, as evidenced by a report noting that the BSU agent's findings "remain as foundational knowledge for many FBI concepts, methods, and research models" (Turvey, 2000, p. 4).[6] In a review of the FBI's work, the Director of the Behavioral Science Section of the Michigan State Police stated that "law enforcement should be no less demanding [of good science] than biology, chemistry, physics, or physiology" but we have failed in meeting those demands (Rossi, 2001, p. 765).

The quest to privately analyze serial murder to meet the demands of good science subsided and was replaced by a need to publicly demonstrate knowledge. But the usefulness of this expert commentary reached its pinnacle well before its failings were showcased. During the DC Sniper investigation (Kleinfield & Goode, 2002), serial murder experts realized that their accumulated knowledge about race could not be applied without glaring discrepancies. Race is a contentious topic as it was believed for many decades that most serial murderers were Caucasian and that those of different races were aberrations (Jenkins, 1993). Although results from a comparative study showed that both Caucasian and African American serial murderers share an almost equal percentage of serial homicide offending (Yaksic, 2006), Hickey (2013) argues that featuring African American serial murderers does not sell newspapers with the perception being that these are urban issues. Several studies have since addressed the myth that the typical serial murderer is Caucasian (Branson, 2013; Kuhns & Coston, 2005; Lester & White, 2014; McClellan, 2019; Walsh, 2005). Morton and Hilts (2008) call these discrepancies a byproduct of the "talking head phenomenon" and recommend that such statements be viewed with skepticism. For instance, two stories about the same African American serial murderer called him both "rare" (Welsh-Huggins & Seewer, 2009) and "stereotypical" (Brown, 2009). Another story promulgated the idea that only strangers are victimized by serial murderers, implying that they do not mix their street life with their home life and that those with an intimate connection to the offender are safe from harm (Longa, 2008), a dangerous assertion.

Researchers began to look upon these ideas as antiquated around the 2010s as by then "everything had changed" (Vronsky, 2018, p. 23). Even though recent efforts by the FBI have helped make strides in serial murder research, they do not maintain a running list of serial murderers.[7] As such, the Atypical Homicide Research Group was created as a platform where researchers could combine databases (Boyne, 2014). The resultant Consolidated Serial Homicide Offender Database (CSHOD) (Aamodt, Fox, Hickey, Hinch, Labuschagne, Levin, McClellan, Nelson, Newton, Quinet, Steiger, White, & Yaksic, 2021) contains decades of systematically collected data on serial murderers and is a resource for journalists, police, practitioners, and scholars to help them understand how these offenders behave in the modern world. Around the same time, the Murder Accountability Project was being formed as a means to identify suspicious clusters of serial homicide activity (Hargrove, Witzig, Icove, Harry, Arntfield, Yaksic, Lang, & Wolf, 2017). Similar work is being done around the globe as former Brigadier Gérard Labuschagne (2020) relays in his recent memoir by recounting the progress the field has made oversees over the years while providing a much-needed international perspective.

But this progress has not been consistent. The new generation of researchers author few manuscripts (Dowden, 2005), are often attracted to the study of serial murder due to its popularity, have profit-based motives and high expectations of fame. These self-proclaimed experts believe that proximity to a serial murderer's brain in a jar, a night's stay in Lizzy Borden's house, or a visit to a murder victim's grave can provide insight into the phenomenon of serial murder. Some adopt nicknames such as "serial killer whisperer" or liken themselves to mythological beings, such as a siren who lures information out of murderers. Others are convinced that with enough will, might, and technology, they can solve serial murder series that are half a century old (Busch, 2018; Fagan, 2021; Holbrook, 2017) but only in front of cameras or for the reward money. Oftentimes, these efforts are overwrought with half-truths, overdramatizations, and sensationalism as the individuals involved are revealed to be frauds (Cain, 2019; Marshall, 2020) having been attracted to, and then taken in by, the offenders because they share certain qualities (Yaksic, 2018). Still, there are those who approach the topic with grace and mindfulness: neuroscientist Jim Fallon believes that drawing a direct parallel between himself and psychopaths will help him better understand such offenders (Fallon, 2014), while retired FBI special agent Jeff Rinek recounts his pursuit of a serial murderer with a deep compassion for the victims and without ego or narcissistic overtones (Rinek & Strong, 2019).

In summary, researchers now acknowledge that interest in serial murder was spurred forward by high-profile cases from the 1970s, cases that focused on the deadliest offenders and continue to serve as the base of knowledge. A lack of reliable data has slowed research on serial crime (Petee & Jarvis, 2000). This process began 20 years ago as evidenced by the mere seven pages dedicated to the study of serial murder found across two volumes of writings compiled by the FBI's BSU (Behavioral Science Unit, 1999, 2002). Given that little has changed since then, this review aims to use data to recalibrate serial murder research by refocusing attention away from the ultra-rare "deadliest" offenders to the more common murderers who pose a more consistent threat to day-to-day life.

Notes

1 Table 1.1 shows that the biographies of many serial murderers have been recycled in books written between 1986 and 2020. Bundy is the most popular serial murderer, featured 71% of the time, followed by Wuornos, Kemper, and Dahmer at 57%, and DeSalvo, Gacy, and Bianchi at 50%.

2 Dennis Nilsen, James DeBardeleben, Gary Ridgway, Leonard Lake, and Jerry Brudos.

3 The logo for Depue's The Academy Group was inspired by Thomas Harris' *Red Dragon* (IMDb, 2004).

4 This was the first study to find that half of all serial murderers since 1995 have been African American.

5 FBI Special Agent Mark Hilts Chief of the FBI's BAU #2. Interviewed by Thomas Hargrove of the Scripps Howard News Service April 22, 2010 at Quantico, VA. Author's files.

6 A survey administered to researchers and FBI personnel in 2005 asked if inferences made by the FBI were outdated. Each researcher responded affirmatively while the FBI unanimously disagreed. Author's files.

7 BAU Major Case Specialist Timothy Keel (personal communication, 2015) and FBI crime analyst Thomas Dover (personal communication, 2020) confirmed that the FBI does not maintain a running list of serial murderers. Results from a Freedom of Information/ Privacy Act request (Hardy, 2011) confirmed that the NCAVC does not maintain a running list of serial murderers.

References

7News Staff. (2021). How cops linked a man charged with killing his mother this week to 3 DC cold case murders. 7News. Retrieved from https://wset.com/newsletter-daily/how-police-linked-a-man-charged-with-killing-his-mother-this-week-to-3-cold-case-murders

Aamodt, M., Fox, J., Hickey, E., Hinch, R., Labuschagne, G., Levin, J., McClellan, J., Nelson, B., Newton, M., Quinet, K., Steiger, C., White, J., & Yaksic, E. (2021). Consolidated serial homicide offender database. Harvard Dataverse. Retrieved from https://dataverse.harvard.edu/dataverse/serial_homicide

Adjorlolo, S., & Chan, H. C. (2014). The controversy of defining serial murder: Revisited. *Aggression and Violent Behavior.* 19(5):486–491.

Allely, C., Wilson, P., Minnis, H., Thompson, L., Yaksic, E., & Gillberg, C. (2017). Violence is rare in autism: when it does occur, is it sometimes extreme? *The Journal of Psychology.* 151(1):49–68.

Allely, C. (2020). The Psychology of Extreme Violence: A Case Study Approach to Serial Homicide, Mass Shooting, School Shooting and Lone-Actor Terrorism. Routledge.

Arluke, A., Levin, J., Luke, C., & Ascione, F. (1999). The relationship of animal abuse to violence and other forms of antisocial behavior. *Journal of Interpersonal Violence.* 14(9):963–975.

Beasley, J. (2004). Serial murder in America: Case studies of seven offenders. *Behavioral Sciences & the Law.* 22(3):395–414.

Behavioral Science Unit. (1999). Selected Readings for the Next Millennium. Federal Bureau of Investigation.

Behavioral Science Unit. (2002). Selected Readings for the Next Millennium: Vol. 2 (2000–2002). Federal Bureau of Investigation.

Boyne, E. (2014). Serial homicide collaborative brings research data together. *Criminal Justice Update, An Online Newsletter for Criminal Justice Educators.* 43(1):2. Routledge and Anderson. Retrieved from https://tandfbis.s3.amazonaws.com/rt-files/docs/SBU3/Criminology/CJ%20UPDATE%20FallWinter%202014.pdf

Branson, A. (2013). African American serial killers: Over-represented yet underacknowledged. *The Howard Journal of Criminal Justice.* 52(1):1–18.

Brown, T. (2009). Imperial Avenue strangler a stereotypical sexually sadistic serial killer, experts say. The Plain Dealer. Retrieved from www.cleveland.com/metro/2009/11/imperial_avenue_strangler_is_a.html

Busch, A. (2018). "Most dangerous animal of all" bestseller about author's father as the zodiac killer picked up. Deadline. Retrieved from https://deadline.com/2018/05/zodiac-killer-most-dangerous-animal-of-all-gary-l-stewart-campfire-entertainment-ross-dinerstein-1202400219/

Cain, S. (2019). True crime author's claims to have interviewed serial killers contested. The Guardian. Retrieved from www.theguardian.com/books/2019/jul/15/true-authors-interviewed-serial-killers-paul-harrison

Calhoun, B. (2017). Yesterday's crimes: Conversations with Ed Kemper. SF Weekly. Retrieved from www.sfweekly.com/news/yesterdays-crimes-news/yesterdays-crimes-conversations-with-ed-kemper/#:~:text=Before%20the%20FBI%20and%20Mindhunter,for%20analyzing%20'70s%20serial%20killers.&text=June%2020%2C%201973%20was%20a,Cruz%20from%201972%20to%201973

Deepak, S., & Ramdoss, S. (2021). The life-course theory of serial killing: A motivation model. *International Journal of Offender Therapy and Comparative Criminology*. 65(13–14):1446–1472.

DeFronzo, J., Ditta, A., Hannon, L., & Prochnow, J. (2007). Male serial homicide: The influence of cultural and structural variables. *Homicide Studies*. 11(1):3–14.

DeLisi, M., Bunga, R., Heirigs, M., Erickson, J., & Hochstetler, A. (2019). The past is prologue: Criminal specialization continuity in the delinquent career. *Youth Violence and Juvenile Justice*. 17(4):335–353.

Depue, R., & Schindehette, S. (2005). Between Good and Evil: A Master Profiler's Hunt for Society's Most Violent Predators. Grand Central.

Douglas, J., & Olshaker, M. (1997). Journey into Darkness. Simon and Schuster.

Douglas, J., Burgess, A., Burgess, A., & Ressler, R. (2013). Crime Classification Manual: A Standard System for Investigating and Classifying Violent Crime. John Wiley.

Dowden, C. (2005). Research on multiple murder: Where are we in the state of the art? *Journal of Police and Criminal Psychology*. 20(2):8–18.

Egger, S., & Doney, R. (1990). Serial Murder: An Elusive Phenomenon. Praeger.

Egger, S. (2002). The Killers among Us: An Examination of Serial Murder and Its Investigation. Prentice Hall.

Fagan, K. (2021). Zodiac killer case solved? "Case Breakers" group makes an ID, but police say it doesn't hold up. San Francisco Chronicle. Retrieved from www.sfchronicle.com/bayarea/article/Zodiac-Killer-case-solved-Case-Breakers-16514228.php

Fallon, J. (2014). The Psychopath Inside: A Neuroscientist's Personal Journey into the Dark Side of the Brain. Current.

Felton, D. (2021). Monsters and Monarchs: Serial Killers in Classical Myth and History. University of Texas Press.

Geberth, V. (1981). Psychological profiling. *Law and Order*. 29(2):46–52.

Giannangelo, S. (1996). The Psychopathology of Serial Murder: A Theory of Violence. Greenwood.

Gill, J. (2000). Missing children: How politics helped start the scandal. FatherMag.org. Retrieved from www.fathermag.com/006/missing-children/abduction_3.shtml

Gleiberman, O. (2020). "Crazy, Not Insane" review: Alex Gibney's fascinating documentary about what makes a serial killer. Variety. Retrieved from https://variety.com/2020/film/reviews/crazy-not-insane-review-alex-gibney-dorothy-lewis-1234767669/

Gurian, E. A. (2021). Serial and Mass Murder: Understanding Multicide through Offending Patterns, Explanations, and Outcomes. Routledge.

Haggerty, K. (2009). Modern serial killers. *Crime, Media, Culture*. 5(2):168–187.

Hall, S., & Wilson, D. (2014). New foundations: Pseudo-pacification and special liberty as potential cornerstones for a multi-level theory of homicide and serial murder. *European Journal of Criminology*. 11(5):635–655.

Harbort, S., & Mokros, A. (2001). Serial murderers in Germany from 1945 to 1995: A descriptive study. *Homicide Studies*. 5(4):311–334.

Hardy, D. M. (2011). FOIPA Request No.: 1171394-000. Names & Demographics of All Serial Killers Known to NCAVC. Freedom of Information/Privacy Act Request.

Hargrove, T., Witzig, E., Icove, D., Harry, B., Arntfield, M., Yaksic, E., Lang, H., & Wolf, I. (2017). Accounting for murder: A new tool for homicide investigators. White Paper.

Harrison, M., Hughes, S., & Gott, A. (2019). Sex differences in serial killers. *Evolutionary Behavioral Sciences*. 13(4):295–310.

Hickey, E. (2013). Serial Murderers and Their Victims. Cengage Learning.

Hickey, E., Walters, B., Drislane, L., Palumbo, I., & Patrick, C. (2018). Deviance at its darkest: Serial murder and psychopathy. In C. J. Patrick (Ed.), Handbook of Psychopathy (pp. 570–584). The Guilford Press.

Holbrook, D. (2017). "The hunt for the zodiac killer" is on in 5-part history docu-series. TVInsider. Retrieved from www.tvinsider.com/649554/hunt-for-the-zodiac-killer-history-channel-bay-area/

Holmes, R., & DeBurger, J. (1985). Profiles in terror: The serial murderer. *Federal Probation*. 44(3):29–34.

Holmes, R., & Holmes, S. (2001). Murder in America. Sage.

Homant, R., & Kennedy, D. (2014). Understanding serial sexual murder: A biopsychosocial approach. In W. Petherick (Ed.), Profiling and Serial Crime (3rd ed., pp. 341–372). Anderson.

IMDb. (2004). Chasing the Dragon: Academy Group Inc. Retrieved from www.imdb.com/title/tt0421967/

James, J. & Proulx, J. (2016). The modus operandi of serial and nonserial sexual murderers: A systematic review. *Aggression and Violent Behavior*. 31:200–218.

Jenkins, P. (1993). African Americans and serial homicide. *American Journal of Criminal Justice*. 17(2):47–60.

Kleinfield, N., & Goode, E. (2002). Retracing a trail: The sniper suspects; Serial killing's squarest pegs: Not solo, white, psychosexual or picky. The New York Times. Retrieved from www.nytimes.com/2002/10/28/us/retracing-trail-sniper-suspects-serial-killing-s-squarest-pegs-not-solo-white.html

Kraemer, G., Lord, W., & Heilbrun, K. (2004). Comparing single and serial homicide offenses. *Behavioral Sciences & the Law*. 22(3):325–343.

Kuhns, J., & Coston, C. (2005). The myth that the typical serial murderer is a white male. In J. Walker & R. Bohm (Eds.), Demystifying Crime and Criminal Justice . Roxbury. Retrieved from https://pages.uncc.edu/ccoston/wp-content/uploads/sites/10/2011/09/myths.pdf

Labuschagne, G. (2020). The Profiler Diaries: From the Case Files of a Police Psychologist. Penguin Books.

Leach, G., & Meloy, J. (1999). Serial murder of six victims by an African American male. *Journal of Forensic Science*. 44(5):1073–1078.

Leary, T., Southard, L., Hill, J., & Ashman, J. (2017). The Macdonald triad revisited: An empirical assessment of relationships between triadic elements and parental abuse in serial killers. *North American Journal of Psychology*. 19(3):627–640.

Lester, D. (1995). Serial Killers: The Insatiable Passion. Charles Press.

Lester, D., & White, J. (2014). A study of African American serial killers. *Journal of Ethnicity in Criminal Justice*. 12(4):308–316.

Leyton, E. (2001). Hunting Humans: The Rise of the Modern Multiple Murderer. McClelland & Stewart.

Longa, L. (2008). Serial killer could be anyone, experts warn. News Journal Online.

Malizia, N. (2017). Serial killer: The mechanism from imagination to the murder phases. *Sociology Mind*. 7: 44–59.

Marono, A., Reid, S., Yaksic, E., & Keatley, D. (2020). A behaviour sequence analysis of serial killers' lives: From childhood abuse to methods of murder. *Psychiatry, Psychology and Law*. 27(1):126–137.

Marshall, A. (2020). Death becomes him. Air Mail. Retrieved from https://airmail.news/issues/2020-5-30/death-becomes-him

McClellan, J. (2019). African American Serial Killers: The Neglected Investigative Profile. Self-Published.

Michaud, S. (1986). The F.B.I.'S new psyche squad. The New York Times Magazine. Retrieved from www.nytimes.com/1986/10/26/magazine/the-fbi-s-new-psyche-squad.html

Mitchell, E. (1997). The aetiology of serial murder: Towards an integrated model. Unpublished Thesis. University of Cambridge.

Morton, R., & Hilts, M. (2008). Serial murder: Multi-disciplinary perspectives for investigators. National Center for the Analysis of Violent Crime.

Muller, D. (2000). Criminal profiling: Real science or just wishful thinking? *Homicide Studies*. 4(3):234–264.

Newton, M. (2006). The Encyclopedia of Serial Killers. Infobase.

Norris, J. (1989). Serial Killers. Anchor.

O'Neill, M. (2021). There are four different types of serial killers—Here's how experts describe them. Health.com. Retrieved from www.health.com/condition/mental-health-conditions/serial-killers-types

Osowski, K. (2018). Investigating a serial killer: The development of the FBI's role told through public documents. *DttP: Documents to the People*. 46(4):19–24.

Ostrosky-Solís, F., Vélez-García, A., Santana-Vargas, D., Pérez, M., & Ardila, A. (2008). A middle-aged female serial killer. *Journal of Forensic Sciences*, 53(5):1223–1230.

Ozimek, T. (2018). Serial killer admits he murdered '10 times more' victims than police know about. The Epoch Times. Retrieved from www.theepochtimes.com/serial-killer-admits-he-murdered-10-times-more-victims-than-police-know-about_2431221.html

Palermo, G. (2002). Criminal profiling: The uniqueness of the killer. *International Journal of Offender Therapy and Comparative Criminology*. 46(4):383–385.

Petee, T., & Jarvis, J. (2000). Analyzing violent serial offending: Guest editors' introduction. *Homicide Studies*. 4(3):211–218.

Pino, N. (2005). Serial offending and the criminal events perspective. *Homicide Studies*. 9(2):109–148.

Porter, B., (1983). Mindhunters: Tracking down killers with the FBI's psychological profiling team. *Psychology Today*. 17:44–52.

Quinet, K. (2011). Prostitutes as victims of serial homicide: Trends and case characteristics, 1970-2009. *Homicide Studies*. 15(1):74–100.

Reavis, J. (2011). Serial murder of four victims, of both genders and different ethnicities, by an ordained Baptist minister. *Case Reports in Psychiatry*. 2011:1–9. Retrieved from www.hindawi.com/journals/crips/2011/163403/

Ressler, R., & Shachtman, T. (1993). Whoever Fights Monsters: My Twenty Years Tracking Serial Killers for the FBI. Macmillan.

Rinek, J. L., & Strong, M. (2019). In the Name of the Children: An FBI Agent's Relentless Pursuit of American's Worst Predators. Quercus.

Rossi, D. (2001). Review of geographic profiling. *Journal of Forensic Science*. 46(3):765.

Seltzer, M. (1998). Serial Killers: Death and Life in America's Wound Culture. Psychology Press.

Shanafelt, R., & Pino, N. (2013). Evil and the common life: Towards a wider perspective on serial killing and atrocities. In R. Atkinson & S. Winlow (Eds.), *New Directions in Crime and Deviancy* (pp. 252–273). Routledge.

Shanafelt, R., & Pino, N. (2014). Rethinking Serial Murder, Spree Killing, and Atrocities: Beyond the Usual Distinctions. Routledge.

Smith, V. (2010). Police release confession in W.VA. serial killings. Charleston Gazette-Mail. Retrieved from https://killerscrawlspace.files.wordpress.com/2020/11/transcript_of_childers.pdf

Stefanska, E. B., & Tehan, S. (2021). After a storm comes a calm: International expert decision-making process regarding abstract definitions of emotional cool-off periods in sexual homicide. *Psychology, Crime & Law*. In press. Retrieved from www.tandfonline.com/doi/full/10.1080/1068316X.2021.1962869

Stone, M. (2009). The Anatomy of Evil. Prometheus Books.

Turvey, B. (2000). The Estate of Sam Sheppard v. State of Ohio, Case No. 312322. Knowledge Solutions, LLC.

Vronsky, P. (2004). Serial Killers: The Method and Madness of Monsters. Penguin Books.

Vronsky, P. (2018). Sons of Cain: A History of Serial Killers from the Stone Age to the Present. Penguin Books.

Walsh, A. (2005). African Americans and serial killing in the media: The myth and the reality. *Homicide Studies*. 9(4):271–291.

Welsh-Huggins, A. & Seewer, J. (2009). Unusual method for Ohio slaying suspect. Monterey Herald. Retrieved from www.montereyherald.com/2009/11/08/unusual-method-for-ohio-slaying-suspect/

Wiest, J. B. (2011). Creating Cultural Monsters: Serial Murder in America. CRC Press.

Williams, D. (2021). Forensic behavioral science of serial and mass murder with an addition of leisure research: A descriptive synthesis. *Forensic Sciences*. 1(1):16–24.

Wilson, C. (2007). The Serial Killers: A Study in the Psychology of Violence. Virgin Books.

Wilson, D. (2003). Profiler can't recall why he said letter wasn't from Green River killer. Seattle Times. Retrieved from https://archive.seattletimes.com/archive/?date=20031126&slug=greenriver26m

Wilson, D., Yardley, E., & Lynes, A. (2015). Serial Killers and the Phenomenon of Serial Murder: A Student Textbook. Waterside Press.

Wolf, B., & Lavezzi, W. (2007). Paths to destruction: The lives and crimes of two serial killers. *Journal of Forensic Sciences*. 52(1):199–203.

Yaksic, E. (2006). Can a demographic make you psychopathic? The Northeastern University Research, Innovation, Scholarship and Entrepreneurship Expo. Retrieved from www.northeastern.edu/rise/presentations/can-demographic-make-psychopathic/

Yaksic, E. (2015). Addressing the challenges and limitations of utilizing data to study serial homicide. *Crime Psychology Review*. 1(1):108–134.

Yaksic, E. (2018). The perpetual influence of dark traits on alienists. In In M. DeLisi (Ed.), Routledge International Handbook of Psychopathy and Crime (pp. 301–318). Routledge. Retrieved from www.taylorfrancis.com/chapters/edit/10.4324/9781315111476-19/perpetual-influence-dark-traits-alienists-enzo-yaksic

Yaksic, E. (2019). Serial murder. In E. McLaughlin & J. Muncie (Eds.), *The SAGE Dictionary of Criminology* (4th ed., pp. 476–479). SAGE.

Yaksic, E., Harrison, M., Konikoff, D., Mooney, R., Allely, C., De Silva, R., Matykiewicz, B., Inglis, M., Giannangelo, S., Daniels, S. & Sarteschi, C. (2021). A heuristic study of the similarities and differences in offender characteristics across potential and successful serial sexual homicide offenders. *Behavioral Sciences & the Law*. 39(4):428–449.

3

SERIAL MURDER

2011–2021

Overview

Recent research suggests that serial murderers have evolved beyond the situational factors that contributed to the success of their counterparts from the past. Potential serial murderers, who are ignored for being boring and predicable, often fail at their first attempts at building a killing career[1] because they must take invariably greater risks to achieve the same benchmarks as Golden Age serial murderers. Our heavily surveilled society, the proliferation of technology, better prepared and connected police, and an aware and vigilant public[2] have driven some would-be serial murderers to adopt the tactics of the spree murderer (Yaksic, 2019), others to eliminate their targets in a mass outburst, and a few to placate themselves via alternative outlets. Some offenders continue forward and take advantage of lucky breaks, conceptualized in *Killer Data* as undue opportunities provided by systemic deficiencies (Department of Veterans Affairs Office of Inspector General, 2021; Epstein, 2021; Yaksic, Allred, Drakulic, Mooney, De Silva, Geyer, Wills, Comerford, & Ranger, 2021).

This review challenges the common conceptions of the serial murderer by relying on an expanded definition to show that the difference between other violent offenders and serial murderers is narrowing (Culhane, Hilstad, Freng, & Gray, 2011). Thinking broadly about serial murder has determined that offenders engage in violence in a furtive "other life" as a secondary activity and that they are also akin to "thugs" cycling in and out of prison who mix serial murder into a wide offending pattern (DeLisi, 2015). The findings of two studies place the modern serial murderer closer in relation to one-off murderers who kill acquaintances and family members out of anger (Pakkanen, Zappalà, Bosco, Berti, & Santtila, 2015): Salfati and Bateman (2005) found that the majority of serial murderers were expressive, while Hodgkinson, Prins, and Stuart-Bennett (2017) proclaim that serial

DOI: 10.4324/9781003130567-3

murder victims are often not random and can be people with whom the offender shares a relationship. Hall and Wilson (2014) explain that the serial murderer is distinguished from the one-off killer only by the unusual strength of the former's drive. DeLisi, Drury, and Elbert (2018) observed that one-off homicide offenders experience adverse childhood experiences, emotion and behavioral regulation problems, involvement in the criminal justice system, and other forms of violent, property, and drug offending, while Kraemer, Lord, and Heilbrun (2004) show one-offs commit emotion-based crimes – both profiles similar to the serial murderers in this review.

While some researchers acknowledge that serial murders can be the result of situational factors such as relationship strife and parole release (Osborne & Salfati, 2015; Reale, Beauregard, & Martineau, 2020), many continue to segment offenders based on whether they fulfilled a deviant sexual fantasy and killed primarily for sex. Morton, Tillman, and Gaines (2014), for example, conducted a study on a convenience sample of 92 serial murderers whose crimes occurred between 1960 and 2006 and found that serial murderers were mostly Caucasian males who killed for sex using strangulation – in line with previous studies by the FBI. Warwick (2006) warns that efforts to succinctly classify serial murderers lead to confusion and, conversely, a variety of views on different perpetrators. But the framing of serial murder as an extreme, otherworldly form of violence lessens the impact of the more common two-victim serial murderers (TVSMs) who are often overlooked because of their failure to attain a prolific status. Differentiating serial murderers on their level of lethality discounts offenders who avoid the label based on situational variables and differential circumstances such as a misplaced bullet and/or the survival of victims (DeLisi, Drury, & Elbert, 2018). Because offenders responsible for all victim counts share characteristics not reflected by this metric, definitions should focus on the serial murderer's mindset and intent. In the end, research of this nature is limited because we have only begun to explore serial murder in an organized manner (Hickey, 2013).

Parameters

This review analyzes the incidence of known serial murder series that concluded between 2011 and 2021 and compares them to data from the sixth edition of *Serial Murderers and Their Victims* (SMATV). Both the current review and SMATV utilized a portion of data from the CSHOD, a resource compiled by the Atypical Homicide Research Group (AHRG).[3] Because both *Killer Data* and SMATV used the same inclusion criteria and classification of variables, it was possible to compare the data. Case studies will be used to provide narrative depth. The serial murder definition is operationalized here as: the unlawful killing of two or more victims by the same offender(s) in separate events in the United States (Morton & Hilts, 2008). The broadness of this definition allows for a variety of persons who kill over time to be included, (e.g., those who kill for altruistic purposes, as the byproduct of gang violence, to fulfill professional contacts, and persons motivated primarily for financial gain) (Hickey, 2013). Gang members have been included, but they do not represent an exhaustive list given that many researchers have only just begun to consider them to be serial murderers and therefore have not been judicious in including them in their logs over the years. This review incorporates spree murderers into the overall serial murder definition using Lester's 30-day cutoff. Serial and spree murderers have been reported on separately in order to follow historical categorization trends. TVSMs were included after considering their intention and attempts at additional homicides.

A nonrandom sampling method was utilized given that the goal of this review is to be as exhaustive as possible. Certain demographic and psychological records may not be available at the time of writing given that many of the individuals in the database have been convicted only recently. For that reason, information on childhood experiences, psychiatric records, and crime scene details were not consistently available for review. The motivations, lives, and personalities of serial murderers are not fully understood, a byproduct of a distortion of perception from a focus on horrific crimes (Hickey, 2013). For that reason, lesser-known offenders are the focus of the biographies. Serial murderers who were extensively written about elsewhere (i.e., Israel Keyes, Todd Kohlhepp), while studied in the analysis, were not included in the case vignettes. Given the subjectivity of using typologies, their likelihood of reinforcing stereotypes (Hinch & Hepburn, 1998), and the disadvantage they present as blunt instruments that "attempt to provide a one size fits all explanation" (Morton & McNamara, 2005, pp. 48), the offenders included in this review have not been assigned a traditional typology. While many researchers disagree with assigning motive (given the subjectivity of the process and the numerous reasons offenders can have for perpetrating a crime), offenders were assigned a motive after careful review of all available materials. The motives considered in this review were derived from Morton and Hilts's (2008) report: anger, financial gain (criminal enterprise), sexual, psychosis (mental illness), and enjoyment (thrill, excitement, and power).

Findings

The characteristics of all serial murder subtypes that were apprehended between 2011 and 2021 are shown in Table 3.1a.

To summarize:

- The average modern serial murderer is an African American male, without a criminal record, who kills locally, in the Midwest, beginning and ending in early adulthood, after using a firearm to kill two to three victims out of anger.
- TVSMs are generally African American men, who have a criminal record, kill locally, in the Midwest, over an 11–20-year period starting in their youth and ending in midlife, after using multiple methods to kill their victims out of anger.
- Serial murderers who kill three or more victims are generally African American men, who have a criminal record, kill locally, in the Midwest, over a 2–5-year

TABLE 3.1A Characteristics of serial murderers, 2011–2021

Factor	*Level*	*Male Two Victims (N=104)*	*Male ≥3 Victims (N=115)*	*Male Spree (N=115)*	*Female (N=20)*	*Male/Female Teams (N=27)*	*Total (N=381)*
Paroled	**Y**	67.3	53.9	24.3	15	37	45.4
	N	32.6	46	75.6	85	62.9	54.5
Moniker	**Y**	1.9	6.9	4.3	5	3.7	4.4
	N	98	93	95.6	95	96.2	95.5
Number of days	**0**	0.0	0.0	33.9	5	14.8	21.7
	1–10	0.0	0.0	49.5	0.0	18.5	30.6
	11–50	4.8	8.6	16.5	10	11.1	19.3
	51–100	7.6	8.6	0.0	0.0	11.1	10.3
	101–150	5.7	3.4	0.0	0.0	7.4	5.9
	151–200	0.0	1.7	0.0	0.0	11.1	2.4
	201–250	1.9	3.4	0.0	0.0	0.0	2.9
	251–300	1.9	2.6	0.0	10	0.0	2.9
	301–364	1.9	4.3	0.0	0.0	0.0	3.4
Number of years	**1**	2.8	4.3	0	25	0.0	7.2
	2–5	12.5	15.6	0	25	14.8	22.3
	6–10	5.7	9.5	0	10	3.7	11.1
	11–20	22.1	13.9	0	15	3.7	24
	21–30	21.1	14.7	0	5	3.7	22.9
	31–40	10.5	6.9	0	0.0	0.0	10.6
	41–60	0.9	1.7	0	0.0	0.0	1.6
Race	**Caucasian**	35.5	39.1	40.8	80	N/A	40.9
	African American	56.7	49.5	46	15		48.5
	Hispanic	6.7	9.5	8.6	5		8.1
	Other	0.9	1.7	4.3	0.0		2.2

Race (teams)	**Caucasian**	N/A	N/A	N/A	N/A	51.8	51.8
	Caucasian/African American					7.4	11.1
	African American					25.9	25.9
	Hispanic					3.7	3.7
	Caucasian/Other					3.7	3.7
	Other					3.7	3.7
Start age	**10–20**	38.4	24.3	11.3	0.0	18.5	22.5
	21–30	33.6	37.3	39.1	35	40.7	37
	31–40	20.1	23.4	29.5	20	22.2	24.1
	41–50	4.8	7.8	13	30	14.8	10.2
	51–60	2.8	3.4	4.3	10	3.7	3.9
	61–70	0.0	2.6	1.7	5	0.0	1.5
	71–80	0.0	0.8	0.8	0.0	0.0	0.5
Capture Age	**13–20**	9.6	7.8	11.3	0.0	14.8	9.4
	21–30	17.3	26	39.1	20	33.3	27.8
	31–40	22.1	19.1	29.5	20	29.6	23.8
	41–50	25.9	19.1	12.1	30	18.5	19.4
	51–60	20.1	15.6	5.2	25	3.7	13.3
	61–70	3.8	9.5	1.7	5	0.0	4.7
	71–80	0.9	2.6	0.8	0.0	0.0	1.3
Motive	**Anger**	**39.4**	**29.5**	**45.2**	**30**	**33.3**	**37.2**
	Arguments	26.8	11.7	3.8	0	0.0	11.9
	General/Basic	29.2	35.2	42.3	50	44.4	37.3
	Domestic disputes	26.8	26.4	25	0	11.1	23.9
	Argument and domestic	7.3	5.8	3.8	0	0.0	4.9
	Hatred	2.4	14.7	9.6	0	33.3	9.8
	General	0	40	0	0	33.3	21.4
	Government/Police	0	0	40	0	33.3	21.4

(continued)

TABLE 3.1A Cont.

Factor	*Level*	*Male Two Victims (N=104)*	*Male ≥3 Victims (N=115)*	*Male Spree (N=115)*	*Female (N=20)*	*Male/Female Teams (N=27)*	*Total (N=381)*
	Homeless	0	20	0	0	0.0	7.1
	Honor	100	0	0	0	0.0	7.1
	Racial	0	40	40	0	33.3	35.7
	Sex offenders	0	0	20	0	0.0	7.1
	Revenge	7.3	5.8	15.3	50	11.1	11.9
	Convenience	**0**	**0**	**2.6**	**10**	**0.0**	**1.3**
	Avoid apprehension	0	0	100	0	0.0	60
	Eliminate discomfort	0	0	0	100	0.0	40
	Enjoyment	**.9**	**12.1**	**5.2**	**10**	**3.7**	**6.2**
	Financial Gain	**13.4**	**22.6**	**18.2**	**15**	**40.7**	**19.6**
	General	7.1	38.4	4.7	100	0.0	20
	Residential burglary	0	0	4.7	0	0.0	1.3
	Collect/avoid debt	14.2	0	4.7	0	0.0	4
	Contract	0	7.6	0	0	0.0	2.6
	Drugs	14.2	15.3	4.7	0	9	10.6
	Street robbery	64.2	38.4	80.9	0	91	61.3
	Gang violence	**0.0**	**3.4**	**0.0**	**0.0**	**0.0**	**1**
	Mental illness	**0.9**	**0.8**	**6**	**0.0**	**0.0**	**2.3**
	Multiple	**17.3**	**20.8**	**3.4**	**5**	**14.8**	**13.3**
	Anger/financial gain	72.2	33.3	0	100	50	47
	Anger/convenience	22.2	20.8	0	0	25	19.6
	Anger/sex assault	0	25	0	0	0.0	11.7
	Anger/enjoyment	0	0	25	0	0.0	1.9
	Enjoyment/convenience	0	4.1	0	0	0.0	1.9
	Enjoyment/mental illness	0	0	25	0	0.0	1.9
	Financial gain/enjoyment	5.5	4.1	0	0	25	5.8

	Financial gain/sex assault	0	4.1	25	0	0.0	3.9
	Financial gain/negligence	0	4.1	0	0	0.0	1.9
	Financial gain/random	0	4.1	0	0	0.0	1.9
	Anger/sex/financial gain	0	0	25	0	0.0	1.9
	Negligence	**0.9**	**0.0**	0.0	**30**	**3.7**	**2**
	Random	**0.9**	**0.8**	**6**	**0.0**	**0.0**	**2.3**
	Sexual assault	**25**	**9.5**	**8.6**	**0.0**	**3.7**	**12.5**
	Unknown	**0.9**	0.0	**4.3**	**0.0**	**0.0**	**1.5**
Method	**Bludgeon**	5.7	6.9	3.4	5	3.7	5.2
	Drugs	0.0	3.4	0.8	20	0.0	2.3
	Explosion	0.0	0.0	0.8	0.0	0.0	0.2
	Multiple	38.4	26.9	16.5	30	25.9	27
	Neglect	0.0	0.0	0.0	5	3.7	0.5
	Shake	0.9	0.0	0.0	0.0	0.0	0.2
	Shoot	27.8	41.7	63.4	20	55.5	44.3
	Stab	14.4	9.5	8.6	0.0	3.7	9.7
	Strangle	12.5	11.3	6	20	7.4	10.2
Location	**Local**	92.3	84.3	93	80	88.8	89.2
	Regional	2.8	6	4.3	5	11.1	4.9
	National	4.8	9.5	2.6	15	0.0	5.7
Region	**East**	4.8	10.4	6	10	7.4	7.3
	Northeast	17.3	16.5	11.3	20	7.4	14.6
	Northwest	2.8	0.8	2.6	5	0.0	2
	West	9.6	14.7	20.8	10	25.9	15.7
	Midwest	26.9	26	18.2	20	11.1	22.5
	National	4.8	9.5	2.6	15	0.0	5.7
	South	3.8	5.2	13	10	14.8	8.1
	Southcentral	7.6	6.9	13	0.0	11.1	8.9
	Southeast	22.1	8.6	11.3	10	22.2	14.1
	Southwest	0.0	0.8	0.8	0.0	0.0	0.5

period beginning and ending in young adulthood, after using a firearm to kill three victims out of anger.

- A spree killer is more likely to be an African American man, without a criminal record, who kills locally, in the West, over 1–10 days beginning and ending in young adulthood, after using a firearm to kill two victims out of anger.
- Female serial murderers (FSMs) are generally Caucasian, without criminal records, who kill locally, in the Midwest, over a 1–5-year period beginning in young adulthood and ending in midlife, after using multiple methods to kill two victims out of anger or negligence.
- Team-based serial murderers (TSMs) are generally Caucasian, without criminal records, who kill locally, in the West, over a 2–5-year period beginning and ending in early adulthood, after using a firearm to kill two victims for financial gain.

The characteristics of the victims who were killed by all serial murderer subtypes are shown in Table 3.1b.

To summarize:

- The modern serial murderer selected both adult male and female victims, aged 21–30 years old, from a mixture of races. These offenders sometimes shared a cursory relationship with their victims but also targeted strangers. Killings were generally intra-racial.
- TVSMs selected adult female victims, aged 21–30 years old, who were Caucasian. These offenders sometimes shared an intimate relationship with their victims but also targeted strangers. Killings were generally intra-racial.
- Serial murderers who kill three or more victims selected both adult male and female victims, with a preference toward men, aged 21–30 years old, from a mixture of races. These offenders targeted strangers. Killings were generally intra-racial.
- Spree killers selected both adult male and female victims, in a wide age range of 31–50 years old, from a mixture of races. These offenders targeted strangers as often as a mixture of victims with whom they sometimes shared a cursory relationship.
- FSMs selected both male and female Caucasian victims, aged 1–10 years old. These offenders killed family members. Killings were generally intra-racial.
- TSMs selected Caucasian adult male victims, in a wide age range of 31–50 years old. These offenders targeted strangers. Killings were generally intra-racial.

How Are Serial Murderers Portrayed Across Seminal Studies?

In the annals of serial murder research, there have been three seminal studies that influenced succeeding research. The first was conducted by Dr. Steven Egger, the second by retired FBI Special Agent James O. Beasley, and the third by Dr. Eric

TABLE 3.1B Characteristics of victims, 2011–2021

Factor	*Level*	*Male Two Victims (N=104)*	*Male ≥3 Victims (N=115)*	*Male Spree (N=115)*	*Female (N=20)*	*Male/Female Teams (N=27)*	*Total (N=381)*
Victim count	**2**	100	0.0	41.7	55	37	45.4
	3	0.0	46.9	22.6	10	25.9	23.3
	4	0.0	26	22.6	25	22.2	17.5
	5	0.0	14.7	4.3	5	3.7	6.2
	6	0.0	4.3	4.3	0.0	7.4	3.1
	7	0.0	2.6	1.7	5	0.0	1.5
	8+	0.0	5.2	1.7	0.0	3.7	2.6
Victim sex	**Male**	34.6	**22.6**	**28.6**	**35**	**51.8**	**30.4**
	Female	**37.5**	**20**	**13**	**10**	**7.4**	**21.2**
	Both	**27.8**	**57.3**	**58.2**	**55**	**40.7**	**48.2**
	Equal	100	7.5	35.8	72.7	27.2	37.5
	Mainly men	0.0	51.5	34.3	18.1	63.6	35.8
	Mainly women	0.0	40.9	29.8	9	9	26.6
Victim type	**Adult**	88.4	79.1	67.8	50	74	76.6
	Children	0.9	0.0	0.0	5	3.7	0.7
	Elderly	0.0	5.2	3.4	5	0.0	2.6
	Infants	0.9	0.0	0.0	25	0.0	1.5
	Teens	0.9	0.0	0.8	0.0	7.4	1
	Various	8.6	15.6	27.8	15	14.8	17.3
Victim/ offender relation	**Stranger**	**33.6**	**38.2**	**40.8**	**5**	**48.1**	**36.7**
	Intimate (family)	**14.4**	**12.1**	**5.2**	**40**	**7.4**	**11.8**
	Cursory (acquaintances)	**11.5**	**15.7**	**13.0**	**30**	**7.4**	**13.9**

(continued)

TABLE 3.1B Cont.

Factor	*Level*	*Male Two Victims (N=104)*	*Male ≥3 Victims (N=115)*	*Male Spree (N=115)*	*Female (N=20)*	*Male/Female Teams (N=27)*	*Total (N=381)*
	Mixed	**40.8**	**33.9**	**40.8**	**25**	**37**	**37.5**
	Stranger/cursory	33.3	28.2	44.6	0	40	34.9
	Stranger/intimate	35.7	41	21.2	0	50	32.1
	Cursory/intimate	30.9	23	27.6	100	10	28.6
	Stranger/cursory/intimate	0.0	7.6	6.3	0	0	4.1
Victim race	**Caucasian**	37.5	31.3	34.7	75	37	36.7
	African American	25	24.3	14.7	15	18.5	20.7
	Hispanic	2.8	4.3	0.8	0.0	3.7	2.6
	Other	0.0	0.8	0.8	0.0	3.7	0.7
	Mixed	34.6	39.1	48.6	10	37	39.1
Average victim age	**1–10**	1.9	0.0	0.8	30	3.7	2.6
	11–20	7.6	5.2	4.3	5	11.1	6
	21–30	29.8	27.8	20	10	22.2	24.6
	31–40	27.8	20	24.3	5	25.9	23
	41–50	19.2	23.4	24.3	15	25.9	22.3
	51–60	8.6	14.7	15.6	25	3.7	13.1
	61–70	2.8	3.4	6.9	5	3.7	4.4
	71–80	0.0	2.6	3.4	0.0	3.7	2
	81–90	1.9	2.6	0.0	5	0.0	1.5
Inter/intra racial	**Interracial**	6.7	8.6	11.3	0.0	14.8	8.9
	Intra-racial	58.6	52.1	40	90	48.1	51.9
	Mixed	34.6	39.1	48.6	10	37	39.1
Sex worker	**Y**	5.7	5.2	3.4	0.0	7.4	4.7
	N	93.2	91.3	95.6	100	92.5	93.7
	Y/N	0.9	3.4	0.8	0.0	0.0	1.5

Hickey. Each of these authors carried forth the most critical aspects of serial murder research from their respective generations while adding their own expert insight. Their perspectives have led to many breakthroughs over the past several decades. This review is built upon their efforts.

Dr. Steven Egger

In a cross-case analysis of seven serial murderers, Egger (2002) reports on offenders who killed in the Golden Age.[4] Childhood trauma, family histories of alcoholism, and parents who had emotional problems were common. Due to their strong embrace of hatred and resistance to authority, serial murderers had difficulty establishing relationships with others, and all had been married and divorced. Each serial murderer used strangulation as their primary means of killing. Six of the seven men had criminal records and antisocial personalities. Each offender knew how to work around police efforts to capture them, and many of their victims were vulnerable to assault or abduction because of their lifestyle or perceived powerlessness. Although all of these offenders had concerns about their masculinity, each offender viewed themselves as able to overtake their victims through physical force. In Egger's follow-up study of serial murderers who killed between 1900 and 1999, the majority were Caucasian males who victimized young females. In a small number of cases, victims knew their murderer. Elderly women and children were routinely targeted, as were patients in hospitals. College campuses, red light districts, and highways were frequent hunting grounds, and home invasion homicides were common. Serial murderers changed their victim criteria 13% of the time and for-profit motives appear in 7% of the cases. Firearms were used in 20% of the offenses. Little information is offered about FSMs beyond an acknowledgment that they are primarily motivated by financial gain and most had a prior relationship with their victims.

FBI Special Agent James O. Beasley (retd.)

In a study of seven serial murderers who killed between 1969 and 1998, Beasley (2004) found that motives included sexual desires, financial gain, and anger. Murders committed by the same individual were dissimilar in that there were varied circumstances among the homicides and a diversity in methods and victim selection. Four offenders killed across multiple states, and females were killed 72% of the time. In 70% of the homicides, the victim's ethnicity matched that of the offender; two of the offenders had victims of varied races. Victims were mostly sex workers (36%), the elderly (15%), and students (19%). The methods used by three of the serial murderers to perpetrate the homicides varied, while four remained loyal to one method. Four serial murderers had extensive criminal histories that were indicative of their antisocial nature, low self-esteem, self-destructiveness, and lack of self-concern. Although family problems were common, the frequency of physical and/or sexual abuse and animal torture was low.

Dr. Eric Hickey

In SMATV, Hickey (2013) presents data on serial murderers who killed between 1800 and 2011, but most new cases did not carry the social drama, social class, or high body counts from previous years. After the male-on-male killings in the Wild West subsided, sadistic rapists used sex as a means of degrading young female strangers. Serial murderers shifted from confronting their victims to taking them by surprise, isolating them to "act out their aggressions on those perceived to be weak, helpless, and without power and control" (Hickey, 2013, pp. 322). Killing strangers provides offenders with a measure of anonymity, the ability to derive satisfaction from furtive selection, and ease of objectification. Serial murderers destroy what they cannot have and aim to eliminate those who represent what they fear or despise. Hickey notes that many social indices such as employment, lifestyle socio-economic status, and where victims live can put them in the orbit of a serial murderer. Every state has now seen at least one serial murderer, and their distribution is always in flux (see Table 3.2). Those who are unlucky enough to select the wrong location may expose themselves to the risk of victimization. As the population ages, SMATV warns of more elderly victims.

Serial murderers are subdivided into male, female, and team categories in SMATV:[5]

- Male serial murderers (MSMs) in SMATV killed three or more victims. They preferred to victimize young female strangers, rather than acquaintances or family members, and focused particular attention on sex workers. Many victims were hitchhikers and women who engaged in certain professions like modeling. In contrast to Egger's study, the SMATV MSMs tended not to kill children and teens exclusively. SMATV's MSMs do not use firearms as the main mode of death (18%). The typical stereotype of the MSM is the lust murderer whose primary motivation is sexual, but some MSMs never become sexually involved with their victims, and only 8% consider it to be their sole reason for killing. As one study found, there is no empirical foundation to the claim that all serial homicides are sexual in nature (Pakkanen et al., 2015). Enjoyment and money are infrequently the primary motivations for MSMs. In spite of figures released by the FBI's Highway Serial Killing Initiative, 74% of MSMs since 1975 have been local offenders. The perception held of the MSM is that they embark on a unique form of criminal activity, but since 63% of MSMs had a prior incarceration, it is more likely that the criminal justice system failed to adequately deal with offenders before their serial homicide career began (Hickey, 2013).
- FSMs are as lethal as MSMs, and their killings are often of low visibility. Many SMATV FSMs were 'black widows', and care providers who operated in hospitals, nursing homes, and care facilities. FSMs were responsible for 14% to 15% of all victims. SMATV recorded a rise in the total number of victims and the extended time span over which FSMs kill. Few FSMs were found to have a criminal career, and they more often kill in response to unfulfilled

TABLE 3.2 Comparison of the distribution of cases of serial murderers by state over time

State	*1800–2004 (SMATV)*	*2011–2021*
California	53+	44
New York	34	21
Texas	16–30	34
Florida		32
Illinois		17
Ohio	11–15	22
Michigan	6–10	21
Pennsylvania		18
Georgia		15
New Jersey		14
Indiana		10
Washington		10
Nevada		9
Massachusetts		7
North Carolina		7
Alabama		6
Oklahoma		5
Connecticut		3
Wisconsin		1
Louisiana	1–5	13
Missouri		12
Virginia		11
Tennessee		9
Maryland		9
South Carolina		8
Oregon		7
New Mexico		7
Nebraska		7
Minnesota		6
Kentucky		6

needs, mainly for financial gain. One fourth of FSMs killed only strangers, and one third killed only family members. FSMs have specific age-groups of victims: 20% killed only children and one third targeted only adults. Few FSMs killed from all age-groups. Males were more likely to be an FSM's victim. FSMs generally did not kill their victims using violent methods and were highly likely to use poison.

- TSMs represent 26% of offenders in SMATV, and Hickey surmises that more will arise in the 21st century. TSMs were responsible for 14% to 15% of all deaths. TSMs operate symbiotically, and the team is usually masterminded by one person. When women are part of a team, they are generally not the decision-makers, but become equal participants. Not all participants in teams share the same desires, reasons, or skills. Having more than one offender involved does not increase the number of victims. There is a rank order to the relationship groupings of TSMs: spouses are the most frequent pairing, followed by fathers and sons, brothers, mothers and sons, cousins, and male friends. MSMs and FSMs caused more destruction than TSMs. TSMs maintained local proximity to kill sites. Strangers were the most common type of victims with very few killings of family members or acquaintances. TSMs preferred adult victims over children. TSMs were not gender specific and selected both males and females equally. Firearms were used as the sole method of killing in 27% of cases. More than half (54%) used two or more methods to kill their victims. Sex and money were frequent motives of TSMs. TSMs had prior incarcerations 43% of the time.

How Do the Current Review's Findings Compare to the Seminal Studies?

This review's findings challenge much of what Egger surmised about serial murderers:

- The majority of modern serial murderers are African American males who victimized both men and women almost half of the time and, of that proportion, the victims were more likely to be male.
- The victims of serial murderers are now likely to know their murderer in 26% of instances. Elderly women and children are no longer routinely targeted, nor are patients in hospitals. College campuses, red light districts, and highways are no longer frequent hunting grounds. Home invasion killings are nowhere near as prevalent (1%) as lethal street robberies (61%).
- Financial gain appears in 20% of cases as opposed to Egger's 7%.
- The share of serial murderers who use manual means to kill their victims has been halved and stands at 25%, down from Egger's 50%. Victims were killed with a firearm 20% of the time in Egger's study, while 44% of victims in this review were felled by a firearm.
- The 13% of serial murderers who change their victim type in Egger's data is similar to the 17% in this review's data.

The serial murderers in Beasley's study are both similar to and different from their modern-day counterparts:

- There are far fewer serial murderers motivated by sexual desires (57% then versus 13% today) and financial gain (20% today versus 43% then), but the proportion who kill out of anger is similar (37% today versus 43% then).
- The methods and victim selection of modern-day serial murderers are as varied as Beasley indicates, with 27% of offenders using multiple methods, 17% selecting victims from various ages, 48% from both the male and female gender, and 37% targeting victims from a variety of relationships to the offender.

- The percentage of serial murderers killing across multiple states is low (57% then versus 11% today).
- The ethnicity of serial murderers and their victims has become more mixed today as only 52% of ethnicities matched (versus 70% then) and 48% of series had victims of varied races (versus 30% then).
- 36% of victims were sex workers, and 15% were elderly compared to the 5% of sex worker victims and 3% of elderly victims in this review.
- Offenders today used one method of death more often (57% then versus 73% today).
- More serial murderers had criminal histories (57%) than in this review (45%).

While Hickey's findings are similar to this review's, there are a few differences:

- With regard to MSMs who kill alone, victimization has shifted away from a singular focus on strangers over the past decade to offenders who are acquainted with each of their victims a quarter of the time and know at least one of their victims a little more than a third of the time.
- The victimization of sex workers has declined significantly. Only 5% of serial murderers kill sex workers exclusively.
- The incidence of victims who hitchhike or model is almost nonexistent today given societal shifts outlawing the former and professionally organizing the latter.
- MSMs no longer avoid firearms as the main mode of death as 44% used firearms.
- Serial murderers are motived by financial gain with 20% killing solely for money.

Data from this review support several assertions made in SMATV:

- MSMs tended not to kill children and teens exclusively as these victim pools shrank.
- Serial murderers whose sole motive is sex remains low (13% compared to SMATV's 8%).
- Serial murderers citing enjoyment as their motive remains low (6%).
- MSMs who kill locally rose from 74% since 1975 to 89% today.[6]
- A large proportion of serial murderers may be versatile criminals: 63% of the SMATV cohort had a prior incarceration while 48% of MSMs in this review had previously been in prison.
- Overall, MSMs were responsible for 86% of deaths in this review

Male Serial Murderers

Race

As shown in Table 3.3a., the share of Caucasian serial murderers has remained relatively stable over the past 20 years. The prevalence of Caucasian TVSMs is within

TABLE 3.3A Comparison of male serial murderers in the United States 2004–2021

Years	*2004–2011 (SMATV)*	*2011–2021*		
Offender type	*≥3 Victims*	*≥3 Victims*	*2 Victims*	*Spree*
	N=146	*N=115*	*N=104*	*N=115*
Race of offender				
Caucasian	38%	39.1%	35.5%	40.8%
African American	57%	49.5%	57%	46.0%
Hispanic	3%	9.5%	6.7%	8.6%
Other	2%	2%	1.0%	4.3%
Offender year of birth range	1937–1992	1936–2004	1941–1998	1947–2001
Average age of offender at first killing	30	30	26	32
Average age at apprehension	38	40	40	32
Average age of victims	-	40	36	41
Average span of offender killing	7 years	4 years w/o parole; 11 years with parole	4 years w/o parole; 14 years with parole	5 days
Total number of victims	482–618	497–522	208	372–379
Average number of victims per offender	4 to 6	4	2	3
Span of offender killing	1965–2011	1962–2021	1963–2020	2011–2021
Offenders who killed all their victims in same year	31%	33%	24%	100%
Offenders who killed in more than 1 year	69%	67%	76%	0%
1–2 years	12%	4%	3%	0%
2–5 years	18%	16%	13%	0%
6–9 years	15%	10%	6%	0%
10+ years	24%	37%	54%	0%
Method of killing				
Shoot only	30%	42%	27.8%	63.4%
Strangle only	29%	11%	12.5%	6.0%
Stab only	8%	10%	14.4%	8.6%
Beat/blunt force only	7%	7%	5.7%	3.4%
Combination	26%	27%	38.4%	16.5%
Victims of male solo killers				
Adults only	82%	79.1%	88.4%	67.8%
Elderly only	7%	5.2%	0.0%	3.4%
Children only	2%	0.0%	0.9%	0.0%
Various	10%	15.6%	8.6%	27.8%
Strangers only	93%	38.2%	33.6%	40.8%
Sex workers	23%	8.6%	6.6%	4.2%
Males only	19%	22.6%	34.6%	28.6%
Females only	53%	20.0%	37.5%	13.0%
Male and female victims	29%	57.3%	27.8%	58.2%
Mobility				
Involving more than one state	22%	16%	8%	7%

2% to 3% of the incidence of Caucasian serial murderers who kill ≥3 victims. While half of MSMs are African American, those who murder ≥3 victims became slightly less prominent. The incidence of African American TVSMs matches their ≥3 victim counterparts from the past. The incidence of Hispanic serial murderers who kill ≥3 victims has tripled. Hispanic TVSMs are twice as prominent as their counterparts from the past who killed ≥3 victims. The incidence of serial murderers from other races remained stable across time.

Age

The age of MSMs who kill ≥3 victims both at the beginning and end of their series were similar over the past 20 years: late 20s, early 30s at the start, and late 30s and early 40s at the conclusion. Both male TVSMs and those who kill ≥3 victims killed victims who were, on average, older than them.

Timespan

The average span of killing for serial murderers killing ≥3 victims increased by 4 years, but that can be mainly attributed to the high proportion of offenders who were paroled. The average span of killing for TVSMs is nearly double that of their counterparts from the past who killed ≥3 victims, but that can be mainly attributed to the high proportion of offenders who were paroled. Without including paroled offenders, the average span of killing fell to 4 years for both categories. The lower estimate of the total number of victims of serial murderers killing ≥3 victims is similar over the past 20 years, but the upper estimate fell by almost 100 victims. MSMs killing ≥3 victims killed all of their victims in the same year about a third of the time, a 2% increase over the past decade. The majority of MSMs operated across several years, with the highest incidence being 10+ years for both MSMs killing ≥3 victims and TVSMs. TVSMs were the most likely to operate across several years, but this is somewhat due to a high number of these offenders being incarcerated after their initial homicide and then being paroled before their subsequent homicide. Still, MSMs killing ≥3 victims are starting to kill for greater periods of time than in the past.

Kill Method

MSMs killing ≥3 victims used firearms as the sole method of death more frequently than in the past, while TVSMs used firearms slightly less so. The use of strangulation as the sole method of death fell substantially among both MSMs killing ≥3 victims and TVSMs. MSMs killing ≥3 victims and TVSMs stabbing as the sole method of death were slightly more frequent over the past decade, while the use of bludgeoning remained the same for those killing ≥3 victims and decreased 1% for TVSMs. Both MSMs killing ≥3 victims and TVSMs used a combination of methods of death, with a 1% increase for the former and a 12% increase for the latter.

Victim Selection

MSMs were just as likely to kill adults exclusively today as in the past (TVSMs more so than serial murderers killing ≥3 victims). MSMs killing ≥3 victims targeted the elderly slightly less often (5%) while TVSMs did not kill any elderly victims. Children were infrequent victims of MSMs. MSMs killing ≥3 victims selected victims from various ages at an increased rate, while the rate among TVSMs fell by 1%. Male TVSMs and serial murderers killing ≥3 victims were far less likely to select only strangers or sex workers as victims. MSMs killing ≥3 victims and TVSMs both killed only males more frequently with a respective 4% and 16% increase. MSMs killing ≥3 victims and TVSMs both killed females exclusively far less frequently with a respective 33% and 15% decrease. MSMs killing ≥3 victims were far more likely to select victims from both genders while TVSMs did so at almost the same rate as offenders from SMATV.

Serial-Spree Murderers

Race

The racial breakdown of serial-spree murderers (SSMs) is similar to that of TVSMs and of those killing ≥3 victims both from SMATV and from 2011 to 2021. The average age of SSMs at their first killing is a bit older than TVSMs but is similar to the average age of those killing ≥3 victims both from SMATV and from 2011 to 2021.

Age

Similar to both TVSMs and those killing ≥3 victims, SSMs victimize individuals who are older than them. The average number of victims is similar to the number of victims of both TVSMs and those killing ≥3 victims both from SMATV and from 2011 to 2021.

Kill Method

The incidence of SSMs who use firearms as their sole method of death far surpasses both TVSMs and those killing ≥3 victims both from SMATV and from 2011 to 2021. As such, their use of other methods is far lower than that of TVSMs and those killing ≥3 victims both from SMATV and from 2011 to 2021. SSMs tend not to combine methods as much as TVSMs do and those killing ≥3 victims both from SMATV and from 2011 to 2021.

Victim Selection

SSMs selected only adults as their victims less frequently than TVSMs and those killing ≥3 victims both from SMATV and from 2011 to 2021. Instead, SSMs chose victims from various age-groups at almost triple the rate of serial murderers killing

≥3 victims from SMATV, slightly less than double the rate of serial murderers killing ≥3 victims from 2011 to 2021 and triple the rate of TVSMs. The incidence of SSMs selecting only strangers is similar to that of both TVSMs and those killing ≥3 victims from 2011 to 2021 but less than half of the rate of serial murderers who killed ≥3 victims from SMATV. The rate of victimization of sex workers among SSMs is lower than, but similar to, that of both TVSMs and those killing ≥3 victims from 2011 to 2021 but far lower than that of serial murderers who killed ≥3 victims from SMATV. When looking at gender, SSMs most closely resembled serial murderers who killed ≥3 victims from 2011 to 2021 but differed substantially from serial murderers who killed ≥3 victims from SMATV and TVSMs. Only TVSMs killed more men exclusively than SSMs, while SSMs killed the fewest women exclusively. While SSMs were the most likely of the groups to kill both male and female victims, there is only 1 percentage point separating them and serial murderers who killed ≥3 victims from 2011 to 2021.

Mobility

Although the data seem to indicate that SSMs were erratic in their choices when considering the victim's gender and age, SSMs are the least mobile when comparing them to TVSMs and those who killed ≥3 victims both from SMATV and from 2011 to 2021. This finding runs contrary to the image of the highly traveled, "run-and-gun" killer.

Female Serial Murderers

While FSMs are responsible for only 6% of the deaths in this review, they were just as efficient as their male counterparts. For the most part, the killings committed by FSMs were, as in SMATV, of low visibility. The FSMs were especially devious and concocted intricate plans (one offender killed a victim to steal their identity and another offender framed a person and donned the persona of a television producer to do so). There were a few instances where FSMs were known to police due to their criminal past or outward display of animosity and threats toward their victims. In contrast to SMATV, FSMs were not (aside from a nursing assistant and a woman posing as a nurse) employed as nurses or care providers. In this review, males were far more likely to be caregiving serial murderers.[7] Only one FSM killed her husband and an intimate partner and could be thought of as a "black widow." With regard to a rise in the total number of victims and extended timespans over which FSMs killed, the FSMs in this review did not hold to the SMATV profile.

Race

As shown in Table 3.3b, the share of Caucasian FSMs has fallen by 13%, while the incidence of African American and Hispanic FSMs has increased by 8% and 5%, respectively.

TABLE 3.3B Comparison of female serial murderers in the United States: 2004–2021

Years	*2004–2011 (SMATV)*	*2011–2021*
	N=14	*N=20*
Race of offender		
Caucasian	93%	80%
African American	7%	15%
Hispanic	0%	5%
Other	0%	0%
Offender year of birth range	1931–1975	1949–1992
Average age of offender at first killing	40.7	38
Average age at apprehension	47.4	43
Average age of victims	-	33
Average span of offender killing	7.1 years	4 years w/o paroled; 5 years with paroled
Total number of victims	39–55	60–81
Average number of victims per offender	3.1–4.2	3
Span of offender killing	1952–2008	1986–2019
Offenders who killed all their victims in same year	29%	20%
Offenders who killed in more than 1 year	71%	80%
1–2 years	14%	25%
2–3 years	14%	10%
4–5 years	7%	15%
6–9 years	21%	10%
10+ years	14%	20%
Method of killing:		
Poison only	21%	20%
Shoot only	7%	20%
Strangle/smother only	21%	20%
Stab only	7%	0%
Beat/blunt force only	7%	5%
Combination	37%	30%
Victims of female solo killers		
Adults only	93%	50%
Children only	7%	30%
Elderly	14%	5%
Patients	14%	10%
Various	0%	15%
Strangers Only	50%	5%
Sex Workers	7%	0%
Males only	43%	35%
Females only	21%	10%
Male and female victims	36%	55%
Mobility		
Involving more than one state	29%	20%

Age

The average age of offenders at both the beginning and end of their career has fallen by about 3–4 years. FSMs tend to kill victims who are younger than them.

Timespan

The average span of an FSM's career has shortened by about 2 years. The longest time span of nonparoled FSMs (23 years) belonged to an offender whose first homicide was misclassified as an accident. The second longest time span (15 years) belonged to an offender who took forensic countermeasures. The third longest time span (8 years) belonged to an offender who benefited from the misclassification of the death of her son as sudden infant death syndrome. Similar to those in SMATV, FSMs were the least likely of the categories to have had a criminal career (with only 15% having been incarcerated). The percentage of FSMs who killed all of their victims in 1 year decreased by 9%, while those killing in more than 1 year increased by 9%. The greatest increase came among those killing over 1–2 years with an 11% increase. While the percentage of FSMs killing between 6 and 9 years fell by 11%, those killing over 10 or more years increased by 6%.

Kill Method

As in SMATV, FSMs tended not to use violent methods such as bludgeoning or stabbing to kill their victims, instead using drugs, strangulation, and firearms equally (20%). Unlike in SMATV, FSMs killed mainly to appease their emotions and kill out of anger or negligence rather than unfulfilled needs like FSMs of the past. FSMs have begun to use firearms much more frequently, while their rate of poisoning and rate of strangling victims have remained stable. The frequency of FSMs that stabbed and bludgeoned their victims both fell alongside the percentage of FSMs who combined multiple methods together over their career.

Victim Selection

Similar to SMATV, FSMs were more likely to kill males. A small percentage of FSMs killed strangers exclusively (5% compared to the 25% in SMATV). The 40% of FSMs who killed family members is similar to the 33% in SMATV. Unlike SMATV, the FSMs in the present study selected children as victims only 5% of the time, but they did kill infants a quarter of the time. Half of the time, FSMs targeted adults exclusively, an increase over the 33% in SMATV. After adults and infants, FSMs killed from all age-groups 15% of the time. Victims have become younger as FSMs targeted children more often and lessened their interest in the elderly and patients. FSMs selected victims across multiple ages more often. The number of FSMs who murdered strangers fell substantially as they focused more attention on killing family, friends, and acquaintances over the past decade. No FSMs targeted sex workers. The incidence of FSMs selecting males exclusively fell by 8%, while FSMs who targeted females exclusively fell by 11%. The majority of FSMs murdered both male and female victims, a percentage that rose substantially from 36% to 55%. The average victim count was three, with the highest count of seven belonging to the nursing assistant. The average number of victims per FSM has remained about the same over the years.

Team Serial Murderers

The incidence of TSMs has declined from 26% who were responsible for 14% to 15% of deaths in SMATV to just 7% responsible for 7.5% of deaths between 2011 and 2021. The rank order of the relationship groupings in this review differs from the SMATV cohort in that male friends represented the majority of TSMs at 51%, and familial relationship groupings made up 49% (spouses (15%), boy/girlfriends (15%), siblings (15%), and a pair of cousins (4%)). TSMs did cause less destruction than those who killed alone. While sex is no longer a frequent motive of TSMs, financial gain is 41% of the time. The percentage of TSMs who have been previously incarcerated in this review (37%) is similar to the share of TSMs in the SMATV cohort with a prior incarceration (43%). As shown in Table 3.3c, the makeup of TSMs has changed with an increase in male participants and a decrease in female participants. SSM teams look like TSMs from SMATV.

TABLE 3.3C Comparison of team serial murderers in the United States: 2004–2021

Years	*2004–2011 (SMATV)*	*2011–2021*	
Offender type	*Serial*	*Serial*	*Spree*
	N=29	*N=16*	*N=11*
Gender of killers	M: 76% F: 24%	M: 85% F: 15%	M: 73% F: 27%
Average number of accomplices	1	1	1
Race of offender			
Caucasian	55%	50%	55%
African American	38%	25%	27%
Hispanic	7%	6%	0%
Other	0%	19%	18%
Offender year of birth range	1931–1991	1960–2002	1973–1997
Average age of offender at first killing	30.6	28	28
Average age at apprehension	33.4	31	28
Average age of victims	-	34	37
Average span of offender killing	3.1 years	1 year w/o paroled; 3 years with paroled	6 days
Total number of victims	73–91	56–63	34
Average number of victims per offender	2.5–3.1	4	3

TABLE 3.3C Cont.

Years	*2004–2011 (SMATV)*	*2011–2021*	
Offender type	*Serial*	*Serial*	*Spree*
	N=29	*N=16*	*N=11*
Span of offender killing	1994–2010	1994–2019	2011–2019
Offenders who killed all their victims in same year	41%	56%	100%
Offenders who killed in more than 1 year	59%	44%	0%
1–2 years	14%	19%	0%
2–3 years	17%	0%	0%
4–5 years	7%	6%	0%
6–9 years	7%	6%	0%
10+ years:	14%	13%	0%
Method of killing			
Shoot only:	40%	50%	64%
Strangle only:	13%	13%	0%
Stab only:	0%	6%	0%
Beat/blunt force only	13%	6%	0%
Combination	34%	25%	36%
Victims of team killers			
Adults only	100%	75%	73%
Elderly only	0%	0%	0%
Children only	0%	6%	0%
Teens only	0%	13%	0%
Various	0%	6%	27%
Strangers only	100%	50%	55%
Sex workers	7%	13%	0%
Males only	33%	50%	55%
Females only	13%	6%	9%
Male and female victims	53%	44%	36%
Mobility			
Involving more than one state	20%	0%	27%

Race

The prevalence of Caucasian TSMs fell by 5%, but spree killing teams matched TSMs from SMATV. The frequency of African American TSMs decreased for both serial and spree killers.

Age

TSMs are getting younger as the average age of offenders at their first killing decreased by 3 years to 28. The average age of offenders upon capture fell by 2 years to 31. The age of spree killing teams at the start and end of their killings matched the TSMs' start age. Both serial and spree killing teams killed victims who were older than them, on average.

Timespan

The average span of killing for TSMs remained stable, while the total number of victims killed decreased. The average number of victims per offender increased by one. The frequency of TSMs who killed all of their victims in the same year increased by 15%. Although TSMs who killed their victims across multiple years fell by 15%, the frequency of those killing between 1 and 2 years rose by 5%.

Kill Method

Serial and spree killing teams both used firearms more frequently as firearms now represent the most used weapon. TSMs used strangulation at the same rate as the previous decade. Spree killing teams did not use strangulation, stabbing, or beating as their primary method of death. The incidence of TSMs combining methods across their series fell by 9%. Spree killing teams that combined methods across their killings almost matched TSMs from SMATV. Different from the SMATV cohort, TSMs used firearms twice as often, or 56% of the time. With the increased use of firearms comes a decrease of TSMs who used two or more methods to kill their victims, from a high of 54% in the SMATV cohort to a low of 26% in this review.

Victim Selection

The frequency of TSMs killing adults exclusively decreased by 25%. TSMs were more likely to choose children, teens, and victims from various age-groups than were offenders from SMATV, but adults made up the vast majority of victims. Trends from the SMATV cohort regarding victim type and relationship to the offender have continued as strangers were the most common type of victim, with very few killings of family members or acquaintances, and there was a preference for adults over children. TSMs killed strangers only 50% of the time compared to 100% in SMATV. The incidence of sex workers being selected as victims increased by 6%. TSMs were more likely to select men exclusively as victims than in the past and less likely to select female victims exclusively. The frequency of TSMs selecting both male and female victims fell by 9%.

Mobility

No TSMs killed outside one state between 2011 and 2021. Spree killing teams were similar in racial makeup, age, weapon use, and victim selection, aside from the higher likelihood that they would select victims from various age-groups and their high degree of mobility. TSMs have remained within local proximity to kill sites.

TABLE 3.3D Comparison of all serial murderers in the United States: 2004–2021

Years	*2004–2011 (SMATV)*	*2011–2021*
	N=146	*N=381*
Estimated number of victims	584–730	1,143–1,524
Gender of killers	M: 90% F: 10%	M: 93% F: 7%
Average span of offender killing	7 years	3 years w/o paroled; 11 years with paroled
Average number of victims per offender	4–5	3–4
Offenders who killed victims within		
Same year	34%	53%
Multiple years	66%	47%
1–4 years	29%	12%
5–9 years	18%	6%
10+ years	19%	29%
Method of killing		
Shoot only	31%	44%
Strangle only	26%	10%
Stab only	8%	10%
Beat/blunt force only	7%	5%
Poison only	2%	2%
Other	1%	1%
Combination	25%	27%
Offenders murdered		
Adults only	91%	77%
Children only	9%	1%
Strangers only	93%	37%
Sex workers	21%	6%
Males only	22%	30%
Females only	46%	21%
Male and female victims	32%	49%
Mobility		
Involving more than one state	23%	11%

Overall, Table 3.3d shows that the share of FSMs has fallen by 3% over the last decade. The overall span of a serial murderer's career has fallen substantially from 7 years to 3 years. The average number of victims per offender fell by one victim. The number of serial murderers who are apprehended within 1 year represents the majority of offenders having grown by 19% to 53%. The number of serial murderers who killed across multiple years fell 19%, with the greatest change being those killing between 1 and 4 years. The number of serial murderers who kill over more than a 10-year span rose by 10% and is mostly due to those who have been paroled. Without including those who have been paroled, the average span of an offending career is 3 years. The overall use of firearms as the sole method of death rose by 13% to 44%, while the use of strangulation fell 16% to 10%. Each of the other methods is around where they were in the past. The overall number of adults and children who were victimized fell substantially, by 14% and 8%, respectively. The overall number of serial murderers who solely victimize strangers and sex workers fell substantially over the past decade from 93% to 37% and 21% to 6%, respectively. This has occurred as serial murderers have begun to victimize friends, family, and acquaintances at an increasing rate both separately and by mixing those victim types together with strangers. The percentage of serial murderers selecting males has risen by 8% alongside a substantial decrease, by a quarter, in the number of offenders who select female victims exclusively. The percentage of serial murderers who target both male and female victims increased by 16% to almost half.

As shown in Table 3.4, the killing of family and acquaintances by MSMs, which according to SMATV had disappeared in the years leading up to 2011, has seen a reversal in rates of victimization. Data from 2011 to 2021 demonstrate that rates of victimization of strangers fell dramatically among all serial murderer subtypes, while rates of victimization of acquaintances more than doubled for ≥3 victim offenders. The rate of victimization for TVSMs was similar to their ≥3 victim counterparts. The rate of victimization of strangers by FSMs is low and would have been zero if the offender who killed "johns" had been classified as having a cursory relationship with her victims, instead of the homicides being coded as stranger killings. The rate of victimization of acquaintances by FSMs was close to doubling, while victimization of family members remained stable with only a 5% increase. The rate of victimization for FSMs who killed a mixture of strangers, acquaintances, and family was also stable, having risen only 3%. The victimization style of SSMs was most like TSMs except for the victimization of acquaintances where they were more like TVSMs. TSMs selected more victims from a range of categories at more than double their previous rate while their selection of strangers as victims fell by a little more than a quarter.

TABLE 3.4 Comparison between male, female, and team serial murderers murdering family, acquaintances, and strangers in the United States, 1826–2021

Years	*1975–2011 (SMATV)*	*2011–2021*	*2011–2021*	*1826–2004 (SMATV)*	*2011–2021*	*1975–2011 (SMATV)*	*2011–2021*	*2011–2021*
Offender type	*≥3 Victims*	*≥3 Victims*	*2 Victims*	*Females*		*Teams*		*Spree*
	N=287	*N=115*	*N=104*	*N=64*	*N=20*	*N=48*	*N=27*	*N=115*
Strangers	91%	38%	33%	25%	5%	75%	48%	41%
Acquaintances	7%	16%	12%	18%	30%	4%	7%	13%
Family/ friends	2%	12%	15%	35%	40%	2%	7%	5%
Mixed	0%	34%	40%	22%	25%	15%	37%	41%

TABLE 3.5 Comparison of serial murderers killing victims in specific victim age and gender categories in the United States, 1800–2021

Years	*1800–2011 (SMATV)*	*2011–2021*	*1850–2004 (SMATV)*	*2011–2021*	*1800–2011 (SMATV)*	*2011–2021*
Offender type	*Males*		*Teams*		*Females*	
	N=491	*N=334*	*N=49*	*N=27*	*N=64*	*N=20*
Age only						
Children	3%	0.6%	2%	4%	20%	30%
Teens	4%	0.6%	8%	7%	0%	0%
Adults	55%	78%	42%	74%	31%	50%
Elderly	4%	3%	0%	0%	13%	5%
Gender only						
Females	45%	23%	28%	7%	10%	10%
Males	21%	28%	26%	52%	17%	35%
Both	35%	49%	46%	41%	67%	55%
Unknown	0%	0%	0%	0%	6%	0%

As shown in Table 3.5, the incidence of MSMs targeting children and teens shrank to almost half a percent while the rate of victimization of the elderly also decreased. MSMs killed more strangers when compared to the past. TSMs targeted children and adults with greater frequency and killed teens at almost the same rate as in the past, but they stayed away from killing elderly victims. FSMs targeted children and adults with greater frequency, but their rate of victimizing the elderly fell substantially and they continued to ignore teens as potential victims. The incidence of MSMs targeting only females has decreased by almost half. There has been an increase in the victimization of males and offenders who select victims from both genders over their series. TSMs targeted only females far less frequently than in the past as the rate fell by a multiple of 4 but the rate of TSMs selecting only males rose by a multiple of 2. There has been a small decrease in offenders who select victims from both genders over their series. The percentage of FSMs killing exclusively female victims remained the same, while their selection of only male victims rose by a multiple of 2. FSMs who selected victims from both genders over their series decreased by 12%.

As shown in Table 3.6a, there were several shifts in the methods used by serial murderers to bring about death. The use of so-called "hands-on methods" (bludgeoning, stabbing, strangulation) fell among MSMs and TSMs, while FSMs beat and strangled their victims with slightly more regularity. More specifically, TSMs embraced the use of firearms as their sole method of killing at a multiple of 2, and they almost completely abandoned the singular use of bludgeoning and strangulation across their series. The incidence of serial murderers who utilized firearms as their sole method of killing rose by a multiple of 2.5 across both MSMs

TABLE 3.6A Comparison of methods of serial murderers in the United States, 1800–2021

Years	*1800–2004 (SMATV)*	*2011–2021*	*1800–2004 (SMATV)*	*2011–2021*	*1826–2004 (SMATV)*	*2011–2021*
Offender type	*Males*		*Teams*		*Females*	
	N=367	*N=334*	*N=45*	*N=27*	*N=64*	*N=20*
Firearms	18%	45%	27%	56%	8%	20%
Bludgeoning	9%	5%	29%	4%	0%	5%
Stabbed	13%	11%	32%	4%	3%	0%
Strangulation	12%	10%	45%	7%	11%	20%
Poison	5%	1%	7%	0%	34%	20%
Other	2%	1%	5%	0%	0%	5%
Combination	43%	27%	54%	26%	32%	30%

TABLE 3.6B Percentage comparison of motives of serial murderers in the United States, 1800–2021

Years	*1800–2004 (SMATV)*	*2011–2021*	*1800–2004 (SMATV)*	*2011–2021*	*1826–2004 (SMATV)*	*2011–2021*
Offender type	*Males*		*Teams*		*Females*	
	N=367	*N=334*	*N=49*	*N=27*	*N=64*	*N=20*
Sex	8%	14%	49%	4%	0%	0%
Money	7%	18%	31%	41%	26%	15%
Mental	6%	3%	0%	0%	0%	0%
Enjoyment	2%	6%	25%	4%	3%	10%
Anger	11%	38%	9%	33%	0%	30%
Combination	51%	14%	60%	15%	15%	5%

and FSMs. The use of multiple methods across the series of both MSMs and TSMs fell by a multiple of 1.5 and 2, respectively.

As shown in Table 3.6b, there were several shifts in the motivations of serial murderers over the past decade. MSMs were more likely to be singularly motivated by sex, money, enjoyment, and anger (at multiples of 1.7, 2.5, 3, and 3.4, respectively) and far less interested in combining motives over the past decade. Offenders who had a diagnosed mental illness at the time of the offense pattern fell by half. TSMs were far less likely to be singularly motivated by sex and enjoyment or to combine motives. TSMs were greatly motivated by both financial gain and anger with rates for both motives increasing over the past decade. FSMs were never motivated by sex or mental illness, less interested in financial gain and combining motives than in the past, a bit more interested in enjoying themselves, and far more interested in

TABLE 3.7 Comparison of mobility classification of male, female, and team serial murderers in the United States, 1826–2021

Years	*1975–2011 (SMATV)*	*2011–2021*	*2011–2021*	*1826–2004 (SMATV)*	*2011–2021*	*1850–2004 (SMATV)*	*2011–2021*	*2011–2021*
Offender type	*≥3 Victims*	*≥3 Victims*	*2 victims*	*Female*		*Teams*		*Spree*
	N=331	*N=115*	*N=104*	*N=64*	*N=20*	*N=49*	*N=27*	*N=115*
Multistate	26%	16%	8%	22%	20%	39%	11%	7%
One state	74%	84%	92%	78%	80%	61%	89%	93%

appeasing their emotions through anger. The rise of anger as a motivating factor among all categories of serial murderers (by a multiple of 3) is certainly concerning and mirrors the increase among other homicide offenders over the past decade.

As shown in Table 3.7, serial murderers from each category have become more place-specific over the past decade as the incidence of multistate offenders fell. The most dramatic shift occurred among TSMs whose rate of killing across multiple states fell by a multiple of 3.5. According to SMATV, rapid urbanization, a lessening need to travel to maintain anonymity, and familiarity with the area have contributed to serial murderers offending within only one state.

Notes

1 The television show *Clarice* and movie *The Little Things* are purposefully set in the 1990s since following the exploits of today's serial murderers would prove boring to modern viewers.
2 For example, the "Netflix and chill" generation has removed themselves from the victim pool, forcing serial murderers to expend more energy when trolling for targets.
3 The AHRG is a thinktank comprised of scholars, practitioners, police, and journalists who are dedicated to the study of serial murder.
4 Five of the seven selected serial murderers can be found in Table 1.1.
5 While "spree serial killings" are not tabulated, they are mentioned as occurring in a short time frame.
6 In the past decade, one long-haul trucker killed serially but his crimes were unrelated to his employment as a trucker.
7 There were five males that killed patients under their care (either by negligence during surgery or by over-prescribing drugs). Another offender posed as a caregiver to gain access to elderly victims.

References

Beasley, J. (2004). Serial murder in America: Case studies of seven offenders. *Behavioral Sciences & the Law*. 22(3):395–414.

Culhane, S., Hilstad, S., Freng, A., & Gray, M. (2011). Self-reported psychopathology in a convicted serial killer. *Journal of Investigative Psychology and Offender Profiling*. 8(1):1–21.

DeLisi, M. (2015). Mayhem by occupation: On the relevance of criminal careers to sexual homicide offenders. In A. Blockland & P. Lussier (Eds.), Sex Offenders: A Criminal Career Approach (pp. 219–229). John Wiley.

DeLisi, M., Drury, A., & Elbert, M. (2018). The homicide circumplex: A new conceptual model and empirical examination. *Journal of Criminal Psychology*. 8(4):314–332.

Department of Veterans Affairs Office of Inspector General. (2021). Care and oversight deficiencies related to multiple homicides at the Louis A. Johnson VA Medical Center in Clarksburg, West Virginia. Retrieved from www.oversight.gov/sites/default/files/oig-reports/VA/VAOIG-20-03593-140.pdf

Egger, S. (2002). The Killers among Us: An Examination of Serial Murder and Its Investigation. Prentice Hall.

Epstein, G. (2021). Missing and missed: Report of the independent civilian review into missing person investigations. Retrieved from https://carl-acaadr.ca/wp-content/uploads/2021/04/Missing-Persons-Report.pdf

Hall, S., & Wilson, D. (2014). New foundations: Pseudo-pacification and special liberty as potential cornerstones for a multi-level theory of homicide and serial murder. *European Journal of Criminology*. 11(5):635–655.

Hickey, E. (2013). Serial Murderers and Their Victims. Cengage Learning.

Hinch, R., & Hepburn, C. (1998). Researching serial murder: Methodological and definitional problems. *Electronic Journal of Sociology*. 3(2):1–11.

Hodgkinson, S., Prins, H., & Stuart-Bennett, J. (2017). Monsters, madmen … and myths: A critical review of the serial killing literature. *Aggression and Violent Behavior*. 34:282–289.

Kraemer, G., Lord, W., & Heilbrun, K. (2004). Comparing single and serial homicide offenses. *Behavioral Sciences & the Law*. 22(3):325–343.

Morton, R., & McNamara, J. (2005). Serial murder. In J. Payne-James & R. Byard, T. Corey, & C. Henderson (Eds.), Encyclopedia of Forensic and Legal Medicine (pp. 47–53). Elsevier.

Morton, R., & Hilts, M. (2008). Serial Murder: Multi-disciplinary Perspectives for Investigators. National Center for the Analysis of Violent Crime.

Morton, R., Tillman, J., & Gaines, S. (2014). Serial Murder: Pathways for Investigations. Federal Bureau of Investigation, US Department of Justice.

Osborne, J., & Salfati, C. (2015). Re-conceptualizing "cooling-off periods" in serial homicide. *Homicide Studies*. 19(2):188–205.

Pakkanen, T., Zappalà, A., Bosco, D., Berti, A., & Santtila, P. (2015). Can hard-to-solve one-off homicides be distinguished from serial homicides? Differences in offence behaviours and victim characteristics. *Journal of Criminal Psychology*. 5(3):216–232.

Reale, K., Beauregard, E., & Martineau, M. (2020). Is investigative awareness a distinctive feature of sexual sadism? *Journal of Interpersonal Violence*. 35(7–8):1761–1778.

Salfati, C., & Bateman, A. (2005). Serial homicide: An investigation of behavioural consistency. *Journal of Investigative Psychology and Offender Profiling*. 2(2):121–144.

Warwick, A. (2006). The scene of the crime: Inventing the serial killer. *Social & Legal Studies*. 15(4):552–569.

Yaksic, E. (2019). Moving past sporadic eruptions, discursive killing, and running amok: Recognizing the convergence of the serial and spree killer. *Journal of Criminal Psychology*. 9(3):138–146.

Yaksic, E., Allred, T. B., Drakulic, C., Mooney, R., De Silva, R., Geyer, P., Wills, A., Comerford, C., & Ranger, R. (2021). How much damage do serial homicide offenders wrought while the innocent rot in prison? A tabulation of preventable deaths as outcomes of sentinel events. *Psychology, Crime and Law*. 27(1):76–88.

4

AN OVERVIEW OF THE MODERN SERIAL MURDERER

The Importance of Narrative Context

Ferguson, White, Cherry, Lorenz, and Bhimani (2003, p. 292) proclaim that the study of serial murder is "likely to remain an inexact science," mainly due to unclear definitions that inhibit researchers from being able to distinguish between offenders. Hickey and Harris (2013, pp. 197–198) identified such discrepancies within the serial murder definition by introducing ten scenarios that challenged the "typical stereotypes purported by the media and immortalized by Hollywood." Providing a narrative context is critical to overcoming this definitional discordance as the process allows for proper categorization while highlighting nuances within data that are lost among the descriptive statistics (Yaksic, 2018). Skrapec (2001) urges researchers to look for the kinds of experiences that define serial murderers as human, act as motivational forces, and provide emotional meaning. This can only be accomplished by becoming familiar with the details of an offender's crimes and the surrounding events. Detailed below are vignettes related to 210 series (55% of this review's sample). Through random selection, the modern serial murderer was revealed as being criminally active, paroled, and having experienced relationship strife.[1] The following case vignettes are organized by perpetrator type, motive, and case-specific factors.

Perpetrator Type

Several perpetrator types were identified in the data, reported on in the following section, and arranged based by distinguishing characteristics: number of victims (e.g. two, and three or more), gender (e.g. female), partnerships (e.g. teams), chosen role in society (e.g. caregiver, survivalist), and method (e.g. in a spree-like fashion, committed a mass murder during their series, failed to attain their desired victim count, serial shooters).

DOI: 10.4324/9781003130567-4

Traditionally Defined Serial Murderers

Some of the leading thinking on how serial murderers are defined has been challenged over the past two decades (Yaksic, 2015). There is significant variation due to the use of different inclusion and exclusion criteria by researchers and police (Allely, 2020). Serial murderers have been segmented based on the timing of their killings, their motivation, their body count, and their inferred deadliness (Yaksic, 2018). Such variation has led to the misinterpretation of data, errors in classification,[2] and difficulty in making generalizations of, and comparisons between, studies (Kiger, 1990). DeLisi and Scherer (2006) note that resolving these semantic issues would hasten the understanding of serial murder.

Homant and Kennedy (2014) detail the exploits of Robert, a serial murderer determined to overcome the setbacks he encountered in his attempts to commit five sexual assaults over a 14-month period, a case that encompasses much of what is supposedly "typical" of serial murderers. Some researchers found that measuring the offender's intent better differentiates between types than a temporal component (Adjorlolo & Chan, 2014; Harbort & Mokros, 2001). Others have found that while there is frequent instability in the households of serial murderers, they are neither consistently victims of physical or sexual abuse as children, nor do they always engage in animal torture, take souvenirs or leave signatures, escalate in their violence as they continue killing, improve their methods and change their strategies over their careers, kill in a sadistic fashion strictly for sexual gratification, become more evidence conscious over time, allow media coverage to alter their criminal intentions, or perform the same crime scene behaviors throughout their series (Beasley, 2004; Schlesinger, Kassen, Mesa, & Pinizzotto, 2010). To remain historically consistent, traditionally defined serial murderers (TDSMs) are defined in this review as those who killed ≥3 victims over a period of time for personal gratification.

Some TDSMs used sexual violence as a means to control not only victims who they killed but others in their lives. Some murders can be sexual in nature without displaying obvious signs (one TDSM did not kill for overtly sexual reasons, yet the sexual overtones of his crimes were apparent):

- Lucius Crawford stabbed four women who rebuffed his sexual advances.
- While Lucky Ward did not sexually assault his victims, one was strangled with her own bra, and another was found naked from the waist down.
- William Gibson claimed that he wanted to have sex with his victims.
- Deangelo Martin offered one surviving victim a place to sleep but raped her instead.
- Antonio Rodriguez killed three women during what he described as "rough fantasy sex."
- Robert Rembert raped a woman in a bus station bathroom where they both worked.
- Ali Irsan raped his first wife and his oldest daughter.

- Edward Acquisto had served lengthy prison sentences for the rape of an ex-girlfriend.
- Darren Vann raped a sex worker.
- Stewart Weldon raped 11 women and left them alive.

Several of the TDSMs assaulted and attempted to kill additional victims but were unsuccessful:

- Lucius Crawford attempted to murder a coworker.
- Johnny Avalos has claimed that at least 20 intended victims escaped.
- Deangelo Martin committed nonfatal attacks, a sexual assault and stabbing of one woman, and the kidnapping and assault of another.
- Antonio Rodriguez is a suspect in the sexual assault of three other women who survived.
- James Ritchie's mother labeled him a 'time bomb' and he was arrested for a home invasion with plastic handcuffs and two firearms.
- A home alarm system caused Anthony Garcia to flee the house of one would-be victim.
- In an extensive plot to kill five people, Ali Irsan wanted to eliminate all those whom his daughter loved so that she would suffer before she died.
- In front of police, Darren Vann threatened to blow up the home of a man he thought was sheltering his girlfriend, held her hostage, and stated that he would burn her alive.
- Todd West shot at a car without killing anyone.
- Police said 11 other women survived being attacked by Stewart Weldon.
- Kendrick Johnson intended to kill a victim but ran out of bullets.

Some TDSMs behaved in the manner expected of them by leaving calling cards, keeping trophies, taking forensic countermeasures, posing, or stalking their victims:

- Deangelo Martin positioned each victim and left a victim's sock behind as a calling card.
- Robert Rembert displayed his victims to shock whoever discovered them.
- William Gibson cut the breast off of one victim and kept it with him.
- Cedric Marks removed the hands and teeth of a victim to delay identification.
- Khalil Wheeler-Weaver wore gloves and condoms.
- Johnny Avalos stated that he would stalk victims in the middle of the night.
- Billy Chemirmir took trophies and pawned many of his victim's possessions.

Many TDSMs understood their victims to be vulnerable:

- Lucky Ward killed the homeless as he knew targeting them would not arouse suspicion.

- Expert testimony in the case of James Bradley referred to him as a narcissist who loves control and who chose vulnerable victims to wield power.
- Timothy Crumitie was called a "wolf in sheep's clothing" given his use of his role as a pastor to victimize congregants.
- Darren Vann targeted women who were involved with sex work and drugs.
- Shaun Gallon noted the vulnerability of his victims and thought of them as prey.
- Michael Mullins targeted women living in the margins, beat, and raped them, left them partially nude, and covered them with a blanket.
- Shawn Grate targeted women who slipped through the social cracks or were vulnerable from drug use.
- Jose Martinez attributed his success to the selection of victims who are poor, immigrants, and criminals – those who, in his words, "don't matter."
- Billy Chemirmir targeted older residents who lived alone.
- Handyman Kevin Gavin killed three neighbors at a senior housing development.

Some of the TSMs offered explanations for their crimes:

- William Gibson claimed that an "evil" came over him when he killed.
- Kevin Sweat shot two girls alongside a road claiming he mistook them for "monsters."
- Lucius Crawford killed after becoming enraged that his victim was unfaithful.
- Jon Guerrero told his surviving victim that he stabbed him because he is a "bum."
- Aeman Presley claimed to have become addicted to murder after the first homicide.
- Itzcoatl Ocampo blamed his desire to kill on a "kill gene."
- Robert Gleason stated that killing is the same as "going to the fridge or tying a shoe."

The victim selection of some TDSMs was highly varied:

- Robert Rembert killed a coworker, shot a man in a parking lot, went to prison and, 12 years after his release, strangled and raped another woman, then shot his cousin and another woman whom he lived with 3 months later.
- Timothy Crumitie, who is suspected in the death of his wife, killed his former business partner, an intruder, and an older woman he lived with after he became appointed as the woman's power of attorney.
- Edward Acquisto beat a bartender to death because he would not serve any more drinks and beat another man into a coma in a separate incident.
- Aeman Presley purchased a firearm to commit robberies but instead targeted the homeless.
- Jamie Walter killed his father and, in a separate incident, used a hammer to kill two other men as they were sitting around a campfire at a homeless encampment.

Several TDSMs had financial motives:

- Edward Acquisto shot a fundamentalist Bible group's leader as they argued over a loan.
- Zachery Franklin was called the "most dangerous criminal" for the homicides of a man for his gold chain, and another for a motorcycle.
- David Nelson stole silver from a man and killed him and his mother.
- Billy Chemirmir stole the valuables of his victims to resell.
- Kevin Gavin got into arguments with his victims over finances.

Revenge featured as a central component in the lives of some TDSMs whose motives were highly personal and unique to their particular character disorders:

- Kevin Sweat blamed the family of one of the victims for the death of his brother as he believed that they sold his brother bad drugs.
- Ali Irsan was a domineering patriarch who fatally shot his daughter's friend and, 11 months later, his son-in-law in honor killings, in retribution for his daughter leaving home, converting to Christianity, and marrying a Christian.
- Anthony Garcia was motivated by hatred and revenge when he killed four people, including the son of a physician who helped fire him from a residency program two decades ago. Five years later, Garcia killed two others related to his firing.
- Charles Severance engaged in a bitter custody battle and had a general hatred for the elite, which motivated him to shoot his victims after knocking on their doors.

The body disposal methods of TDSMs were varied:

- James Ritchie killed five people in parks and along bike paths.
- Deangelo Martin killed four women and left their bodies in vacant homes.
- David Nelson dumped his victim's bodies out of town.
- Robert Rembert left one victim's body in a field, close to the road.
- Darren Vann left his victim's bodies in abandoned structures.
- Christopher Scheibe stabbed and dumped two women in the woods.
- Jamie Walter burned his victim's bodies in a barrel.
- Antonio Rodriguez grew up blocks from where he strangled his victims.

When others were suspected or convicted of the crimes TDSMs were responsible for and that resulted in the offender gaining the freedom to continue killing, those TDSMs benefited from lucky breaks. In other instances, offenders were not charged for their crimes or the medical examiner did not list the cause of death as homicide.

- Two other men were convicted of David Nelson's crimes.
- Another man spent 4 years in prison for one of Antonio Rodriguez's crimes.

- Leon Means was a suspect, but those charges were dropped for further investigation because a victim's brother-in-law was considered a suspect.
- After stabbing the mother and brother of a former classmate, Itzcoatl Ocampo caught a break when the classmate became a suspect.
- Jose Martinez was suspected of numerous murders but never charged.
- The medical examiners initially identified the cause of death of Billy Chemirmir's victims as natural causes.

Drugs and alcohol played a role in the lives of some offenders as they coped with their lives:

- James Ritchie was a promising student, but his life descended into drugs.
- Michael Mullins became an addict after both his parents died when he was young.
- Aeman Presley wanted to be an actor but spent his time drinking and using drugs.
- Michael Madison abused drugs and alcohol to cope with repressed anger toward women.
- Troy Whisnant had a history of drug abuse.
- After his friend died, Itzcoatl Ocampo developed post-traumatic stress disorder (PTSD), became depressed, and abused alcohol and could not find work. His family fell apart because of his father's drug use.
- An evaluation of Robert Gleason found a history of substance abuse and depression.

Other TDSMs suffered setbacks in life:

- Zachery Franklin's parents were drug addicts who were often incarcerated.
- Leo Boatman spent time in the juvenile justice system.
- Michael Mullins is illiterate with intelligence tests noting an intellectual disability.
- Lucky Ward was homeless.
- Michael Madison had an abusive and unstable childhood and "hated the female species."
- Johnny Avalos was determined by the court to be intellectually disabled.
- Darren Vann was terminated from his job.
- Jamie Walter is a repeat offender as he used violence in the past against others.
- Casey Pigge told himself not to care about anything, to embrace his "two sides," to gain acclaim by virtue of antisocial acts, and to use fantasy to escape the brutality of his childhood and the deep sense of insecurity and fears of abandonment.

Some offenders had backgrounds that should have precluded them from engaging in serial murder:

- After recovering hundreds of thousands of dollars during the homicides, Jose Martinez gave it to his mother and threw a party for one of his daughters. One of Martinez's lawyers said, "The human side outweighed the monster side" as he surrendered himself after learning that his granddaughter was going to be questioned about a homicide he committed.
- Shawn Grate was called a charmer with his own mother stating, "He's good looking but the Devil's good looking too."
- Charles Severance, who saw himself as a "noble exposer of truth," earned a mechanical engineering degree, was briefly married, and campaigned for political office.
- Cedric Marks was a former mixed martial arts fighter.

Suicide among TDSMs was rare:

- Edward Acquisto and James Ritchie confronted police with a firearm and were subsequently killed.

Two-Victim Serial Murderers

Although TVSMs have historically been ignored by serial murder scholars due to the belief that a pattern of behavior is established only after a third murder, that logic is beginning to erode. Homant and Kennedy (2014) observed that someone who has "only" killed once may psychologically be a serial murderer who simply has not yet acted on impulses or was arrested after their first homicide. One study found that all that separates TVSMs from other subgroups is a lack of opportunity to act on subsequent intentions (Adjorlolo & Chan, 2014). Another study found that classifying serial murderers by body count, and then inferring deadliness, unnecessarily segments a population of offenders who share similar pathologies with other subgroups. Concluding that TVSMs should be excluded from research studies neglects the narrative factors responsible for homicidality, namely, formative events, intent, markers associated with serial murder, and the relationship between victim and attacker. Excluding TVSMs also gives agency to offenders able to take advantage of favorable circumstances to become successful (Yaksic, 2018). In more basic terms, the commission of one homicide is rare enough, but once an offender has murdered, "the likelihood of doing it again increases nearly 1,500%" (DeLisi, Bunga, Heirigs, Erickson, & Hochstetler, 2019, p. 345). As serial murderer Lucius Crawford so eloquently stated, "...kill once, you'll kill again" (Kochman, 2015).

TVSMs were the most likely of the subgroups to fit the stereotype of the repeat sex offender:

- Sex offender Brandon Lavergne kidnapped and sexually assaulted a woman.
- Jeffrey Moreland raped a woman in his home after giving her a ride and left behind DNA evidence that connected him to two similar homicides.

- Jesse Matthew has a history of sexually assaulting women. One woman came forward and provided a DNA sample that would eventually link Matthew to the homicides of two college students, committed 5 years apart.
- Edward Mero killed a girlfriend and then killed a woman during a sexual experience.
- Telyith Hopkins had just raped and strangled a housekeeper when he killed a man who picked him up at a bus stop.
- John Gardner had an insatiable sex drive, which he fused with anger toward women.

Like other subgroups, several of the TVSMs assaulted and attempted to kill additional victims:

- Patrick Watkins is responsible for dozens of attempted murders.
- James Maxwell filmed himself raping and trying to kill a third victim, and tried to get rough with another but she was able to escape.
- Joseph Danclair forced a victim to disrobe and perform a sex act, but she escaped.
- John White stabbed a woman with the intent to do great bodily harm.
- Shawn Jarrett raped a woman who survived, and he was interrupted assaulting another.
- Kenneth Lumpkin tried to sexually assault and kill a woman he knew.
- Shaun Gallon fought with a man in a bar and tried to kill him with an explosive device.
- Steven Hobbs is accused of raping sex workers, some of whom survived.
- Jeffrey Willis kidnapped a girl after she became lost after leaving a party, but she escaped.
- Leeroy Rogers raped and shot a woman and left her for dead, but she survived.

Like other subgroups, many TVSMs understood their victims to be vulnerable:

- Mark Beebout sexually assaulted and strangled a 15-year-old girl who had run away and encountered him at a parish. Beebout was instructed to take the girl to another location that could better assist her. He also strangled a woman he met while she was volunteering at a homeless outreach program.
- Jesse Matthew abducted one woman who was locked out of a concert and another who had texted a friend about being lost after a night of partying.
- Jeffrey Moreland raped a woman after telling her he knew she was vulnerable and chastised her for getting in his vehicle.
- Maintenance man James Harris waited in his victim's apartment to sexually assault and strangle her since he knew she would be alone.
- Aaron Glee took advantage of a victim who confided in him about her recent sexual assault, giving her a place to bathe and sleep but warehoused her for 5 days, raped her, and then killed her to silence her efforts to escape.

- Jeffrey Willis attempted to kidnap a 16-year-old girl who was lost after leaving a party.
- Tyrone Walker strangled two young women who had crack cocaine habits.

Others abducted their victims:

- Jeffrey Willis kidnapped a woman who worked at a business he frequented 2 years after he shot a jogger near her home.
- Brandon Lavergne followed a victim as she rode her bike from her friend's home, rammed her off the bike, and fought with her.
- Kenneth Lumpkin had been friends with a woman he kidnapped and strangled to death after he got into an argument with her.

Like other subgroups, TVSMs understood how to destroy evidence to inhibit investigations:

- Derek Richardson covered both victims with bleach to try to destroy evidence.
- Brandon Lavergne disposed of evidence in various locations, burned his truck, and bought an identical one to cover his tracks.
- John White cleaned up the crime scene and disposed of items along with his victim's body and drove her car to another location to give the appearance that she was abducted.
- Edward Mero set fire to a house to cover his crime.

A few TVSMs displayed interest in underage victims:

- John Gardner pleaded guilty to sex crimes against children under 14 and was deemed to be a danger to the community.
- Jeffrey Willis recorded girls who were under the age of 14 and who used his bathroom.
- James Maxwell was jailed for the rape of a 9-year-old neighbor.

Few TVSMs were known to keep trophies:

- Jeffrey Willis had a folder titled "VICS" on his hard drive that contained information on his victims and was considered to be a digital trophy. There were 15,000 videos of girls in swimsuits and nighttime videos of neighbors undressing. Police found photos of women bound and gagged, handcuffs, chains, ropes, and syringes of powerful sedatives.

Some of the TVSMs offered explanations for their crimes:

- Joseph Danclair claimed that both victims died after using marijuana and cocaine.
- Telyith Hopkins claimed that one victim made sexual advances toward him.

- John Gardner, who killed his victims to avoid apprehension, thought he would like the memory of stabbing his victim but only enjoyed the memory of her assault.
- Matthew Guzman thought his victims were gay and "coming on to him."
- Tyrone Walker claimed that his first victim blackmailed him so that his girlfriend would not find out they were romantically connected.

Some of the methods used by TVSMs are just as violent as those of TDSMs:

- Reginald Riggins put a shirt in a victim's mouth and shoved it down her throat with a stick after she declined to have sex with him.
- Steven Hobbs strangled one woman to death and bound another victim with handcuffs.
- Telyith Hopkins wrapped phone cords around victims' necks and placed bags over their heads.
- John White thought about killing his victim for weeks and watched necrophilia pornography before beating her with a mallet, strangling her, and undressing her.

Some TVSMs benefited from lucky breaks:

- Leeroy Rogers was suspected of a shooting, but the case was dismissed.
- The police ruled the fire set by Edward Mero as accidental, which allowed him to kill another woman 2 years later.
- John Gardner told his psychiatrist that he was a danger to others but was ignored.
- Examiners had ruled James Lynn's first wife's death a suicide.
- By resigning, the hospital did not report Christopher Duntsch to the National Practitioner Data Bank that flags problematic doctors, allowing him to continue hurting patients.

Like other subgroups, the body disposal methods of TVSMs were varied:

- Steven Hobbs dumped one of his victims in the woods five miles from his house.
- Derek Richardson dumped two sex workers on the side of roads nearly a year apart.
- Leeroy Rogers shot and killed two women and dumped their bodies under bridges.
- Patrick Watkins left his victim's bodies at the scene of the crime.
- Jeffrey Moreland assaulted a woman, shot her to death, and left her in a bathtub.
- Tyrone Walker dumped two women in wooded or grassy areas.
- John White strangled a woman he was acquainted with and dumped her in the woods.
- Shawn Jarrett dumped a coworker's body near their place of employment.

Serial-Spree Murderers

Although serial and spree murderers were integrated together after attendees of an FBI symposium deemed the separate classifications to be of little use (Morton & Hilts, 2008), some authors continue to stratify offenders using temporal parameters (Safarik & Ramsland, 2020) even though spree homicide may not be distinct enough to classify separately (Osborne & Salfati, 2015). Schlesinger, Ramirez, Tusa, Jarvis, Erdberg (2017) found support for such claims since a sizeable number of serial murderers killed in a rapid-sequence manner[3] either all in one spree, or in one or two clusters. Pollock (1995) wrote about a "spree serial murder," and there were serial-spree murderers (SSMs) within Gurian's (2017) research sample. Another study determined that serial and spree murderers are beginning to converge due to the constraints put upon them by a more aware society and better police practices (Yaksic, 2019). There appears to be only a quantitative difference between serial and spree killers representing different aspects of the same phenomenon (Yaksic, Simkin, & Roychowdhury, 2021). To avoid controversy, SSMs were studied as a separate subgroup.

Although their attacks were carried out in "spree-like" fashion, several SSMs were called serial murderers:

- According to police, Jeremy Harris, whose crimes took place over the span of 18 days, fit the "definition of a serial killer."
- James Wright was referred to as a serial killer even though his killings took place over only 17 days.
- Nathaniel Petgrave, whose crimes spanned 7 days, was labeled a "serial murderer" by the police chief.

Several SSMs killed for sexual reasons:

- Ali Syed went on an hour-long rampage that spanned 25 miles and five locations after killing an escort in his parent's house.
- Cleophus Cooksey, who shot and killed nine people (including his own mother) over a 21-day span, rapped about leaving a woman to die in the dirt after sex, which was how one of his victims was found.
- Reginald Kimbro raped and killed two women, one of whom was his former girlfriend.

Several SSMs assaulted and attempted to kill additional victims:

- Nathaniel Petgrave set out to kill five people and was successful in only three attempts.
- James Willie was captured after a woman that he abducted escaped his apartment.
- Jeremy Harris who killed three people by shooting them from inside his own vehicle shot and wounded others who survived.

- Joshua Mebane stated, "My only regret from that night was that I allowed the husband to live."
- Jonathan Cruz threatened to kill a girl to whom he had sold drugs, but she escaped.
- While riding a bicycle, Jon Guerrero attacked nine people by whacking them on the back of the head as they sat at bus stops or stood on sidewalks.
- Esteban Smith had hundreds of rounds of ammunition in his vehicle and shot at several people who survived their wounds.
- Kiernan Brown was arrested before he could kill two other women on his hit list.

A few SSMs behaved like TDSMs:

- Nathaniel Petgrave scrawled a message in blood that referred to his kill count.
- James Brown set a vehicle on fire to destroy evidence.
- Nikko Jenkins lured two with a ruse claiming that women would have sex with the victims.
- James Willie was described as a regular guy, but he was responsible for the killings of a man and a woman whom he stalked on dark stretches of highways.
- Stanley Mossburg used bleach and an air conditioner to slow his victims' decomposition.
- Cosmo DiNardo lured four men to his family's farm under the guise of selling them marijuana and shot each to death in two separate incidents.

Many SSMs understood their victims to be vulnerable:

- Nathaniel Petgrave killed homeless men because they were easy targets.
- Methamphetamine-addicted transients Morrison Lampley and Lila Alligood targeted a tourist because she was foreign and alone.

Several SSMs utilized online services to post their viewpoints or request services:

- Dwight Jones' activity on Twitter offered a window into his mindset of persecution, with efforts to discredit his ex-wife by posting hours of videos that outlined what he saw as a conspiracy to take his son away from him.
- Mark Conditt spouted homophobic abuse online and defended sex offenders before killing two and injuring four with explosives.
- Drew Maras' Facebook posts are full of conspiracy theories.
- Jonathan Cruz posted messages over Facebook Messenger regarding the sale of a gun.

The victim selection of some SSMs was varied:

- Jeremy Harris' victims were waiting for a ride, sitting at a traffic light, or panhandling.

- Evan Ebel killed a chief of prisons and a pizza delivery man.
- Dwight Jones targeted a forensic psychiatrist who had testified against him, two paralegals and a counselor who supported his ex-wife, and a couple he played tennis with.
- Ramon Escobar killed his aunt and began attacking homeless men during robberies.

Many of the time frames over which SSMs killed were short and their crimes spastic in nature:

- While the first victim of Ramon Escobar survived, he attacked another man 2 days later, and 6 days after that, he attacked three men with a baseball bat. Four days later, Escobar killed a man under the Santa Monica Pier. Four days later, he attacked another man.
- Peter Manfredonia, who killed a man with a samurai sword, had several interactions with police for suicidal and homicidal ideation, stole, and then crashed a truck after a home invasion and then walked to his drug dealer's house, shot and killed him, and kidnapped his girlfriend.
- Jason Nightingale went on a random shooting spree, killing three and wounding four.
- James Brown killed his first two victims 6 days before another two.
- Drew Maras fatally shot a couple and then a sheriff's deputy days later.
- Over a 12-day period, Juan Ortiz shot four sex workers to death, two of whom he knew.
- Jonathan Cruz committed three random murders over a 4-day period.
- Reginald Kimbro killed two women within 4 days of each other.
- Dwight Jones shot and killed six people over 5 days after stewing for 9 years with resentment and self-pity following his divorce.
- William Boyette left four women dead over a 7-day period.
- Sean Barrette indiscriminately targeted drivers of vehicles during a 2-week killing spree.

Some of the SSMs offered explanations for their crimes:

- Jonathan Cruz texted his girlfriend that he was going "purging," a reference to the movie where murder is legal for one night a year.
- James Wright claimed that the three deaths of women he killed were accidental.
- Christopher Speight thought his sister was plotting to kick him out of the house.
- Mark Conditt recorded a confession without showing empathy or remorse and called himself a psychopath.
- Joshua Mebane stated that he derived emotional and physical gratification from killing.
- Evan Ebel wanted to kill so many people that Hitler would be jealous.
- Patrick Drum, who shot two convicted sex offenders to death, stated that he would have continued killing people if he was not captured.

- Morrison Lampley and Lila Alligood dreamed of starting a marijuana farm and robbed their victims for money and resources.
- Shannon Lamb killed a colleague who he believed was an obstacle to tenure.
- Juan Ortiz confessed to having a hatred for sex workers and desired to be killed by police after posting two goodbye messages on Facebook.
- Peter Manfredonia claimed his homicides resulted from the victim's triggering language.
- Stanley Mossburg stated that his victims were chosen by God and that he was a prophet.

The life circumstances of SSMs were highly variable:

- Authorities described Ali Syed as a "loner" and "gamer" who would spend a lot of time alone in his room. Syed stated that it was his "last day" before killing himself.
- Drew Maras, a self-styled UFOologist whose book about ancient aliens and the end of the world was titled *Open Your Eyes: To 2012 and Beyond*, was living out of his van and thought the world was going to end.
- Evan Ebel came from privilege, but after his sister died in a car accident, he became numb, volatile, with a "bad streak," and constantly angry at everyone, and was deemed to be a risk to the prison community.
- Friends described Mark Conditt as a deep thinker who liked to argue and would become combative in conversation, was recently terminated from his job, lacked direction due to the insularity of being home schooled, and might have been struggling with his sexuality, which conflicted with his staunch religious background.
- Cleophus Cooksey, whose rap name was King Playbola, wrote love songs to women.
- Ramon Escobar has a criminal record and was deported six times.
- Jon Guerrero has been in and out of jail and institutions for much of his life.
- Nikko Jenkins comes from a family of violent criminals, and his childhood was filled with abuse and criminal activity.
- Marc Carr suffers from an intellectual disability, his parents were addicted to crack cocaine, and his illiterate grandmother raised him and largely ignored his mental illness.
- Years of drug abuse are blamed for Randy Santos' volatile and paranoid behavior.
- Jody Hunt had a breakdown and was overwhelmed by grief and had money problems.
- Rodrick Dantzler was bipolar, was abusing alcohol, and had a temper.

The employment history and future goals of SSMs were varied:

- Juan Ortiz was a member of the US Border Patrol.
- James Wright was a carnival worker.

- Shannon Lamb was a well-liked geography professor and an active musician.
- Erbie Bowser was a Maverick ManiAAC dancer.
- Eulalio Tordil was a Homeland Security officer.
- A neighbor described Kenneth Gleason as a "clean-cut American kid."
- Some stated that Sean Barrette was a good kid who wanted to be a football player.

Some SSMs benefited from lucky breaks:

- Police had confiscated the gun used in Nathaniel Petgrave's homicides a month before the killings but had returned it to him 5 days later. Police detained Petgrave after finding him driving a stolen vehicle but released him.
- Reginald Kimbro was twice accused of assaulting women, but no charges were filed.
- Intel supervisor Juan Ortiz used his position to monitor leads and avoid arrest.

Female Serial Murderers

Two decades ago, Hinch and Hepburn (1998) warned that excluding FSMs from research samples would limit scholarly inquiry. Clark and Palattella (2017), who craft an impeccable narrative of an FSM's disordered mind and calculated crimes, noted that Hickey was perhaps the first researcher to acknowledge the threat posed by FSMs. Since then, the inclusion of FSMs has shown that there is more to the explanation of serial murder than individual pathology. Schechter and Schechter (2010) draw a contrast between the heightened qualities of ruthlessness, egotism, and masculinity within the MSM and a distortion of caretaking, nurturing, and romantic devotion traits within the FSM. Farrell, Keppel, and Titterington (2011) also observed that there are differences between female and male serial murderers. Tully and Smith-Inglis (2018) confirmed these differences, noting that MSMs and FSMs differ on modus operandi, harder to detect methods, and the desire to achieve notoriety, which explains why females appear to be more successful at serial homicide than males, and enjoy longer killing careers. Gurian (2011) found that FSMs were more likely to target adult family members using single methods for purpose-oriented motives. When FSMs do kill strangers, those victims are typically weak, helpless, and confined to a hospital bed or nursing care facility. White and Lester (2012) discovered that serial homicides by females seem to be less brutal with less use of torture and more use of drugs to subdue a victim. Gurian (2017) surmises that FSMs kill for a longer time frame due to a smaller number of victims, selecting intimates and family as victims, and use of poison. Harrison, Murphy, Ho, Bowers, and Flaherty (2015) wrote that FSMs kill over a longer period of time than their male counterparts, have more victims, and are frequently nurses or serve some caretaker role. Like with MSMs, data on psychological measures collected through firsthand accounts demonstrated that there is no single comprehensive profile of FSMs (Hildebrand & Culhane, 2015).

Accordingly, the FSMs in this review did not fit every aspect of the profiles from previous scholars.

Some FSMs are more devious and cunning than their male counterparts:

- Lois Reiss struck up a friendship with her victim specifically because she looked like her and killed her to steal her identity.
- Michele Kalina claimed that each of her four pregnancies were cysts that were drained and reoccurred.
- Pamela Hupp stabbed her best friend to death to gain access to her life insurance policy and orchestrated a ruse that involved luring a disabled man to her home by pretending to be a producer of NBC's Dateline to frame the woman's husband. Instead, she shot and killed him and planted a knife and kidnapping note on his body.

The motives of some FSMs were similar to those of their male counterparts:

- Susan Monica made several excuses for the shooting deaths of two men and stated that she does "not value human life very much … the only thing wrong with the planet is there's people on it."
- Jody Herring, who shot and killed two cousins, an aunt, and a social worker in a plot for revenge, blamed her relatives for calling the Department of Children and Families, which led to the loss of custody of her daughter.
- Kelly Cochran made a pact with her husband on their wedding night to kill anyone involved in their extramarital affairs.

Some FSMs disposed of their victim's bodies in gruesome ways:

- Kelly Cochran served her lover's remains to her neighbors at a barbecue.
- Jennifer Berry threw her newborn baby out the window.
- Susan Monica killed two handymen who worked on her property a year apart from one another, dismembered them, and fed them to her pigs at her farm.
- Michele Kalina killed her newborns and kept bones in a cooler and others in concrete.

The life circumstances of FSMs were highly variable:

- Angelina Barini was a sex worker who supplied drugs containing fentanyl to three men.
- Reiss forged checks to steal $11,000 from her husband's account, fled to Florida, and stopped at casinos along the way earning her the nickname "Fugitive Grandma."
- Michele Kalina was a nurse's aide.
- Jennifer Berry devoted her career to helping others and aiding troubled families and worked for charities.

- Tracy Garner posed as a nurse and injected two women's buttocks with a silicone substance, which led to their deaths.
- Christine Sanchez shot and stabbed her acquaintance to death 3 years before shooting 3 of her roommates to death.

Team-Based Serial Murderers

Until recently, TSMs have been studied sporadically. Gurian (2011) found that mixed-sex partnered serial offenders are more likely to target adult strangers, use a variety of weapons and methods to kill their victims, and kill locally within 2 years or less for pleasure-oriented motivations. Gurian (2013) offers several explanations for the mechanisms behind mixed-sex-partnered serial murders: (1) convincing another to become a killer offers its own sense of power, (2) the feeling of responsibility is diminished when tasks are shared, (3) group dynamics heighten the level of commitment, (4) older leaders are gratified by dolling out commands while younger followers are happy to comply, (5) the interdependency of partnerships is appealing, (6) romantic attraction compels some female partners to go along with their male counterpart's plans, (7) trust and emotional connectedness between bonded pairs is powerful, (8) there is fear of abandonment, (9) there is desire to attain stimulation through thrill or excitement, (10) inhibitions lessen among teams as one allays the fears of another, (11) reluctant partners comply out of need for survival of relationship, and (12) there is shared belief in persecutory delusions and superiority complexes. Gunn, White, and Lester (2014) found that TSMs were less likely to be mentally ill, and more likely to kill acquaintances, with more brutality and deviancy, and record their murders for the thrill. MSMs partnered with a friend whereas women more often killed with a significant other. Chai, Yaksic, and Chopin (2021) found that TSMs were more likely to be composed of older males who were more likely to kill adult employees or customers for financial reasons, and use firearms, over a short period of time.

The TSMs in this review were highly symbiotic:

- Franc Cano and Steven Gordon used a coded language to speak and coaxed one another into maintaining their motivation to kill.
- Mary Rice went along with William Boyette's crusade against women.
- Kim Williams was a willing participant in her husband Eric's quest for revenge against two lawyers.
- Elwyn and Candice Crocker both equally participated in starving, tasing, and beating their own children, keeping them naked in dog crates, and zip tied so they would not escape.
- An older Richard Beasley, a self-styled street minister and ex-convict, was a spiritual mentor to fellow killer Brogan Rafferty.
- Brandon Lyons and Jerrett Allen were cousins who strangled one victim whose body was found only five miles from his home.

- Jerard and Amanda Miller dressed up as the anarchic Joker and Harley Quinn, and their bond only tightened as they left their hometown after people found out about Jerad's criminal record.

The life circumstances of TSMs were highly variable:

- Eric Williams was a former attorney and justice of the peace.
- Herbert and Catherine Schaible believed in faith-healing rather than modern medicine and withheld medical care for two of their eight children.
- Sex offenders Franc Cano and Steven Gordon strangled their first victim after the elder Gordon heard that she shared his daughter's name.

TSMs perceived their victims to be worthless:

- Franc Cano and Steven Gordon left the body of their last victim at a trash sorting facility in an outward display of what they felt about her worth to society.
- Elwyn and Candice Crocker bathed their children by hosing them down while crated, withheld food as a punishment, put items in their food to make it taste as if it were inedible, and duct taped one child to a pool ladder to straighten her joints.
- Eric and Kim Williams had an elaborate plan of goring their victims with a crossbow and filling their stomachs with napalm. The Williams scouted out their victim's houses and Eric planned on posing as a police officer to gain access, but the plan was abandoned.

Multiple-Event Murderers

Offenders who commit a mass murder during their serial homicide career have not been thoroughly studied. These offenders have been named multiple-event murderers (MEMs) in this review given the multiple events over which their killings take place. Schlesinger (1998) reported on an offender who killed an acquaintance to silence her from divulging their sexual relationship to his girlfriend, then another acquaintance and her children in a similar scenario 6 months later, and finally two additional victims. Although not labeled as an MEM, this offender had severe anger toward women and presented himself as powerful and in control.

Given that anger is increasingly becoming a common driver for serial murder, the one-time distinctions between serial and mass murder are beginning to erode. Many serial murderers, like mass murderers, encounter stressful and triggering situations in life that set them on the course toward multiple murder. Both sets of offenders also fixate on misogynistic deviant fantasies (Murray, 2017) with a newer group of entitled "involuntary celibate" men yearning to obtain sexual experiences at the cost of other's lives (Williams, Arntfield, Schaal, & Vincent, 2021). The existence of MEMs highlights that the ever-narrowing distinctions between certain categories of offenders may not be useful.

A recent study found that MEMs more often killed for situational reasons (arguments, false perceptions, delusions, opportunistic robberies, or escape from apprehension) than targeted ones (gaining access to a particular victim, revenge against a specific person, enjoyment, or elimination of obstacles to a goal) (Yaksic, Harrison, & Hood, 2021). Three offenders in this review killed multiple victims at one time for situational reasons: two due to an argument while another killed to avoid apprehension. Two offenders killed multiple victims at one time for targeted reasons: both for revenge against a specific person. Of the six MEMs, four (67%) had been paroled after having killed before. These MEMs overwhelmingly selected victims with whom they shared a close relationship.

- Michael Ballard murdered a man and served 17 years in prison before being released to kill his ex-girlfriend, her father, her grandfather, and a neighbor who heard their screams and tried to help.
- Paul Gilkey, who had served a decade in prison for killing a man, was upset with how his terminally ill ex-wife was being cared for by her two sisters and his own son. He shot them to death after an argument that arose over whether or not his ex-wife should have been given tea and toast or an orange.
- Morris McCabe had been released from a 30-year prison sentence for the shooting death of a man in 1979. Ten months after his release, McCabe killed his ex-girlfriend's new boyfriend, and two other victims after stealing a rifle from a friend. McCabe had threatened to kill his ex-girlfriend's children if she broke up with him after she described him as obsessive and jealous.
- Curtis Davis was sentenced to 40 years in prison for killing a man but was freed 3 years before he shot three friends to death over an argument about a jacket.
- Avtar Singh killed his wife, three children, and himself 15 years after he had been an Indian Army Major in Indian-held Kashmir where he had killed a human-rights lawyer who had spoken out against the army's abuses.
- Martin Martinez was about to be charged for the killing of his ex-girlfriend's 2-year-old child that occurred a year before he stabbed her and his mother to death and then suffocated her two daughters and his niece using plastic bags fastened around their necks. Martinez was arrested later in the day while attending a family barbecue.

Caregivers

A District Attorney prosecuting a nurse for four deaths caused by air embolisms proclaimed that "…a hospital is the perfect place for a serial killer to hide" (Priser, 2021). Patients are perhaps the most vulnerable type of victim given their inherent immobility and trust in their caregivers. There is no true safe place in a health care institution if a serial murderer is employed there. While the article *When Healers Do*

Harm: Women Serial Killers in the Healthcare Industry (Pearson, 2021) stated that of the 90 serial murderers who have been convicted after operating in hospitals, long-term care facilities, and private residences most have been nurses (half of whom are female, overprescribe drugs, or induce heart attacks or strokes). The serial murderers in this review do not fit that profile as they are mostly medical doctors:

- Billy Chemirmir is a former health care worker who posed as a maintenance person to gain access to the properties of at least 18 elderly women and smothered them with a pillow.
- Christopher Duntsch is a former neurosurgeon who has been nicknamed "Dr. Death" after killing two patients and injuring and maiming 33 out of 38 patients in less than 2 years. Duntsch turned to neurosurgery because it is a lucrative field. Colleagues noted that he boasted about his skills in the operating room even after being new to the area and that his abilities left much to be desired. Duntsch emailed a colleague that he was ready to "become a cold-blooded killer."
- Reta Mays, a nurse's assistant, killed eight patients by injecting them with lethal doses of insulin. Mays worked the night shift in a ward that housed many patients who had diabetes. A doctor noticed that the patients suffered unexplained hypoglycemic episodes.
- William Valuck prescribed drugs to eight patients who died of overdoses. One patient received 510 pills, another 470 pills, another 330 pills. One patient, who had been prescribed 450 pills that day, killed a person while driving under the influence.
- William Husel had administered at least 25 lethal doses of fentanyl designed to hasten the death of patients.
- Dzung Pham wrote prescriptions for at least five people who died of drug overdoses. Victims had text messaged Pham, and their prescriptions were filled without being seen. Pham charged between $100 and $150 per office visit. A man to whom Pham provided drugs ran over and killed someone. A mass murderer had also taken drugs prescribed by Pham.

Potential Serial Murderers

Not all serial murderers set out with the expressed goal of becoming a serial murderer. For one, the crime of serial murder is not the gateway to immediate fame that it once was, given that only 4% of offenders in this review were given enough media coverage to be allotted a nickname. There are also many other outlets where disenfranchised men can obtain vicarious thrills.[4]

The younger generation of potential serial murderers may also lack the skills, abilities, and patience to carry out decade's long campaigns of violence. Of those who do desire to become a serial murderer and set out to do so, not all are successful (Williams & Vincent, 2018). A recent study of potential serial murderers revealed the commonalities and differences among both aspiring and probable serial murderers (Yaksic, Harrison, Konikoff, Mooney, Allely, De Silva, Matykiewicz, Inglis, Giannangelo, Daniels, & Sarteschi, 2021). Aspiring serial murderers yearned to become successful serial murderers and attempted to kill their victim but failed to cause their death. They were inexperienced and had an immature grasp of what it means to be a serial murderer, journaled to work out the merger of pre-offense fantasies into the execution of crime, preferred blunt force injuries and stabbing weapons over strangulation, used serial murder to seek a controlled means of satisfying a need for power, were open to introspection, self-analysis, inspiration and influence, engaged in excessive ideation that prematurely exhausted their energy, and failed to formulate the necessary components of a successful homicide. Probable serial murderers desired to become serial murderers and killed one victim but could not reach the minimum threshold of two or more victims. They were obsessed with and influenced by serial murderers, cognizant of their pursuit of a "serial killer" identity, motivated to act on urges to "self-actualize" and become a successful serial murderer, preoccupied with killing as a byproduct from consuming popular media, fixated on the idea that anyone could be a victim at any time, less interested in the process of homicidal ideation and fantasy, and invested in the process of killing and allowed it to consume their identity.

The aspiring serial murderers below exhibited at least one of these characteristics that were either detectable by those around them or were made known by the individual themselves:

- A former girlfriend of Brendan McMichael stated that he felt like a serial murderer and said, "I'm prepared to kill you tonight." The stabbing was a deliberate progression.
- Austin Lehman claimed to be a sociopath with anger issues who idolized serial murderers, enjoyed watching the terror inflicted by mass-casualty incidents, and watched videos of school shootings online. He wrote "I'm gonna have so many bodies. A lot of suffering. I plan on making others hell a reality."
- Tyler Benson, who wanted to be like Theodore Bundy, enjoyed the power he felt while beating sex workers, desired to be feared, and wanted total compliance from his victims.
- Daniel Spain followed a woman for several blocks and stabbed her because he wanted to be a serial murderer. Spain was open in his admission that "being able to find someone alone and hurt them without any witnesses is really hard."
- In her diary, Pearl Moen wrote that murder provides "a high unlike any other" so she stabbed a stranger 21 times, but the victim survived. She wanted to kill to see what it felt like and describes herself as a homicidal psychopath with a deep hatred toward people.
- Amy Brown attempted to kill a man she met on Craigslist, but the man survived. Brown told police she is a psychopath who has been plagued by homicidal thoughts since middle school. She intended to rip out her date's heart and eat it. Police found a life-sized coffin in her bedroom and a journal outlining her plans to become a serial murderer.

- A search of Neal Falls' car found a machete, axes, knives, a shovel, a sledgehammer, bleach, plastic trash bags, bulletproof vests, clean socks, and underwear. Falls had an alter ego online where he solicited sex workers.

The probable serial murderers below exhibited at least one characteristic that was either detectable by those around them or were made known by the individual themselves:

- Gregory Hale wanted to emulate his role model, the Nightstalker, and to fulfill an obsession with killing a person and dismembering them. Hale's Facebook page contained sexually explicit images, references to Scandinavian mythology, and cannibalism.
- Fabian Rubio raped and mutilated his underage victim who he met with under the pretense that he would buy her cigarettes. Prosecutors stated that Rubio is a budding serial murderer and regarded him as a psychopathic sexual predator with no remorse.
- Gauvin Monaghan beat his victim, tied him up, and put him in a drum. Prosecutors stated that he had the earmarks of a serial murderer, but he got caught after his first homicide.
- Daniel Bartelt had articles about serial murderers on his computer. Days before he snuck into his victim's home, tied her up, raped, and strangled her, Bartelt attacked another woman but she fought him off. He was described as psychopathic and narcissistic.
- Timothy Wilsey pretended to take his victim out on a date, strangled her, and left her for dead. He wrote in his journal that he was thinking about killing someone and stated, "I just enjoy killing, simple as that … I wanted to take a life for years." He described himself as homicidal with a year's long "hunger, thirst, and craving" to kill. He picked his victim because she seemed lonely and friendless.
- Daniel Marsh researched serial murderers, daydreamed of torture, and killed his victim "out of morbid curiosity." He had been consumed by homicidal and suicidal thoughts, "couldn't take it anymore," and had to kill. Doing so was "pure happiness" and "the most enjoyable thing" he had ever felt. He had planned on committing another murder.
- Miranda Barbour was fascinated with the fictional serial murderer Dexter and said she is a serial murderer. She lured her victim through an advertisement on Craigslist, where she offered sex in exchange for payment. She teamed with her husband because they wanted to murder someone together for a thrill to celebrate their anniversary.
- Adrian Gonzalez lured his victim into his apartment with ice cream, then choked, raped, and stabbed her. He showed no remorse, had hallmarks of psychopathy, and was declared to be a serial murderer in the making.
- Matthew Phelps was obsessed with the movie American Psycho and even dressed like the main character, Patrick Bateman. His Instagram profile picture

was of a blood-spattered Bateman. One post stated, "There is an evil in my head." Phelps' friends said he wanted to know what it would be like to kill someone. Phelps killed his wife by stabbing her 123 times with some wounds more than four inches deep.

- Cassandra Bjorge and Johnny Rider killed Cassandra's grandparents and planned to kill Johnny's family and Cassie's mother to become serial murderers.
- James Worley abducted his victim and bound, asphyxiated, beat, and buried her. Police found a room on Worley's property with a blood-spattered freezer and mounted restraints, women's underwear, rope, zip ties, and firearms and stated that Worley fits the profile of a serial offender.
- Anthony Rauda shot and killed a camper after having tried to kill ten people over a 2-year period. Rauda had been living off the grid in the wilderness and wore tactical gear while scavenging for food.
- Christopher Parker engaged in random attacks as a serial shooter. He was successful in one homicide attempt but not others. Police found an arsenal of weapons in his home after he made Facebook threats against a local bank.

Potential Serial Murderers Who Were Successful

There were at least four murderers who desired to become a serial murderer and did attain that goal. It is of note that these four offenders were no more successful than other serial murderers who made homicide a part of their criminal offending.

Two of these offenders killed in a "spree-like" fashion, which precluded them from attaining their goals of a long-term killing career:

- Stanley Mossburg wanted to be a serial murderer and said that he likes killing people. He stole one victim's vehicle and drove to his sister's house and she helped him escape. He allowed one person to live, demanded money, and said, if that victim wanted to live, not to fight back like the deceased did.
- Kiernan Brown told a caseworker he wanted to be a serial murderer and killed two women within hours of each other, one in her home and the other in a motel room.

Two of these offenders fell short of the traditional definitional threshold of three or more homicides and killed a fellow inmate specifically to reach the required number of victims:

- Leo Boatman admitted to his friend that he had killed two "preppies" in the Ocala National Forest by using a rifle he stole from his uncle in a quest to become a serial murderer. Boatman was arrested after the man who gave him a ride after the shootings tipped off police. He has since killed a fellow inmate.
- Casey Pigge asked an investigator about how many people needed to be killed before he could be dubbed a serial murderer.

Serial Shooters

Serial shooters used firearms to kill their victims quickly, without haste, and indiscriminately. Three of the four serial shooters used their vehicles to shield themselves from view and as a means of quick escape from the crime scene. Serial shooters share qualities with both TDSMs and SSMs in that two serial shooters sought intimacy with their victims by interacting with them prior to shooting at them, two of the offenders targeted someone known to them some time before killing random victims, and two offenders used the cover of darkness to their advantage by attacking only in the late evening or early morning.

- Patrick Watkins intended to rob his victims when he approached them while they were going about their daily routines in the late evening or early morning. Over a 3-year period, Watkins rode his bicycle or walked up to random people, demanded cash, and then began shooting at them. Watkins was linked to dozens of robberies and assaults, two homicides, and at least six attempted murders. Some of Watkins' crimes were clustered together in time.
- Aaron Saucedo shot and killed his mother's romantic partner 5 months before launching into a 6-month series of homicides of 12 random victims, three of whom survived. The shootings were carried out on a weekend night or early in the morning against people going about their business. Saucedo used multiple vehicles to perpetrate his crimes, many of which were clustered together in time.
- Todd West shot and killed his cousin a month before killing a man at an intersection, and two other men within 24 hours. Ten days later, West shot and killed a man after saying, "See ya later" and emptying his .38-caliber pistol. West killed two others in a vehicle the same day. Damage to his vehicle prevented West from killing more people.
- Alexander Hernandez randomly targeted people to shoot from his vehicle. Hernandez pulled up alongside victims and said, "I am going to kill you." Hernandez fixated on victims who would catch his eye and would follow them. Most of the victims were driving: one home from work, one to work, and one to a fishing trip. His vehicle was unique with spoked rims and had stickers of a white skull and a 666 on the back.

Survivalists

Two offenders lived a survivalist lifestyle, which emphasizes self-reliance, amassing the skills and knowledge necessary to live in the wilderness, and self-defense. Both serial murderers believed in the tenants of survivalism in that they trusted only themselves and aimed to protect what they considered to belong to them. The survivalists acted like TDSMs in that they covertly stalked some of their victims like prey.

- Before he was captured, Shaun Gallon eluded police and hid in the forest for 5 weeks using his survival skills. Gallon was "upset at his own life" when he killed a camping couple "out of spite" because they were sleeping in a location barring camping. Thirteen years later, Gallon shot his brother to death due to a grudge.

- Aaron Bassler led the sheriff's office on a 36-day manhunt on what was described as "his territory." One of Bassler's victims was a city councilman, and another was a land manager looking for a marijuana garden. When they encountered Bassler in separate instances, he shouted and then opened fire. Bassler disappeared into the forestland where he had been living for months, tending to an opium poppy plot.

Motive

In thinking about the critical components of serial murder, Ferguson, White, Cherry, Lorenz, and Bhimani (2003) state that the mind and motives of the perpetrators are more important than broad identifiable behaviors. While there are inherent drawbacks related to classifying serial murderers by motive given the subjectivity involved in parsing out the offender's reasoning from what actually spurred them forward, and the potential of researchers to oversimplify the offender's intentions, attendees of the FBI serial murder symposium agreed that there are five reasons why serial murderers kill: (1) anger; (2) psychosis (mental illness); (3) ideology; (4) enjoyment (thrill, excitement, and power); and (5) financial (criminal enterprise).

Anger

Although Myers, Husted, Safarik, and O'toole (2006) wrote that anger is not a key component of sexual serial murderers, James and Proulx (2016) studied a sample of offenders who reported feelings of strife with a woman and frustration in the hours preceding a homicide. Many serial murderers had contentious relationships with intimate partners due to feelings of powerlessness, insecurity, jealousy, and lack of control over their own lives. They sought to regain their dominance through real or threatened violence. Serial murders are often the result of a toxic mixture of fragile masculinity and the personality traits of narcissism, Machiavellianism, and psychopathy. Rather than being the emotionless automatons they are portrayed to be, serial murderers may feel too deeply and be ill-equipped to deal with such emotions. Many serial murderers have paranoid personalities, which compel them to keep track of casual everyday slights from others and transform them into grudges. Serial murderers then channel those resultant feelings of ill will into their homicides. Without genuine social networks, these offenders cannot properly vent their anger. Although Warf and Waddell (2002) succinctly state that serial murderers represent a version of a broader pattern of male violence against women, this review found that many MSMs also victimize other men as a means to alleviate their feelings of anger.

As the offender's contempt grows, some serial murderers engage in intimate partner violence as a rehearsal for future homicides:

- Dwight Jones verbally and mentally abused his ex-wife because, as her status grew, Jones became jealous, became physically violent, and threatened to kill her and their son if she left him.
- William Boyette had a history of domestic violence and he brutally assaulted girlfriends, avoiding prosecution by threatening his victims.
- William Gibson used the rent money of a former girlfriend to get high and had several violent incidents where he would verbally and physically abuse her.
- Shelby Nealy had a history of domestic violence against his wife.
- Juan Valdez's criminal history includes domestic violence.

If the first victim in a sequence is the offender's girlfriend or spouse, and the subsequent homicides are committed immediately afterwards, they are usually part of a chain of victims spawning from the offender's initial motivation to kill:

- Carroll Tuttle perpetrated what police called an "extreme case of domestic violence" when he fatally shot his wife, son, and neighbor. Tuttle killed his neighbor because he thought he was having an affair with his wife. The neighbor had been trying to help Tuttle's wife escape from the abusive relationship. Tuttle shot at deputies who returned fire and killed him.
- Two months after Eulalio Tordil's wife filed a protective order against him, he fatally shot her. In his journal, Tordil wrote that his marriage had "reached a point of no return." The day after killing his wife, Tordil fatally shot a man coming to the aid of a woman whose car he was trying to steal. He also killed a woman during another carjacking.
- Alto Miles shot four people to death over 1 day in two separate locations. Miles' first two victims were his ex-girlfriend and her friend who were looking at men's pictures on Facebook. Miles became jealous and killed them. Afterwards, he decided to get revenge on a man who had previously beaten him.
- Rodrick Dantzler, a felon who served time for felony assault and domestic violence, shot and killed his wife, their daughter, and his wife's parents. He also killed a former girlfriend, her sister, and her daughter after his wife was planning to leave him. The murders occurred over the course of 1 day in two separate homes while two nonfatal gunshot injuries took place on the road. Dantzler engaged in a chase with police and killed himself.
- Mainak Sarkar, a former doctoral student who had shot a UCLA professor to death, directed police to find a kill list with two other names. One belonged to his estranged wife whom Sarkar had killed before driving 2,000 miles to UCLA. Sarkar was able to locate only one of his intended victims before he killed himself. Sarkar's relationship with his mentors soured after they allegedly stole his computer code.

When the first homicide is a significant other, it can bolster the offender's confidence to victimize others in their orbit:

- Cedric Marks abducted and killed the mother of his children from a domestic violence shelter 11 years before strangling his ex-girlfriend and another man.
- James Lynn killed his first wife in 1990 and his third wife after an argument and dumped her body in a well.
- Kylr Yust, who had a history of volatile relationships with women, killed his girlfriend because she did not love him, and he did not want anyone else to have her. The victim had filed a restraining order against him due to violence. Yust confessed to killing her to four people and told his then-pregnant ex-girlfriend that "I've killed people before, even ex-girlfriends out of sheer jealousy; I will kill you." Ten years after the first homicide, Yust killed a girl after she left a party with him. Her body was found 30 yards away from his first victim.
- Vernon Primus who has been labeled a manipulator and psychopath, strangled his girlfriend to death and left her in a garbage bag in Brooklyn. He then stabbed a real estate agent to death in his home country of Saint Vincent before moving in with his elderly aunt in Vermont. There, he is alleged to have held a woman captive and sexually assaulted her for almost 4 months.

There are instances where significant others are killed by serial murderers in the course of their use of homicide as a conflict resolution tool:

- Maksim Gelman went on a 28-hour stabbing spree that began with the killing of his stepfather after an argument. Gelman claimed that he needed to flee the DEA and his stepfather stood in his way. As Gelman stated before stabbing a victim on a train, "My girlfriend ruined my life!" Some said that Gelman was obsessed with her from afar and that he was stalking and harassing her. Gelman stabbed his ex-girlfriend, her mother, and a pedestrian.
- Warren Birkbeck, who served time in prison for killing a man in 1962, killed his estranged wife in 1999 and admitted that he has "a hard time being rejected" after he stabbed his female roommate to death once he heard her talking to another man on the phone.
- Jody Hunt was an ex-convict who had held a previous girlfriend hostage, held personal and professional grudges, and killed his partner, business rival, ex-girlfriend, and the woman's new boyfriend before killing himself.

Roy Hollander is a prime example of how these factors crystalize into a lethal combination. Hollander was an "anti-feminist lawyer" and member of the National Coalition of Men who fought what he perceived to be feminist oppression by posing as a package deliveryman and fatally shooting a lawyer he viewed as his rival and, 8 days later, the son of a US District Court Judge who presided over one of his many lawsuits. Hollander had drafted a list of more than a dozen names that included judges, doctors, and other targets. Hollander has since been described as a lunatic hiding in plain sight whose misery and grief transformed into rage, an angry and bitter man who felt he had nothing to lose. Hollander also harassed, sued, threatened, and abused many other people and wrote that firearms were the one remaining source of power men still have.

Psychosis

While most serial murderers are "normal in judgment, moral reasoning, inner awareness, and sense of self," mental illness sometimes influences a serial murderer's outlook and subsequent intention to commit criminal acts. Still, the presence of demons or monsters may not be "a fabrication of a delusional mind or a cynical imitation of popular perceptions" but rather a physical representation of the offender's doubled self (Shanafelt & Pino, 2013, pp. 268–269).

Many offenders in this review made statements about the devil, or other deities, and attributed their actions to this influence:

- Jason Dalton stated that a devil head appeared in the Uber app and supplied him with objectives to complete such as random shootings.
- Todd West told police that the devil made him kill random victims.
- Sean Barrette had been committed twice and was once found rocking back and forth with a cross on his head and a pendant in his mouth and screaming that he was the devil.
- Daniel St. Hubert, the so-called Brooklyn Ripper, stated that the devil made him stab a young woman and a 6-year-old boy to death 2 days apart from one another.
- David Contreras' was thought to be a paranoid schizophrenic because he exhibited unusual behavior such as talking to himself, expressing disconnected thoughts, and describing angels in church and demons infesting his body.
- Lucius Crawford is quoted as saying he has "a demon inside."
- Nikko Jenkins claimed he committed four homicides as sacrifices to deity Apophis.
- Joshua Mebane stated that the murder of his cellmate was a "Satanic sacrifice."

Three offenders mentioned that it was their mission to destroy demons:

- Kiernan Brown claimed to be "ridding the demons of some dear friends of his."
- Christopher Scheibe took psychoactive drugs and claimed that his victims, who he knew, were demons.
- Christopher Speight stated that an Egyptian princess told him to shoot his family because they were demons.

Some offenders were suspected of having mental health issues:

- Dwight Jones disliked authority figures, would frequently be depressed, and was suspected of being mentally ill.

- Aaron Bassler's father noted that his son's homicides came after a decade of erratic, strange behavior, and suspected mental illness and that his son "didn't have any empathy" and became "increasingly delusional and antisocial."

Others had vague mentions of histories of psychiatric disturbances without further documentation:

- Troy Whisnant had a history of psychological disturbance.
- Jamie Walter has substantial mental issues.
- Casey Pigge had a litany of psychiatric diagnoses.
- Antonio Rodriguez had a history of mental illness.
- Matthew Guzman has a mental illness.
- Robert Burger had been committed to mental institutions four times over his life.

Others had specific psychiatric diagnoses:

- Daniel St. Hubert is a paranoid schizophrenic who spent time in jail for trying to strangle his mother to death and scrawled the phrase "$ KILLZZ, I WILL" and a winking smiley face on a stop sign.
- Itzcoatl Ocampo showed signs of PTSD, and he became depressed and developed clinical delirium after his friend died.
- Marc Carr, who suffers from schizophrenia, lived two doors down from his victim, strangled another during an attempt to rape his girlfriend, dragged the man's body into the garage, and tried to asphyxiate his girlfriend with a plastic bag.
- In between his homicides, Cosmo DiNardo sought treatment for bipolar disorder, schizoaffective disorder, and schizophrenia for help with violent psychotic episodes.
- Shawn Grate was diagnosed with persistent depressive disorder and bipolar disorder.
- Shaun Gallon blamed lysergic acid diethylamide (LSD) for his schizotypal personality disorder.
- Jon Guerrero suffered from schizophrenia.
- Michael Mullins was diagnosed as bipolar and schizophrenic.
- An expert testified that Charles Severance has a personality disorder with mixed paranoid and schizotypal features.

Others were severely mentally ill:

- Erik Meiser was suffering from a delusional disorder when he killed a man with a machete while burglarizing his house, 2 months after killing his first male victim. Meiser believes that he is the target of conspirators who torment him and turned his son into a cannibal.

- Jeffrey Eady attempted to get treatment after being paroled for armed robbery, but voices in his head instructed him to shoot a neighbor, kill a woman, and steal her car 2 days later. His mental illness prevented him from understanding that his victims were dead.
- Christian Falero stabbed six people with a kitchen knife over 5 minutes because of an earthquake, screamed that it was "the end of the world" while naked, and yelled the word "fire" to compel people to open their apartment doors.
- Peter Manfredonia, a UConn senior, wrote a message on the wall of his apartment referencing Sandy Hook shooter Adam Lanza, "We saw what happened when Adam snapped, now they see what happens when I snap."

Ideology – Extremist Violence and Racial Hatred

Those who advocate for the use of extreme methods like homicide to achieve goals related to their beliefs have increased their violence over the previous decade. It is unsurprising that there is overlap among these groups given that the motivational thrust behind both extremist violence and serial murder is contempt.

Victims were commonly in a position of authority, in these instances police officers:

- Steven Carrillo, an Air Force sergeant, was associated with the extremist anti-government "boogaloo" group and was motivated to kill police officers when he ambushed a sheriff's deputy and, in a separate attack, sprayed bullets across a guard shack in front of a federal building, killing an officer. Carrillo scrawled the phrase "I became unreasonable" in his own blood on the hood of a car.
- Jerad and Amanda Miller were a married couple who held antigovernment views and killed two police officers before killing an armed civilian in a Walmart.
- Scott Greene ambushed two police officers with a rifle while they sat in their vehicles two miles and 20 minutes apart. Greene clashed with police after being removed from a football game for flying the confederate flag and used a derogatory term in reference to an African American man whom he threatened to kill.

Others were killed because of what they represented to the offenders:

- David Pedersen and Holly Grigsby killed Pedersen's father and stepmother on their way to California to "kill more Jews." The pair held white supremacist beliefs and killed a man because his name sounded Jewish. Pedersen's father was killed because he supposedly molested two young relatives.
- Ali Brown stated that his "mission is vengeance, a life for a life." Over a 3-month span, Brown killed three people by shooting them at close range after becoming angry with the United States' actions abroad. Brown believes his

murders were justified shootings in retaliation for actions of the US government in Iraq, Syria, and Afghanistan.

Five offenders were motivated by racial hatred. Two offenders chose to kill others of a different race, one offender made references to Hitler, and another went along with the motivations of his partner. The offender with the weakest reasoning killed over the longest period of time. Those with a delineated goal carried out their attacks in a "spree-like" fashion suggesting that offenders with true racial animus may be fueled and compelled forward by their beliefs:

- Kori Muhammad shot a security guard a week before shooting three Caucasian men in a mass shooting due to racial animus. Muhammad referred to Caucasian people as "grafted devils." In court, Muhammad made demands for slavery reparations and likened his killing of people to a natural process. As an aspiring rapper, Muhammad referred to himself as a black god and made references to violence between African American and Caucasian people. Muhammad stated that white supremacy has to die, and he encouraged "black warriors" to "mount up."
- Jacob England and Alvin Watts engaged in a spate of shootings in 1 day after the 2-year anniversary of the slaying of England's father. England wrote extensively about how upset he was about the death of his father at the hands of an African American man.
- Kenneth Gleason shot and killed two African American men 2 days apart and five miles from one another. Gleason shot at the pedestrians while in his car and only exited once they fell to the ground where he stood over them while continuing to fire shots. A day before the first homicide, Gleason fired several shots into the home of the only African American family on the block where he lived with his parents. Gleason's phone records contained repeated references to Hitler and "cleansing."
- Fredrick Scott threatened to shoot up his high school and "kill all white people" before he shot six people to death near trails within a year. Five of the victims were shot from behind in surprise attacks as they walked dogs and did normal things.

Enjoyment – Thrill, Excitement, and Power

Serial murderers have been known to kill for the power and pleasure derived from dominating others, and the thrill and excitement associated with doing something socially unacceptable and getting away with it. Williams (2021) introduces the concept of "deviant leisure" and conceptualizes enjoyment under four themes: murder as a game, killing for fun, killing for the experience of sensation, and murder as celebration. In the past, serial murderers were thought to kill purely for the excitation related to outsmarting the police, garnering fame for their exploits, and hunting for the "perfect" victim. Today, these objectives typically occur in tandem with other motives. At a base level, most serial murderers in the present review enjoyed killing, but it was infrequently their primary reason for committing homicide.

Two serial murderers in this review spoke of the thrill related to killing: Christopher Scheibe wrote that "There's no thrill like hunting down a human and killing them," and Itzcoatl Ocampo claimed to have a thrill for blood. Although these serial murderers did not kill primarily to obtain a thrill, five others did.

Three of the five serial murderers labeled "thrill killers" killed in a manner similar to that of SSMs:

- Konrad Schafer and David Damus thought it would be fun to kill an older teen as part of a 2-week shooting spree. Schafer used his father's .45 caliber carbine rifle to shoot one victim to death as he walked to catch the bus for work. Days later, Damus used the rifle to shoot another victim, whose house the pair broke into, while Schafer slit the man's throat.
- David Contreras repeatedly stabbed a man while he was out walking his dog. Less than 6 weeks later, Contreras repeated this pattern by stabbing a woman and her daughter while they were walking near their home.

The remaining "thrill killers" spaced out their homicides but killed in a manner similar to that of SSMs:

- Justice Henderson fatally shot his first victim because he wanted to "see the effects of shooting someone" with a new firearm he acquired. Five weeks later, Henderson shot and killed three people within a 3-day period, one because he thought they witnessed him break into a car, another during a robbery, and the third after being rejected when he asked to help the victim walk his dog.
- William Spengler wrote that he wanted "to see how much of the neighborhood I can burn down and do what I like doing best, killing people" shortly before he fatally shot his sister, set fire to his house, and ambushed and killed two of the responding firemen with two long guns. Spengler had spent 17 years in prison for murdering his grandmother with a hammer.

Financial – Criminal Enterprise

Gang Violence

Offenders who perpetrate gang-related homicides have not been named as serial murderers due to strict interpretations of the definition as homicide is thought to be the inevitable byproduct of street violence regardless of offender motivation. There is no denying that gangs are criminal enterprises (given their structure, methods, and motives whose members kill serially from time to time).

While one pair of offenders fit the typical image of the "gang-banger," several serial murderers linked to gangs killed for reasons other than gang warfare:

- Kendrick Johnson talked about wanting to be a professional hit man and bragged about shooting and killing people in drive-by shootings in an ongoing gang war.
- Anthony Foye and Nathaniel Mitchell were motivated by greed, witness intimidation, and revenge for being disrespected when they killed five people in a "killing competition" between gang members. Prosecutors labeled Mitchell as a "remorseless serial killer" who was fueled by a desire to improve his killing statistics and thereby his status in the gang. Both he and Foye were trying to gain a reputation as gang members willing to shoot people.
- While twin brothers Jerone and Tyrone Sotolongo were gang members linked to three homicides and three shootings. One victim was killed over a fight for a gold chain.
- Percy Camel was on a mission to retaliate against Latinos when he fatally shot two victims 2 months apart, one stemming from a fight between clubgoers.

Professional Contracts

Professional contract murderers, who are colloquially known as "hit men," have been largely ignored in the literature given the belief that these types of offenders cannot be personally gratified by murdering a victim whom they did not select. But Morton and McNamara (2005, p. 48) acknowledge that contract killers are serial murderers given that motivation can be a "synthesis of rationales." Schlesinger (2001) warns that contract murder is understudied and could be increasing. The two professional murderers in this review each killed a victim outside their contracts. In both cases, the offender killed to obtain revenge for the death of a relative. The mixture of personal motivations with hired "hits" contradicts most of what has been written on this subset of offenders and suggests that they should be counted among the ranks of other serial murderers:

- Jose Martinez is a confessed drug cartel "hit man" who killed more than three dozen people over 30 years. He killed two victims who had stolen 10 kilos of cocaine from his employers, but his first homicide was to avenge a beloved sister. He also lived by a code and tried to kill only his targets and not their family members.
- Dexter Collins was paid to eliminate a man who witnessed a double homicide. Another highly publicized homicide was carried out on a musician. Collins killed a victim outside a grocery store as retaliation for her having killed his uncle.

Drug Trafficking

Like professional murders and homicides attributed to gang violence, killings associated with drug trafficking often are not labeled as serial murders. If the desire to kill is not born separate from the offender's job description, then their actions are generally not categorized as serial murder. But the four drug traffickers in this review each took part in at least one homicide outside their trafficking lifestyles: one as retaliation, another after an argument, and another during a robbery. Homicide is seen as a reliable tool to eliminate the source of the offender's discomfort:

- Phillip Bryant killed two men as a strong-arm tactic to take over a housing project and use it to grow his drug-dealing enterprise. Both homicides furthered his position in the "New York Boys" and his reputation for violence. Bryant also killed another man as retaliation for having pressed charges against a fellow gang member's brother for robbing him of his necklace.
- Arturo Ibarra and Raul Segura-Rodriguez were members of a violent drug crew whose calling card was the Santa Muerte death cult. The cult's stickers marked their vehicles, and the symbol of the cult adorned the bands to hold their cash, and shrines in their homes. The cult was also the inspiration for their tattoos. One set of murders involved the binding of four men who were shot dead in front of two children in a garage while others involved the robbery of their victims.
- Dontae Morris killed three men related to the drug trade and two police officers when they attempted to arrest him. Morris killed one victim after arguing with him on a basketball court earlier in the day, another for revenge after the victim held him at gunpoint during a drug rip-off, and another to send a message to a drug dealer.

Case-Specific Factors

While an innumerable combination of events can transpire over a serial murderer's career and contribute to vast differences among them, several offenders in this review shared commonalities in behaviors (use of technology, criminal histories, warehousing victim's remains), victims (fellow inmates, witnesses), age (over 50), and stature (parolee, military veteran, "prolific").

The Use of Technology

Alongside tremendous growth within the technology sector, serial murderers who used websites and applications to acquire their victims and social media to vent their frustrations have become much more prevalent in recent years. While this behavior provides serial murderers with wider access to victim pools and the opportunity to draw like-minded people toward them, it also presents increased risk to the offender as police benefit from the near ubiquity of surveillance and new equipment that aids in their ability to respond to crime.

Before its demise, Backpage.com was a popular place for serial murderers to acquire victims:

- James Brown met his victims in pairs via the website.
- Darren Vann used the name "Big Boy Appetite" when searching for escorts to victimize, and he met at least one of his victims using the website.
- Kylan Laurent made an appointment with a sex worker, bound her wrists with zip ties, strangled her, cleaned the crime scene, and placed her in the bed.
- Alberto Palmer met victims online with the intent of having intercourse with them. When it came time for payment, Palmer would beat the victims to death. Palmer placed dozens of calls to women who were advertising their services.

Other websites and applications have been used to lure victims:

- Khalil Wheeler-Weaver used Tagged to arrange sexual encounters with women before strangling them with articles of clothing. One victim texted asking Wheeler-Weaver if he was a serial killer.
- Brandon Lyons and Jerrett Allen used Grindr to lure men to a robbery ambush.
- Brogan Rafferty and Richard Beasley were dubbed the "Craigslist Killers" for their use of the website in targeting four older, single, out-of-work, desperate men with backgrounds that made it unlikely their disappearances would be immediately noticed. The Craigslist ad noted that it was the "job of a lifetime" but served only as a device to lure unsuspecting men to be robbed of their possessions, killed, and discarded.
- Jason Dalton, an Uber driver who shot six people to death, claimed that the app guided him to kill by taking over his mind and body.
- Darnell Braud fatally shot a man during a meeting arranged on a dating app.
- Anthony Robinson, dubbed the "Shopping Cart Killer" due to his method of transporting his victim's remains, used the dating apps Plenty of Fish and Tagged to select and lure his victims to area motels.

Social media has been used to stalk victims, voice opinions, and flaunt their lifestyles:

- After Peter Manfredonia hacked into his ex-girlfriend's social media accounts she broke up with him. He responded by killing a man near her apartment.
- Jason Nightingale hinted at his plans and shared his desire for fame over social media, claiming he would be on television, and posted the following quote, "The tiger and the lion may be more powerful, but the wolf doesn't perform in the circus." Another picture on his Facebook page showed wads of cash and a man pointing a gun at a woman's head.
- In one online post, Amanda Miller wrote, "to the people of the world. your lucky i can't kill you now, but remember one day i will get you because all hell will break lose."
- Steven Carrillo posted in a Facebook group in support of igniting a race civil war.

- Shaun Gallon had been described by a relative as "odd" as he made Facebook posts referencing a world known only to him. One post noted that he recognized someone "from the pliedes star cluster Al Nehosh de Nesser Jeserate" and that the boy thanked him for "saving his world."
- Jacob England and Alvin Watts interacted on Facebook where Watts provided support regarding England's anger.
- Kori Muhammad indicated on social media that his goal was to kill as many Caucasian people as possible.
- Percy Camel bragged in a homemade video about using the same gun in his homicides.
- Jody Hunt posted a message to Facebook that he wanted to see that his victims "received their fair pay of hurt."
- Kendrick Johnson documented his activities as a gang member in posts on social media where he was known as MVP and The Main Sniper.
- Willy Suarez Maceo flaunted a flashy lifestyle on social media filled with cars, crypto investments, and luxary home sales. Meanwhile, Maceo targeted homeless men and shot them to death.

Some serial murderers used technology to mislead others or to find helpful information:

- Stanley Mossburg responded in a vile way to a text the victim received from his wife.
- Shelby Nealy used his wife's phone after killing her to pretend to be her for an entire year before killing her family with a hammer after they became suspicious.
- Cosmo DiNardo Googled the Soup Maker Cartel, a Mexican drug syndicate known for dissolving bodies in acid.
- Khalil Wheeler-Weaver Googled instructions on how to make homemade poison.

Police were able to utilize other forms of technology to capture serial murderers:

- An arrogant Eric Williams sent a tip to police that was traced to his computer.
- The phone records of the victims and items found with their bodies led police to GPS track the devices connected to Franc Cano and Steven Gordon.
- Evan Ebel slipped off his ankle bracelet he received after his release from prison.
- Shannon Lamb was tracked down due to a license plate reader.
- The crimes of Jeremy Harris were linked using cellphone data and license plate readers.
- Police used ShotSpotter technology to quickly respond to the final shootings of Jason Nightingale and, in a separate instance, Kori Muhammad.
- Khalil Wheeler-Weaver was captured after friends of a victim created a fake online profile to lure him to police.

- Michael Mason was apprehended after police used facial recognition software to find images of him on social media. He also tried to sell a .40-caliber firearm on Instagram.
- Police found Alberto Palmer through "live tracking" his cellular phone.
- James Brown's cellular phone led police to tie him to the homicides.
- Darren Vann's cellular phone records contributed to his arrest.
- As a means to fabricate a motive and frame her current boyfriend, Samuel Wright used his victim's phone to send messages to him stating that she was leaving him for a new and better lover, but the boyfriend's phone pinged off a cellphone tower far away from where Wright's victim was and Wright's phone pinged off the same tower as his victims.

The activities of several serial murderers were captured on surveillance images, some of which led to the offender's immediate capture while others served as documentation of their actions:

- Police were able to track Peter Manfredonia through Uber rides, car thefts, and cameras.
- Patrick Watkins was seen on camera wielding a pistol as he walked toward a cashier.
- Morrison Lampley and Lila Alligood were captured on camera using a stolen vehicle.
- Telyith Hopkins was caught on video leaving one of the crime scenes.
- Joseph Danclair was seen on a hotel camera checking in with a victim and leaving alone.
- Brandon Lavergne's truck and Jeffrey Willis' minivan were seen on camera.
- Video showed Darren Vann enter his victim's motel room.
- Aaron Bassler was caught on camera with an assault rifle at a cabin that he burglarized.
- Salvatore Perrone was captured on camera carrying a duffel bag filled with weapons.
- Albert Flick was seen on video waiting for his victim.
- Randy Santos' attack on one man was captured on video.
- Jerard Garrett was caught on video killing a man during a drug transaction.
- Fredrick Scott was caught on camera following one of the victims.
- Kiernan Brown was caught on video with one of the victims as well as buying weapons.
- Video showed Stanley Mossburg pull a gun on his first victim and bind his arms.
- The "Seminole Heights Killer" was seen on a camera walking from a crime scene.
- Eulalio Tordil was captured on video as he fatally shot his victim in an SUV.
- The patrol car dashcam helped identify Dontae Morris.
- Stanley Mossburg was caught on video at the residence of his second and third victims.

- Video captured Kenneth Gleason driving his vehicle into a parking lot, removing the license plate, and placing tape over the vehicle's identifying markings.
- Nathaniel Petgrave, Angelina Barini, and Jeremy Harris' crimes were seen on camera.
- Troy Whisnant's crime spree began to unravel when a highway patrolman asked a store's manager to see the surveillance video from which he was identified.
- Jeffrey Eady's family recognized him from surveillance images published in the news.
- Ali Brown was apprehended after being seen on video.
- Ramon Escobar was seen in the attack area and was arrested after fitting a description.
- John Ewell was caught on camera entering a home after pretending to be a utility worker.
- Willy Suarez Maceo was seen on video driving the same car at two crime scenes. Police traced Maceo's license plate to him the next day.

Refusing to "Age Out" of Crime

Several serial murderers killed their victims while aged 50 (the end of the range of the age-crime curve) (Ulmer & Steffensmeier, 2014). Seventy-eight offenders (19%) were aged 50 or above at the time of their capture. But because an incarceration after an early homicide interrupts a serial murderer's plans, the continuation of their series after parole would artificially inflate the total number of late-term killers. For that reason, it is important to know that 25 of those offenders (32%) had never been incarcerated or paroled and that many of these offenders had long-term killing careers unimpeded by police intervention. Of those 25 nonincarcerated, nonparoled serial murderers, only 7 (28%) did not start killing in close temporal proximity to their initial homicides and had at least a 10-year gap between their first and last homicides.

The motives of these offenders were varied:

- Richard Brooks, age 50, set up his friend with the allure of a drug deal and also killed a high-ranking member of the Pagans gang after another man hired Brooks because he blamed the victim for his arrest.
- John Ewell, age 53, killed his victims, one of which was his own neighbor, after home invasions and pawned some of the jewelry.
- Salvatore Perrone, age 64, who was called "Son of Sal" by his neighbors for his odd behavior and combative personality, claimed that killing three shopkeepers of Middle Eastern descent "has to do with a plan to promote world peace."
- Dennis Stanworth, age 70, committed a string of violent sexual assaults against four women, shot two teenage girls, and killed his 89-year-old mother after being paroled.
- Roy Hollander, age 72, was openly misogynistic and denounced women, having written about "solutions" to feminists that entailed "taking out

those specific persons responsible for destroying their lives." He blamed his shortcomings on others, especially women whom he viewed as controlling modern civilization.

Several of these offenders engaged in intimate partner violence and killed significant others:

- Albert Flick, age 77, killed his wife in 1979, was paroled, and killed a friend whom he was infatuated with because she intended to move away from him.
- Arthur Cain, age 53, who was paroled for a murder and armed robbery, killed a woman he was in a relationship with 7 months after being released, stuffed her body in a suitcase, and hid it in an alley.
- Eugene Johnson, age 61, who was convicted more than 30 years ago of stabbing a former lover to death, killed his girlfriend after writing "If I can't have you, no one can."
- Robert Burger, age 67, who killed his wife days before Christmas, was convicted of stabbing a priest to death after an argument when he was 18 years old.
- Jeremiah Fogle, age 58, shot his wife to death in 1986, called the police, and subsequently received 10 years of probation. Twenty-five years later, Fogle shot and killed another wife after accusing her of infidelity. He went to church and shot and killed a minister.
- Lawrence Banks, age 65, was called a "modern-day serial killer" for having shot a friend to death and killing his own son 8 hours later on the same day. Twenty-eight years later, Banks killed his daughter on Mother's Day and left her dismembered body inside a shopping cart next to a dumpster. He threw his 7-month-old daughter through a glass door during an argument with his wife who herself was found dead shortly after. He choked and threated to kill another wife. His girlfriend and her daughter were killed days after a protective order was taken out against him.

The life circumstances of some of these offenders were filled with criminal activity:

- John Ewell had a long history of property crimes.
- Dennis Stanworth has a long criminal history that includes kidnapping and sexual assault.
- Lawrence Banks has an extensive history of reacting with violence.

The employment histories and aspirations of these offenders were varied:

- Jeffrey Moreland was a former police officer.
- Salvatore Perrone dreamed of making a name for himself in the clothing industry.
- Ali Irsan was a con man who bilked thousands of dollars out of large corporations.
- Jeremiah Fogle stepped down as deacon after women complained about unwanted contact.

Parolees

Egger (2002) surmised that the number of serial murderers who are released from prison to kill again might be increasing. This review shows that 45% of serial murderers had, at some point over their killing career, been released from prison to claim additional victims.

Some of these offenders killed only strangers:

- Lawrence Anderson's first stop after release was to his neighbor's house to cut out her heart. Anderson brought the heart to his aunt and uncle's house, cooked it, and tried to serve it to them before killing his uncle and their 4-year-old granddaughter.
- Edjuan Payne shot and killed a man during an armed robbery in 1987 when he was 17. After being released, the body of another victim was found beaten, stabbed, and strangled behind his mother's house. Payne claimed that an argument had gotten out of hand.
- Tyrone Arnold strangled a woman to death 23 years after doing the same to a neighbor whose nude body was found by her children.
- Ricardo Munoz was convicted of a double homicide in 1986, was paroled in 1997, and was arrested in 2015 for the shooting death of a man.
- Christian Williams was found guilty of murder in 1993, was sentenced to 30 years in prison, but was paroled in 2013. Less than 2 years later, Williams killed again. In the first instance, Williams and his victim were partying when he stabbed them to death, and in the second case, Williams invited the victim into his home before stabbing them.
- Peter Jones stabbed and strangled his elderly neighbor to death in order to steal her belongings and resell them to support a drug habit. Jones had been paroled for the stabbing death of a man in 1997.
- Steven Clippinger was not supposed to have a firearm after being incarcerated for killing a man in 1989 but was able to obtain one with the help of his girlfriend. Clippinger used the firearm to kill his brother and sister-in-law after an argument.
- Damien Torres was 14 when he killed his first victim after firing upon another car. He was paroled from a juvenile facility and had been out for 6 months when he killed again in a shooting outside a bar after getting into a fight inside the establishment.

Others selected victims from different groups:

- Marlon Ricks was on parole for the death of his stepfather when he became convinced that his girlfriend was cheating on him. He stabbed her 17 times and called all of the men in her phone to inquire into what type of relationship they had. Parole records indicated that the circumstances surrounding his first homicide were "very unlikely to re-occur."

- Samuel Wright was convicted of murder for the 1991 shooting of a man after a dispute. After being paroled in 2010, Wright began a relationship with the woman he would eventually kill after she began seeing someone else.
- Zollie Dumas served more than 20 years for stabbing his girlfriend to death in 1988. She was clearing her belongings out of their shared trailer when Dumas hid in the bathroom and attacked her with a steak knife while police officers waited outside. After being paroled, Dumas killed another woman after a domestic dispute.

A few of these offenders targeted only significant others:

- Joseph Oberhansley served 12 years in prison for killing his girlfriend and shooting his mother. Two years after his release, Oberhansley killed another girlfriend, dismembered her, and consumed some of her body parts.
- Tony Degrafreed was imprisoned for 14 years for killing his first wife, and, less than a decade after being released from prison, he was convicted of killing his second wife.
- Andrew Jett was previously convicted of beating a girlfriend to death with a tire iron in 1992 and spent 18 years in prison. Two years after his release, Jett killed a second girlfriend.

Several of these offenders began their killing careers when they were young and killed at least one of their victims during an argument:

- Donte Graves was just 13 years old when he and two other teenagers robbed and beat an attorney to death while he was walking home. After he shot and killed a man over a coat, one prosecutor labeled Graves an "absolute menace" who terrorized the streets after he was released from the juvenile system.
- Juan Valdez was 14 years old when he beat a father (who disapproved of his daughter dating Valdez's older cousin) with a fireplace poker, cut him with a kitchen knife, and choked him with a dog leash. Valdez fatally shot the mother of his children nearly 25 years later after being paroled.
- Steven Pratt was 15 years old when he got into an argument with his next-door neighbor and shot him to death. Thirty years later, Pratt killed his 64-year-old mother 2 days after his release from prison.
- Bennie Dupnik was 16 when he beat his 72-year-old boss to death with a pool cue. He was paroled after serving 32 years for her murder. Two years later, Dupnik stabbed his girlfriend to death and killed himself.
- Darnell Braud was 16 years old when he shot his first victim. After serving 10 years, and 7 months after being paroled, Braud fatally shot a man. Braud then shot and killed another man after having argued with him.
- Eric Tidrick was 17 years old when he bludgeoned a man during a robbery in 1978. Thirty-two years later, after being paroled, Tidrick stabbed his 77-year-old mother to death, covered her body with pillows, and telephoned police to confess.

- Scott Thompson was 17 years old when he was overcome with an unexplainable feeling and stabbed an 88-year-old woman who gave him three dollars and a drink of water. Twenty-four years later, Thompson was free on parole when he randomly beat a young man to death after agreeing to give him a ride.
- Kyle Wilson was 17 when he stabbed a 15-year-old boy to death following an argument about an $80 debt. Five years later, after being paroled, Wilson beat his cousin to death after getting into an argument with him over not paying his share of expenses in their shared apartment.

Extensive Criminal Histories

Several serial murderers have extensive criminal histories and were considered to be predatory, habitual offenders. A recent study suggests that many serial murderers view their patterns of criminality as activities that coalesce into a career (Campedelli & Yaksic, 2021). As the serial murderer's self-concept begins to align more closely with reality, homicide becomes a natural extension of their lifelong exposure to the criminal justice system. One study found that serial murderers had been convicted of other, nonlethal offenses, including rape and attempted homicide (Sturup, 2018), while another notes that they generally have had contact with the criminal justice system and that one third were career criminals before their first homicide (DeLisi & Scherer, 2006). Morton, Tillman, and Gaines (2014) found that almost 80% of offenders had arrest records.

There is some debate about whether or not serial murderers are homicide specialists or if they are versatile offenders who mix homicide into a larger pattern of criminal offending. One study found that serial murderers often commit kidnapping, rape, armed robbery, theft, and other crimes during the course of their homicidal conduct (DeLisi, Bunga, Heirigs, Erickson, & Hochstetler, 2019). Individuals, such as serial murderers, who "recurrently contemplate lethal violence, that view homicide as a viable behavioral option, and whose individual-level traits are conductive to homicidal activity are more likely to kill" (DeLisi, Drury, & Elbert, 2018, p. 6).

In this review, some offenders committed crimes in a pattern where homicide seemed to be the inevitable outcome while other offenders killed in concurrence with other crimes. While the concept of escalation is not well studied, the case histories of some offenders give credence to the idea that homicide can be an act born from the culmination of a long history of relying on violence to resolve conflicts or obtain what they desire. For instance, one review found that some offenders show progression from burglary to sexual assault to murder (Martin, Schwarting, & Chase, 2020).

All but one of the serial murderers who escalated to homicide committed a mix of nonviolent and violent crimes over their careers:

- Randy Santos bludgeoned four homeless men to death with a piece of construction metal as they slept. His criminal history is extensive with six arrests, including charges of punching a stranger on the subway, choking another man at an employment agency, and punching a homeless man inside a shelter. Santos was kicked out of his mother's apartment after assaulting his grandfather.

- Leon Means was referred to as a "walking crime wave" for crimes dating back to 1984 that included unarmed robbery, breaking and entering, and stabbing a man in a robbery attempt. Means spent most of his life in prison but was still able to kill four women whom he knew: his wife and mother-in-law while a prison escapee in 1989 and two women an hour apart in 2014, 4 years after being paroled.
- Stewart Weldon's record includes burglary, unlawful possession of a weapon, assault with a dangerous weapon, breaking and entering, assault and battery on a police officer, breach of peace, kidnapping, and sexual assault.
- Carroll Tuttle's criminal history stretched from 1987 to 2004 and included criminal trespass, disorderly conduct, and assault.
- Dontae Morris' criminal career includes charges for disturbing the peace, vehicle theft, battery, drug possession, carjacking, resisting an officer, attempted murder, aggravated battery, attempted robbery, and possession of a short-barreled shotgun.
- Darren Vann was found guilty of aggravated fleeing police and, years later, he was arrested for threatening his ex-girlfriend. Three years later, he was convicted of aggravated sexual assault and paroled 6 months before the series of homicides began.
- Aaron Glee's criminal record dates back to 1989 and includes convictions for robbery, grand theft auto, credit card fraud, forging bills, suspicion of marijuana possession, burglary, cocaine possession with intent to sell, battery, and providing false identification to police. He was arrested for aggravated battery, weeks before he killed two women.
- Erik Meiser's history of violence dates back to his teens and includes burglary, resisting arrest, false identification to police, possession of narcotics, vandalism, disorderly conduct, battery, trespass, theft, assault, domestic violence, cruelty towards a child, violation of a protective order, obscene phone calls, and ethnic intimidation.
- Richard Beasley's criminal history includes managing sex workers, aggravated menacing, possession of marijuana, tampering with evidence, cultivation of marijuana, and possession of criminal tools.

All but one of the serial murderers whose homicides occurred in concurrence with their crimes committed both nonviolent and violent crimes over their careers:

- Lucky Ward's criminal record dates back to the late 1970s and includes aggravated assault with a deadly weapon, theft, assault causing bodily injury, drug possession, and prostitution. The first homicide attributed to Ward occurred in 1985, in the middle of his offending pattern.
- Patrick Watkins, who has several robbery and firearm convictions dating from 1989, killed two people during a long stretch of robberies.

- Gerardo Hernandez preyed on women business owners, carjacked, raped, and murdered a girl on her lunch break, and lay in wait to bludgeon and stab a woman to death in her own home during a burglary. Hernandez also committed a string of armed robberies on several businesses across several counties. During one of these incidents, Hernandez tried to remove the pants of one victim and put his hand down the shirt of another.
- Jerard Garrett killed a man during a drug transaction that turned into a robbery. Six days later, he shot a man to death over drugs. Garrett has an extensive criminal history that includes drugs, kidnapping, and robbery.
- Shawn Jarrett's criminal background dates back to his teens. In 1979, Jarrett, then 16, was charged with breaking into a home and raping a woman. In 1982, he broke into a neighbor's house, raped and murdered her, and fled with her jewelry. Two months later, Jarrett assaulted a 58-year-old woman. Jarrett was released in 2012 and raped an 85-year-old woman 2 months after having killed a coworker he showed an interest in.
- Troy Whisnant confessed to killing his best friend and was incarcerated for a year and 14 months. Between his release and the murders of his father, stepmother, and a US Forest Service officer, he committed crimes that included stealing credit cards, larceny, possession of narcotics, and assault on a public figure.
- The crime spree of Anthony Foye and Nathaniel Mitchell occurred over 11 days and involved attempted murders, robberies, and firearms offenses.
- Peter Jones was convicted of 15 felonies between 1990 and 2006: two unarmed robberies, a burglary, and, less than a month after his release, an attempted first-degree murder. Just months later, Jones was successful in his next attempt to kill.
- James Harris has been arrested for burglary, assault, theft, trespassing, drug and gun offenses, statutory sexual assault, rape, and corruption of a minor.
- Leeroy Rogers has been arrested at least 10 times for theft, felony burglary, shooting a clerk, trespassing, rape, possession of weapon, assault, attempted capital murder, aggravated sexual assault, and aggravated robbery. Rogers was released 2 years before he shot two women to death within 4 months.

Warehousing Victim's Remains

Serial murderers who warehoused their victim's remains on their property share some unique qualities related to their relationships with women. Each of these offenders preyed on their victim's need for security by offering them attention.

- Over the course of 9 months, Michael Madison lured each of his three victims back to his apartment where he strangled them and disposed of their bodies in garbage bags around his apartment. Madison had several girlfriends, dealt drugs, and partied while his victim's remains rotted. He was inspired by another serial murderer to keep his victims' bodies close to home. Madison invited one of the victims to his apartment but lied via text messages that he was younger and without children.

- Stewart Weldon killed three women whom he preyed on while they were searching for drugs. His female passenger, who shared two children with him, stated that Weldon had been torturing her and holding her captive for a month. Police found three bodies in Weldon's house after his mother called to report a foul order.
- Shawn Grate texted a friend "meet the other me" after receiving a barrage of scathing messages. While being held as Grate's sex slave, a woman who regarded him as a "big brother" was able to call 911 and escape. Grate used the residence where she was held to hide the body of a strangled woman underneath a pile of clothes. The remains of a second victim were in the basement. Grate choked one victim until she admitted that she wanted to live but he claims that she did not. Grate's criminal record is filled with attacks on women who found him to be controlling, jealous, and violent.

Victimizing Fellow Inmates

Each of the serial murderers who killed fellow inmates was initially incarcerated for murder. There were a variety of reasons for these offenders to kill their cellmates:

1. To fulfill a plot to get the death penalty:

- Denver Simmons and Jacob Philip had already killed separately outside prison before meeting inside and teaming up to kill four fellow inmates in an effort to get the death penalty. Simmons and Philip had each separately killed a woman and her child and then together lured men, one by one, into their cell to be strangled and beaten. The pair had much in common and wanted to make a name for themselves.
- Robert Gleason first killed outside prison to cover up his involvement in a drug gang. While inside, he killed his cellmate out of frustration and vowed to continue killing if not given the death penalty. Gleason killed two other inmates before being granted his wish.

2. To avenge their child victims:

- Christopher Fletcher raped and murdered two women 9 years apart and, while incarcerated, killed a fellow inmate who was jailed for child sexual assault due to concerns he would reoffend after release.
- Steven Sandison murdered his girlfriend in 1991 and then his cellmate 16 years later because he was a child molester who would not stop talking about the case.

3. To obtain solitude or a change in cellmate:

- Casey Pigge called himself "Box Cutter" after slitting the throat of his girlfriend's mother. He was dubbed "Hannibal Lecter" by another inmate in a letter complaining about the threat that Pigge posed. Pigge killed one inmate because he wanted his own cell and another because he just felt like killing someone.

- Clinton Powers was serving a life sentence for murdering an inmate in 1996 when he killed a second inmate 15 years later because he wanted a different cellmate. Powers claimed that nothing would stop him from killing, even if he was put on death row, as he would kill death row inmates.

4. To settle personal differences:

- Sheddrick Bentley, who has a tattoo on his arm that says "VICIOUS," stabbed his friend 150 times in an argument over a girl. Bentley strangled his cellmate with a sock for inappropriately touching him.
- Marvin Magallanes, who hated homeless people, stabbed two homeless men to death months after ramming his car into the gate of a reality television star's home. Magallanes soon killed an inmate who was due to be released.

Military Service

Although Henson and Olson's (2010) analysis found a possible connection between military service and serial murder, the link between carrying out justifiable homicides on behalf of the military and the transference of that exposure to killing into the murder of innocent civilians has been long debated. Some offenders may join the military in the hopes of being able to kill with impunity, but participation in the military does not always lead to combat scenarios. But even if the offender had not seen combat, basic training provides enough exposure to death that recruits understand how to carry out a killing.

At least eight serial murderers had served in the military. Three of these offenders killed over a period of time, with two offenders killing strangers, and the other offender killing people he knew:

- Although Itzcoatl Ocampo did not see combat in the Marine Corps, he was said to be jealous of those who did. He did experience a traumatic brain injury and was responsible for bagging up bodies and inspecting the wounded. He killed multiple vagrants, whom he viewed as a "blight," and tracked down a man who gave a disparaging interview about him, stabbed him to death, and was then chased by witnesses.
- Caregiving serial murderer Reta Mays is an army veteran who took medication for PTSD.
- Buford King, an army veteran who served in Iraq, killed three men whom he knew. One victim lived in a trailer on King's property. Police received a tip that a body was buried on King's property and, after extensive digging, unearthed the remains of two men buried nine feet deep. Police had long believed that King was involved in the men's disappearances.

Five other offenders killed in a "spree-like" fashion. All but one killed at least one significant other during their series:

- Juan Ortiz was a combat medic in the Navy who killed four sex workers over a 2-week span 9 years after being discharged. He lived a quiet suburban life with his wife.
- Dwight Jones dropped out of the military after 3 years. He went on to gun down six people in a 4-day rage that stemmed from a divorce and custody battle.
- Erbie Bowser acted out a "military delusion" when he killed his former girlfriend, her daughter, his ex-wife, and a family friend. Bowser used a hand grenade to enter his ex-wife's home and pretended to be a victim when the police responded to the scene.
- Esteban Smith saw two combat tours in Afghanistan before he stabbed his wife to death and went on a shooting "rampage" that claimed the life of one other woman.
- Bradley Stone had one deployment to Iraq as a Marine and had been diagnosed with PTSD. He shot and stabbed his former sister-in-law, her husband, and their 14-year-old daughter to death after a protracted custody battle. He then traveled to another home and did the same to his mother-in-law and grandmother-in-law. Stone then ventured to the apartment of his ex-wife, who lived in fear of him, and fatally shot her.

Victims as Collateral Damage

Several serial murder victims were killed due to their knowledge of homicides or the offender's perception that their anonymity had been compromised.

- Aaron Glee killed his second victim due to her knowledge of his first homicide.
- Jeffrey Moreland killed a victim since she saw him strangle and stab a woman.
- Prentiss Hare killed a woman because she witnessed the death of another person whom Hare killed due to an argument over drugs.
- Kevin Sweat killed his fiancée after she threatened to tell police about his homicides.
- Alto Miles killed a victim to eliminate a witness.

"Prolific" Status

Although several serial murderers with many inter-murder intervals can be explained by parole, there are offenders who could be called "prolific," or those with many victims over uninterrupted, lengthy killing careers. Over the span of a decade, the title of the most prolific serial murderer in California changed hands among four African American offenders: John Floyd Thomas (Bone, 2009); Chester Turner (William-Ross, 2011); Lonnie Franklin (Nestel, 2016); and Samuel Little (Rogers,

2020). These serial murderers pursue this type of longevity by adapting to competing demands that can alter motivation and impact decisions, and disengage from their lifestyle when necessary, neutralize fear, lie to themselves and others, regulate emotions, improve tactics, use principled techniques to persevere, remain receptive to vulnerability, and embrace self-awareness (Yaksic, Comerford, Gordon, Allely, Mooney, Geyer, Taylor, Matykiewicz, Denisov, Vecherin, De Silva, Bulut, Synnott, & Ioannou, 2019). One study found that FSMs, those employing multiple methods, younger serial murderers, and those who acted in more than one state have higher odds of longer careers. This same study found that those offending with a partner and those targeting victims from a single gender have shorter careers (Campedelli & Yaksic, 2021). Another study found that the duration of a serial murderer's series was longer if the offender did not sexually assault the victim, left the body at the crime scene, selected minority victims, used a combination of multiple methods, and had a previous incarceration (Chai, Yaksic, Chopin, Fortin, & Hewitt, 2022).

Only 14 serial murderers (4%) in this review could be considered prolific. There are a variety of circumstances behind how these 14 serial murderers were able to kill for an extended period of time. As seen in Table 4.1, the prolific status granted to these murderers can be attributed to luck in the majority of instances (79%), while the offender's abilities to evade detection can be credited to their freedom to kill just under a quarter of the time (21%). Reale, Beauregard, and Martineau (2020) argue that "rational" offenders pose more of a risk for evading detection because of conscious efforts to hamper investigations. Chan, Beauregard, and Myers (2015) believe that obsessive–compulsive traits help serial murderers strive for perfection and avoid apprehension. But not all offenders have obsessive–compulsive traits or are capable of being rational because serial homicide occurs at the juncture of competing forces – strong emotions and physical desires – that inhibit rationality during the chaotic process of murder (Shanafelt & Pino, 2013). Warf and Waddell (2002) note that serial murderers must contend with local neighborhood social structures, ethnic diversity, the degree of community cohesiveness, and opportunities for surveillance of outsiders. Osborne and Salfati (2015) point out that serial murderers are under various pressures such as the perceived presence of police, geographic factors, and the struggle to maintain social connectedness through marriage and employment, the latter of which influences the length of time intervals within a series by encroaching on the time available to the offender. One offender who struggled with discrepancies within his own self-concept and became paranoid and fatalistic about being apprehended and lost control of his faculties claimed to rely on luck to escape apprehension. More specifically, he benefited from the antiquated attitude of police that sex workers could not be assaulted if they were paid (Pino, 2005).

This review, as well as other research (Balemba, Beauregard, & Martineau, 2014; Yaksic, Allely, De Silva, Smith-Inglis, Konikoff, Ryan, Gordon, Denisov, & Keatley, 2019; Yaksic, Allred, Drakulic, Mooney, De Silva, Geyer, Wills, Comerford, & Ranger, 2021), shows that luck, rather than skill, plays a major role in a serial homicide series. As LePard, Demers, Langan, and Rossmo (2015) demonstrate, there

TABLE 4.1 Circumstances of the prolific, nonparoled, nonincarcerated serial murderer's initial homicide

Offender Name	*Time Span (years)*	*Suspect in First Homicide*	*Circumstances of First Homicide(s) in Series*	*Relation to Victim*	*Factor(s) Allowing Offender to Continue Homicide Series*	*Luck or Skill?*
Jennifer Berry	8	N	Death of first son was thought to be due to sudden infant death syndrome	Familial	Medical examiner misclassified event	Luck
Steven Hobbs	8	N	Booked for failing to appear for a summons, but a DNA sample was not collected	Stranger	Police error	Luck
Prentiss Hare	9	N	Victim was a sex worker whose homicide was considered to be a "cold case"	Stranger	Police allocated resources elsewhere	Luck
William Gibson	9	N	The condition of the body of first victim deteriorated having been outdoors	Stranger	Outdoor elements inhibited the investigation	Luck
Cedric Marks	10	N	Victim's hands and teeth removed to delay or avoid identification	Familial	Offender took forensic countermeasures	Skill
Craig Miller	11	N	Another serial murderer was a suspect	Stranger	Police followed erroneous leads	Luck
Michael Mullins	12	N	First homicide was considered to be a "cold case," DNA from the crime scene had never been submitted	Stranger	Police allocated resources elsewhere, police error	Luck
Shaun Gallon	13	Y	Father lied and destroyed evidence of the double homicide	Stranger	Offender was given assistance	Luck
Michele Kalina	15	N	Victim's body encased in concrete. Hid pregnancies and lied about them being cysts	Familial	Offender took forensic countermeasures and was a convincing liar	Skill
Chris Lovrien	21	N	Left DNA behind at the initial crime scene, but it did not match a sample until a genealogy firm traced lineage	Stranger	Police lacked viable leads	Luck
James Lynn	21	N	Medical examiner ruled the death of first wife a suicide	Familial	Medical examiner misclassified event	Luck
Rosario Melici	22	N	Melici and an accomplice were hired to kill a woman, and he killed the accomplice 2 years later.	Stranger	Intentional lack of connection to victim, eliminated witness	Skill
Amy Bishop	23	Y	Death of brother was ruled an accident/has since been classified as a "miscarriage of justice"	Familial	Police misclassified event as accident	Luck
Stanley Guidroz	28	Y	Fabricated story about a couple who abducted son	Familial	Police followed erroneous leads	Luck

have been several instances where serial murderers benefited from situations outside their control (deleted records, nonreports of missing victims, investigator bias, underresourced and suspended investigations, dismissed charges, and uncooperative witnesses) or, as they are more properly named, "lucky breaks." Conceptualizing these events in this way helps us to recognize that serial murderers are not experts in avoiding or overcoming obstacles. For instance, Brantley and Ochberg (2003) introduced the account of a serial murderer who was released by a judge who determined the offender to harbor no dangerousness, against all contrary evidence. There are also situational and contextual elements of a crime that are beyond the control of the offender (e.g., a broken-down car at the crime scene), which can nullify their post-homicide precautions (Beauregard & Martineau, 2016). Police hope for these factors to help resolve difficult cases and have taken to calling them "strokes of luck" (James & Beauregard, 2020). Both Harbort and Mokros (2001) and Kurkjian (2016) found that a large proportion of serial murderers are apprehended due to chance, while Pakkanen, Zappalà, Bosco, Berti, and Santtila (2015) also acknowledge that some potential serial murderers are unlucky in that they are apprehended after their initial crime.

Notes

1 Several "longreads" (Associated Press, 2020; Callahan, 2016; Cipriano, 2020; Cooperman, 2017; de Acha, Hurd, & Lightfoot, 2021; Friedman, 2014; Garrison, 2018; Hogan, 2018; Ison, 2017; Johnson, 2019; Keefe, 2013; Krauze, 2017; Powers, 2016) and books (Casey, 2018; Porter, 2019; Rother, 2012; Sullivan, 2011) were produced over the study period and were helpful in understanding these offenders.

2 Such as Amy Bishop and Robert Long being labeled as mass shooters rather than the respective classifications of serial murderer and serial-spree murderer.

3 Defined as more than one murder within a 14-day period.

4 The website CrazyShit offers images of sexual deviance and juxtaposes them with videos of actual homicides.

References

Adjorlolo, S., & Chan, H. C. (2014). The controversy of defining serial murder: Revisited. *Aggression and Violent Behavior*. 19(5):486–491.

Allely, C. (2020). The Psychology of Extreme Violence: A Case Study Approach to Serial Homicide, Mass Shooting, School Shooting and Lone-Actor Terrorism. Routledge.

Associated Press. (2020). Detective Trapp, Part 5: A bizarre trial and a new mystery. Texarkana Gazette. Retrieved from www.texarkanagazette.com/news/national/story/2020/jan/04/detective-trapp-part-5-bizarre-trial-and-new-mystery/810757/

Balemba, S., Beauregard, E., & Martineau, M. (2014). Getting away with murder: A thematic approach to solved and unsolved sexual homicides using crime scene factors. *Police Practice and Research*. 15(3):221–233.

Beasley, J. (2004). Serial murder in America: Case studies of seven offenders. *Behavioral Sciences & the Law*. 22(3):395–414.

Beauregard, E., & Martineau, M. (2016). Does the organized sexual murderer better delay and avoid detection? *Journal of Interpersonal Violence*. 31(1):4–25.

Bone, J. (2009). DNA reveals John Floyd Thomas as LA's most prolific serial killer. The Times. Retrieved from www.thetimes.co.uk/article/dna-reveals-john-floyd-thomas-as-las-most-prolific-serial-killer-j0wp7fgd65n

Brantley, A., & Ochberg, F. (2003). Lethal predators and future dangerousness. *FBI Law Enforcement Bulletin*. 72:16–21.

Callahan, J. (2016). Uncovered: The story of a serial killer no one knew existed. The Commercial Appeal. Retrieved from http://projects.commercialappeal.com/uncovered/

Campedelli, G. M., & Yaksic, E. (2021). Survival of the recidivistic? Revealing factors associated with the criminal career length of multiple homicide offenders. *Homicide Studies*. In press. Retrieved from https://journals.sagepub.com/doi/abs/10.1177/10887679211010882

Casey, K. (2018). In Plain Sight: The Kaufman County Prosecutor Murders. HarperCollins.

Chai, A., Yaksic, E., & Chopin, J. (2021). One "two" many: An examination of solo perpetrator vs. team perpetrator in serial homicides. *Homicide Studies*, In press. Retrieved from https://journals.sagepub.com/doi/abs/10.1177/10887679211060030

Chai, A., Yaksic, E., Chopin, J., Fortin, F., & Hewitt, A. (2022). Time after time: Factors predicting murder series' duration. *Journal of Criminal Justice*. Under Review.

Chan, H. C., Beauregard, E., & Myers, W. C. (2015). Single-victim and serial sexual homicide offenders: Differences in crime, paraphilias and personality traits. *Criminal Behaviour and Mental Health*. 25(1):66–78.

Cipriano, R. (2020). The untold tale of Cosmo DiNardo's descent into murder and madness. Phillymag.com. Retrieved from www.phillymag.com/news/2020/02/25/cosmo-dinardo/

Clark, J., & Palattella, E. (2017). Mania and Marjorie Diehl-Armstrong: Inside the Mind of a Female Serial Killer. Rowman & Littlefield.

Cooperman, J. (2017). The unimaginable, infamous case of Pam Hupp. St. Louis Magazine. Retrieved from www.stlmag.com/longform/pam-hupp/

de Acha, G. P., Hurd, K., & Lightfoot, E. (2021). "I felt hate more than anything": How an active duty airman tried to start a civil war. ProPublica. Retrieved from www.propublica.org/article/i-felt-hate-more-than-anything-how-an-active-duty-airman-tried-to-start-a-civil-war

DeLisi, M., & Scherer, A. M. (2006). Multiple homicide offenders: Offense characteristics, social correlates, and criminal careers. *Criminal Justice and Behavior*. 33(3):367–391.

DeLisi, M., Drury, A., & Elbert, M. (2018). The homicide circumplex: A new conceptual model and empirical examination. *Journal of Criminal Psychology*. 8(4):314–332.

DeLisi, M., Bunga, R., Heirigs, M., Erickson, J., & Hochstetler, A. (2019). The past is prologue: Criminal specialization continuity in the delinquent career. *Youth Violence and Juvenile Justice*. 17(4):335–353.

Egger, S. (2002). The Killers among Us: An Examination of Serial Murder and Its Investigation. Prentice Hall.

Farrell, A. L., Keppel, R. D., & Titterington, V. B. (2011). Lethal ladies: Revisiting what we know about female serial murderers. *Homicide Studies*. 15(3):228–252.

Ferguson, C., White, D., Cherry, S., Lorenz, M., & Bhimani, Z. (2003). Defining and classifying serial murder in the context of perpetrator motivation. *Journal of Criminal Justice*. 31(3):287–292.

Friedman, D. (2014). The Craigslist killers. GQ. Retrieved from www.gq.com/story/craigslist-killers

Garrison, J. (2018). The black hand: The life of one of America's bloodiest hitmen. BuzzFeed News. Retrieved from www.buzzfeednews.com/article/jessicagarrison/martinez-hitman-cartel-black-hand-mano-negra-contract-killer

Gunn, J. F., White, J., & Lester, D. (2014). Twice the evil: A comparison of serial killers who killed with a partner and those who killed alone. *American Journal of Forensic Psychology*. 32(1):5–17.

Gurian, E.A. (2011). Female serial murderers: directions for future research on a hidden population. *International Journal of Offender Therapy and Comparative Criminology*. 55(1):27–42.

Gurian, E.A. (2013). Explanations of mixed-sex partnered homicide: A review of sociological and psychological theory. *Aggression and Violent Behavior*. 18(5):520–526.

Gurian, E. A. (2017). Reframing serial murder within empirical research: Offending and adjudication patterns of male, female, and partnered serial killers. *International Journal of Offender Therapy and Comparative Criminology*. 61(5):544–560.

Harbort, S., & Mokros, A. (2001). Serial murderers in Germany from 1945 to 1995: A descriptive study. *Homicide Studies*. 5(4):311–334.

Harrison, M., Murphy, E., Ho, L., Bowers, T., & Flaherty, C. (2015). Female serial killers in the United States: means, motives, and makings. *The Journal of Forensic Psychiatry & Psychology*. 26(3):383–406.

Henson, J., & Olson, L. (2010). The monster within: How male serial killers discursively manage their stigmatized identities. *Communication Quarterly*. 58(3):341–364.

Hickey, E. W., & Harris, B. R. (2013). Serial killing. In Jay A. Siegel, Pekka J. Saukko, & Max M. Houck (Eds.), Encyclopedia of Forensic Sciences (pp. 197–201). Academic Press Waltham.

Hildebrand, M., & Culhane, S. (2015). Personality characteristics of the female serial murderer. *Journal of Criminal Psychology*. 5(1):34–50.

Hinch, R., & Hepburn, C. (1998). Researching serial murder: Methodological and definitional problems. *Electronic Journal of Sociology*. 3(2):1–11.

Hogan, S. (2018). The Cray divorcé. Phoenixmag.com. Retrieved from www.phoenixmag.com/2018/09/01/the-cray-divorce/

Homant, R., & Kennedy, D. (2014), Understanding serial sexual murder: A biopsychosocial approach. In W. Petherick (Ed.), Profiling and Serial Crime (3rd ed., pp. 341–372). Anderson.

Ison, J. (2017). Deadly ambition: Inside the mind of a killer. Chillicothe Gazette. Retrieved from www.chillicothegazette.com/story/news/local/in-depth/2017/09/14/casey-pigge-boasts-murders-claims-he-kill-again/637892001/

James, J., & Proulx, J. (2016). The modus operandi of serial and nonserial sexual murderers: A systematic review. *Aggression and Violent Behavior*. 31:200–218.

James, J., & Beauregard, E. (2020). Murderer vs investigator: Factors influencing the resolution of sexual homicide cases. *Police Practice and Research*. 21(2):172–186.

Johnson, J. (2019). Inside the disturbing mind of Jenner beach killer Shaun Gallon. The Press Democrat. Retrieved from www.pressdemocrat.com/article/article/inside-the-disturbing-mind-of-jenner-beach-killer-shaun-gallon/

Keefe, P. R. (2013). A loaded gun. The New Yorker. Retrieved from www.newyorker.com/magazine/2013/02/11/a-loaded-gun

Kiger, K. (1990). The darker figure of crime: The serial murder enigma. In S. Egger (Ed.), Serial Murder: An Elusive Phenomenon (pp. 35–52). Praeger.

Kochman, B. (2015). Sick serial stabber sentenced to 25 years to life after DNA links him to '93 cold case murder. New York Daily News. Retrieved from www.nydailynews.com/new-york/serial-stabber-sentenced-93-cold-case-murder-article-1.2256700

Krauze, L. (2017). The obsidian serpent. The Atavist Magazine. Retrieved from https://magazine.atavist.com/obsidian-serpent-homeless-murders-california/

Kurkjian, A. (2016). How serial sexual murderers are apprehended. Master's Thesis. Unpublished.

LePard, D., Demers, S., Langan, C., & Kim Rossmo, D. (2015). Challenges in serial murder investigations involving missing persons. *Police Practice and Research*. 16(4):328–340.

Martin, E., Schwarting, D. E., & Chase, R. J. (2020). Serial killer connections through cold cases. Retrieved from https://nij.ojp.gov/topics/articles/serial-killer-connections-through-cold-cases

Morton, R., & McNamara, J. (2005). Serial murder. In J. Payne-James & R. Byard, T. Corey, & C. Henderson (Eds.), Encyclopedia of Forensic and Legal Medicine (pp. 47–53). Elsevier.

Morton, R., & Hilts, M. (2008). Serial murder: Multi-disciplinary perspectives for investigators. National Center for the Analysis ofViolent Crime.

Morton, R., Tillman, J., & Gaines, S. (2014). Serial murder: Pathways for investigations. Federal Bureau of Investigation, US Department of Justice.

Murray, J. (2017). The role of sexual, sadistic, and misogynistic fantasy in mass and serial killing. *Deviant Behavior*. 38(7):735–743.

Myers, W. C., Husted, D. S., Safarik, M. E., & O'toole, M. E. (2006). The motivation behind serial sexual homicide: Is it sex, power, and control, or anger? *Journal of Forensic Sciences*. 51(4):900–907.

Nestel, M. L. (2016). She escaped the "Grim Sleeper" serial killer. Daily Beast. Retrieved from www.thedailybeast.com/grim-sleeper-didnt-sleep-lonnie-franklin-jr-accused-of-30-murders-new-survivor-emerges

Osborne, J., & Salfati, C. (2015). Re-conceptualizing "cooling-off periods" in serial homicide. *Homicide Studies*. 19(2):188–205.

Pakkanen, T., Zappalà, A., Bosco, D., Berti, A., & Santtila, P. (2015). Can hard-to-solve one-off homicides be distinguished from serial homicides? Differences in offence behaviours and victim characteristics. *Journal of Criminal Psychology*. 5(3):216–232.

Pearson, P. (2021). When healers do harm: Women serial killers in the health care industry. The Walrus. Retrieved from https://thewalrus.ca/when-healers-do-harm-women-serial-killers-in-the-health-care-industry/

Pino, N. (2005). Serial offending and the criminal events perspective. *Homicide Studies*. 9(2):109–148.

Pollock, P. H. (1995). A case of spree serial murder with suggested diagnostic opinions. *International Journal of Offender Therapy and Comparative Criminology*. 39(3):258–268.

Porter, B. (2019). The Parable of the Knocker: The True Crime Story of a Prosecutor's Fight to Bring a Serial Killer to Justice. Waldorf.

Powers, A. (2016). The man in the woods. The California Sunday Magazine. Retrieved from https://story.californiasunday.com/aaron-bassler-fort-bragg-manhunt/

Priser, J. (2021). Texas nurse killed 4 patients, prosecutors allege: "A hospital is the perfect place for a serial killer to hide". The Washington Post. Retrieved from www.washingtonpost.com/nation/2021/09/29/nurse-texas-murder-william-george-davis/

Reale, K., Beauregard, E., & Martineau, M. (2020). Is investigative awareness a distinctive feature of sexual sadism? *Journal of Interpersonal Violence*. 35(7–8):1761–1778.

Rogers, J. (2020). Man Called Most Prolific Serial Killer in US History Dies. Associated Press. Retrieved from https://apnews.com/article/us-news-california-samuel-little-3b63489aa94bebe08120a3b76393d7ee

Rother, C. (2012). Lost Girls. Kensington Books.

Safarik, M., & Ramsland, K. (2020). Spree Killers: Practical Classifications for Law Enforcement and Criminology. CRC Press.

Schechter, E., & Schechter, H. (2010). Killing with kindness: Nature, nurture, and the female serial killer. In S. Waller (Ed.), Serial Killers – Philosophy for Everyone: Being and Killing (pp. 115–128). Wiley. Retrieved from https://onlinelibrary.wiley.com/doi/abs/10.1002/9781444324587.ch9

Schlesinger, L. B. (1998). Pathological narcissism and serial homicide: Review and case study. *Current Psychology*. 17(2):212–221.

Schlesinger, L. B. (2001). Is serial homicide really increasing? *Journal of the American Academy of Psychiatry and the Law*. 29:294–297.

Schlesinger, L. B., Kassen, M., Mesa, V. B., & Pinizzotto, A. J. (2010). Ritual and signature in serial sexual homicide. *Journal of the American Academy of Psychiatry and the Law Online*. 38(2):239–246.

Schlesinger, L. B., Ramirez, S., Tusa, B., Jarvis, J. P., & Erdberg, P. (2017). Rapid-sequence serial sexual homicides. *Journal of the American Academy of Psychiatry and the Law*. 45(1):72–80.

Shanafelt, R., & Pino, N. (2013). Evil and the common life: Towards a wider perspective on serial killing and atrocities. In R. Atkinson & S. Winlow (Eds.), New Directions in Crime and Deviancy (pp. 252–273). Routledge.

Skrapec, C. A. (2001). Phenomenology and serial murder: Asking different questions. *Homicide Studies*. 5(1):46–63.

Sturup, J. (2018). Comparing serial homicides to single homicides: A study of prevalence, offender, and offence characteristics in Sweden. *Journal of Investigative Psychology and Offender Profiling*. 15(2):75–89.

Sullivan, I. (2011). The crossover killer: Excerpt from "Raised by the Courts". Youth Today. Retrieved from https://youthtoday.org/2011/02/the-crossover-killer-excerpt-from-raised-by-the-courts/

Tully, T., & Smith-Inglis, M. (2018). Female serial killers: Motives, case studies, and a new typology. *Criminal Justice Research Review*. 19(2):25–56.

Ulmer, J. T., & Steffensmeier, D. J. (2014). The age and crime relationship: Social variation, social explanations. In The Nurture versus Biosocial Debate in Criminology: On the Origins of Criminal Behavior and Criminality (pp. 377–396). SAGE. Retrieved from https://pennstate.pure.elsevier.com/en/publications/the-age-and-crime-relationship-social-variation-social-explanatio

Warf, B., & Waddell, C. (2002). Heinous spaces, perfidious places: The sinister landscapes of serial killers. *Social & Cultural Geography*. 3(3):323–345.

White, J., & Lester, D. (2012). A study of female serial killers. *American Journal of Forensic Psychology*. 30(1):25–29.

William-Ross, L. (2011). L.A.'s "Most Prolific Serial Killer" will be charged for murders of 4 more women. LAist. Retrieved from https://laist.com/news/criminal-justice/las-most-prolific-serial-killer-wil

Williams, D., & Vincent, J. (2018). "It's Going to be Extra Fun!": Analysis of an atypical case of teen homicide as leisure behavior. *Journal of Forensic Sciences*. 63(6):1914–1916.

Williams, D. (2021). Forensic behavioral science of serial and mass murder with an addition of leisure research: A descriptive synthesis. *Forensic Sciences*. 1(1):16–24.

Williams, D., Arntfield, M., Schaal, K., & Vincent, J. (2021). Wanting sex and willing to kill: Examining demographic and cognitive characteristics of violent "involuntary celibates". *Behavioral Sciences & the Law*. 39(4):386–401.

Yaksic, E. (2015). Addressing the challenges and limitations of utilizing data to study serial homicide. *Crime Psychology Review*. 1(1):108–134.

Yaksic, E. (2018). The folly of counting bodies: Using regression to transgress the state of serial murder classification systems. *Aggression and Violent Behavior*. 43:26–32.

Yaksic, E. (2019). Moving past sporadic eruptions, discursive killing, and running amok: Recognizing the convergence of the serial and spree killer. *Journal of Criminal Psychology*. 9(3):138–146.

Yaksic, E., Allely, C., De Silva, R., Smith-Inglis, M., Konikoff, D., Ryan, K., Gordon, D., Denisov, E. & Keatley, D. (2019). Detecting a decline in serial homicide: Have we banished the devil from the details? *Cogent Social Sciences*. 5(1):1–23.

Yaksic, E., Comerford, C., Gordon, D., Allely, C. S., Mooney, R., Geyer, P., Taylor, S., Matykiewicz, B., Denisov, E., Vecherin, A., De Silva, R., Bulut, T., Synnott, J., & Ioannou, M. (2019, November 13–16). Which factors contribute to the serial homicide offender's ability to pursue longevity? Paper presented at the 75th American Society of Criminology Annual Meeting. Retrieved from https://convention2.allacademic.com/one/asc/asc19/index.php?program_focus=view_paper&selected_paper_id=1550081&cmd=online_program_direct_link&sub_action=online_program

Yaksic, E., Allred, T. B., Drakulic, C., Mooney, R., De Silva, R., Geyer, P., Wills, A., Comerford, C., & Ranger, R. (2021). How much damage do serial homicide offenders wrought while the innocent rot in prison? A tabulation of preventable deaths as outcomes of sentinel events. *Psychology, Crime and Law*. 27(1):76–88.

Yaksic, E., Harrison, M., & Hood, B. (2021). Deadly pathways to multiple murder: Comparing serial homicide offenders and multiple-event murderers. *Criminal Justice and Behavior*, Under review.

Yaksic, E., Harrison, M., Konikoff, D., Mooney, R., Allely, C., De Silva, R., Matykiewicz, B., Inglis, M., Giannangelo, S., Daniels, S., & Sarteschi, C. (2021). A heuristic study of the similarities and differences in offender characteristics across potential and successful serial sexual homicide offenders. *Behavioral Sciences & the Law*. 39(4):428–449.

Yaksic, E., Simkin, M., & Roychowdhury, V. (2021). A statistical study of the time intervals between serial homicides. *Journal of Criminal Justice*. 73:1–10.

5

CONCLUDING THOUGHTS

Conclusion

The history of the study and investigation of serial murder is storied as it is filled with rivalries and one-upmanship. Many sought to lay claim to a profitable area of inquiry: scholars with fame-based motives displayed egotistical reasoning for protecting territory while police created obstacles for each other as they jockeyed for jurisdiction (Yaksic, 2019). The unsubstantiated leaps made by many in the early days helped serial murderers tell their stories. Serial murderers received indirect support from the academic and police communities through several myths and stereotypes that are still being promulgated today. But researchers and police are now beginning to work together to counter those inaccuracies. Doing so has led to the understanding that: simplistic categorizations are not useful (given the idiosyncratic pathways to the development of individual psychopathologies), linear models are inadequate, and typologies that overlook various interacting variables are confusing (Shanafelt & Pino, 2014).

As Sarteschi (2016, p. 7) states, when one consumes information about serial murderers in today's world, most available options would be classified as "infotainment … with misinformation about crime." While some offerings are blatantly obscene (Corbett, 2021), it can be difficult to discern the legitimacy of other efforts. The media often capitalizes on victims by positioning their experiences as an opportunity for the vicarious thrill of seeing offenders getting what they deserve (Pedota & Maag, 2021). But these "revenge fantasies" (D'Addario, 2021) provide only temporary comfort and serve to placate those who desire to feel safe and secure in the spurious knowledge that criminals always meet their demise. Televised biographies highlight the most obscure and gruesome details to titillate audiences while focusing on offenders from the "Golden Age" because today's serial murderers are viewed as boring and mundane given that they are more practical

DOI: 10.4324/9781003130567-5

and easier to locate and capture. The serial murder entertainment complex is pervasive and commands a global audience, which introduces the question, "How can our reliance on serial murderers as a source of excitement and jubilation be healthy for us?" No one can claim to know what the impact of long-term exposure to serial murder will be or how it has shaped the minds of those who consume it.

Perhaps societal interest in serial murder will diminish once the media exhausts the wide pantheon of offenders from the "Golden Age." Until then, the present work serves to reframe serial homicide from being viewed as mere bombastic events into what Shanafelt and Pino (2013, p. 253) call a "normal aberration" of violence, which can occur as either targeted, planned attacks or as a momentary response to situational factors. Studies that focus on offenders from the "Golden Age" found that they were extremely deviant (Warren, Dietz, & Hazelwood, 2013) and conformed to the classical characteristics attributed to serial murderers (Kraemer, Lord, & Heilbrun, 2004). But as modern offenders are discovered, fewer incidents of unusual crime scene behaviors have been reported (Morton, Tillman, & Gaines, 2014). This can partly be explained by the apparent normality of African American serial murderers (Lester & White, 2014) as they continue to become more prominent. There are fewer instances today of serial murderers who exhibit the traditional hallmarks such as stalking, paraphilias, communication with the police or the press, ritualistic behavior, sadistic overtones, souvenir and trophy collection, and killing purely for sexual gratification.

Some may argue that this review's findings are a byproduct of attempts to expansively redefine serial murder as a means of creating an artificial paradigm shift. There is urgency in reaching consensus as defense attorneys have begun to capitalize on the state of confusion surrounding serial murder and contest the guilt of offenders based on how they are classified (Etheridge, 2014). We are at a tipping point given that, as of a few years ago, the perception of serial murder seemingly reverted to its 1970's characterization:

> A serial killer is ... not a person. [Serial murder] doesn't have any motive. It doesn't have emotion attached to it. It doesn't fit in the context or anger or revenge or the things that we think people commit homicides for (Jones, 2014)... It seems to become almost an involuntary response ... these are people who kill according to a repetitive pattern, with a similar motivation (McKnight, 2014).

Given these viewpoints, perhaps a shift in thinking is needed. The evidence is beginning to bear out that the old ways that serial murderer's behaved are simply too difficult for modern criminals to replicate under today's stringent environmental conditions. Of course, there is also an inherent contradiction to be navigated when calling attention to the profiteering of the phenomenon while crafting a review about modern-day serial murderers. But any critique of these efforts should be reserved merely for instances where dated information is regurgitated in place of opportunities for new knowledge. *Killer Data* met its expressed goal of acutely summarizing not only how we arrived at where we are in the field today but also where we should be headed. This dual focus on the preceding works of scholars and the inspection of forward-thinking projects hopefully presented a unique and timely perspective.

Recent efforts to expand the definition to include more than serial sexual murderers has brought into view a clearer, yet incomplete, picture of who these men and women are. Today's offenses are seemingly more straightforward and far less atypical than the crimes historically typed as serial murders. Although this review should be referenced with the understanding that trends change over time, there is enough evidence to suggest that society must rethink how we view the modern-day serial murderer in the face of overstated warnings of a surge to occur within the next 15 years (Dangerfield, 2018), the theorized rise in serial murder by 2028 (Oakley, 2019),[1] and astronomical predictions of the range of active serial murderers, which numbers between 2,100 and 4,000 (Chun, 2019). Almost 40 years ago, Holmes and DeBurger (1985) sounded a similar alarm, one that ominously foretold of a rise in the incidence of serial murder after declining murder clearance rates were equated with a supposed increase in related unresolved homicides. But faulty data have hampered both past and future estimates (Gelman & Maltz, 2017; Kiger, 1990) as evidenced by those early predictions that have yet to materialize given the year-over-year decline in serial murder (Yaksic, Allely, De Silva, Smith-Inglis, Konikoff, Ryan, Gordon, Denisov, & Keatley, 2019). We should not need to inflate prevalence estimates or sensationalize these offenders in order to prompt ourselves to reevaluate the current state-of-the-art of serial murder investigation and research.

But issues continue to permeate serial murder research. Although other research has found little difference between foreign and US-based serial murderers (Yaksic, 2022), this review was limited to analyzing the actions of American serial murderers because of a lack of reliable background information on their foreign counterparts and unclear differences in cultures and policing standards. Given the frequent and erroneous supposition surrounding announcements that serial murderers are an ever-present threat to communities (Davis & Hermann, 2017; Dumcius, 2017; Fenton, 2020; Gleiter, 2014; Key, 2018; Kryt, 2017; Robinson, 2018; Sasko, 2018; Sweeney, Williams-Harris, & Nickeas, 2018; Thomas, 2017; Wallace, 2021; Watson, 2021; Whiffen, 2017), it is critically important that researchers and investigators manage their expectations as they search for these offenders using intuition (Saunt, 2021), algorithms (Kolker, 2017), databases (QlikTech, 2011), supercomputers (Bellows, 2019), offender profiling (Yaksic, 2020), geospatial analysis (Comerford, 2021), machine learning (Mariani, 2020), and genetic genealogy (Moon, 2019). Schug (2021) calls for the "next wave" of serial murder research, one that would utilize three assessment techniques (the Structured Clinical Interview for *DSM-IV* (*Diagnostic and Statistical Manual of Mental Disorders*) Axis II Personality Disorders, the Rorschach task, and a comprehensive battery of neuropsychological measures), but until scholars can agree on what constitutes a serial murder series, who the offenders are, and what behaviors they evince, it will be impossible to move beyond semantic discussions and collect that type of data on a wide enough scale for it to have empirical and clinical value.

What is apparent from available data is that serial murderers violate social norms by embracing a self-centered lifestyle punctuated by manipulation, shallow emotion, impulsivity, and pathological lying. These are not good men and women even outside their killing selves. As Hall and Wilson (2014) stipulate, serial murderers do not want to have their drives and desires fully and permanently gratified as they would rather retain the chance of acting out their fantasies as many times as possible in the future. To ensure that the decrease in serial murder holds, it is recommended that we: 1) lessen our addiction to serial murder as a source of entertainment as attempts to produce engrossing products often result in gross mischaracterizations that both empower and cloak these offenders and their followers, 2) move beyond superficial attempts to "get inside the minds" of notorious serial murderers as these efforts only serve to confuse, and 3) identify a new generation of scholars who will continue to make discoveries about this phenomenon. Without a more concerted effort to acknowledge that serial murderers are a combination of "processes that idiosyncratically incorporate emotions, feelings, memories, intentions, fantasies, cultural schema, and plans into a multifaceted whole", multiple interacting variables that are "often too complex for us to completely understand" (Shanafelt & Pino, 2013, pp. 267, 270), we will continue to view them as one-dimensional beings, never truly knowing them, and risk overlooking their activities before further loss of life can be curtailed.

Note

1 This author cites child abuse from the 1990s to 2000s, attitudes toward women, cheap travel and open borders, a toxic legacy of the Iraq War, the lure of social media fame, disconnected living, missing persons, and a rise in violent pornography to explain the supposed coming rise.

References

Bellows, K. (2019). Harrisburg University's supercomputer gives students, school a unique learning experience. Penn Live. Retrieved from: www.pennlive.com/news/2019/06/harrisburg-universitys-supercomputer-not-only-serves-the-students-but-also-the-community.html

Chun, R. (2019). Modern life has made it easier for serial killers to thrive. The Atlantic. Retrieved from www.theatlantic.com/magazine/archive/2019/10/are-serial-killers-more-common-than-we-think/596647/

Comerford, C. (2021). A scoping review of serial homicide geographic mobility literature and four typologies. *Homicide Studies*. In press.

Corbett, K. (2021). You can now watch every episode of "Murder House Flip" for free on Roku. House Beautiful. Retrieved from www.yahoo.com/news/show-called-murder-house-flip-183600380.html

D'Addario, D. (2021). "I'll Be Gone in the Dark" special adds fury, not insight, about Golden State killer: TV review. Variety. Retrieved from https://variety.com/2021/tv/reviews/i-ll-be-gone-in-the-dark-special-1234997008/

Dangerfield, K. (2018). Expect a surge in serial killers in 15 years, Canadian author says. Global News. Retrieved from https://globalnews.ca/news/4388493/surge-serial-killers-15-years/

Davis, A., & Hermann, P. (2017). No, there is no spike in missing girls in D.C.; how tweets created a crisis. The Washington Post. Retrieved from www.washingtonpost.com/local/dc-politics/tweets-stats-and-confusion-the-case-of-dcs-missing-girls/2017/04/02/c35dde3c-161f-11e7-ada0-1489b735b3a3_story.html?utm_term=.23b25ac6b7b6

Dumcius, G. (2017). "There's no one out there killing these kids" found in the water, Boston's top cop says. Mass Live. Retrieved from www.masslive.com/news/index.ssf/2017/05/theres_no_one_out_there_killin.html

Etheridge, J. (2014). De Jager serial killer tag disputed. IOL. Retrieved from www.iol.co.za/news/de-jager-serial-killer-tag-disputed-1692451

Fenton, J. (2020). Rumors of a Baltimore serial killer swirl on social media, but police dismiss them. Here's what we know about the cases. The Baltimore Sun. Retrieved from www.baltimoresun.com/news/crime/bs-pr-md-ci-cr-social-media-rumors-serial-killer-20201211-j4iucvxenrb5ljsqltj4jcw4qm-story.html

Gelman, A., & Maltz, M. (2017). Can you use this data set to find serial killers? Slate. Retrieved from https://slate.com/technology/2017/12/the-data-behind-the-serial-killer-detector-has-some-small-issues.html

Gleiter, D. (2014). Investigator notes similarities between Kortne Stouffer, other missing women; DA doubts there's link. The Patriot-News. Retrieved from www.pennlive.com/midstate/index.ssf/2014/01/florida_investigator_links_kor.html

Hall, S., & Wilson, D. (2014). New foundations: Pseudo-pacification and special liberty as potential cornerstones for a multi-level theory of homicide and serial murder. *European Journal of Criminology*. 11(5):635–655.

Holmes, R., & DeBurger, J. (1985). Profiles in terror: The serial murderer. *Federal Probation*. 44(3):29–34.

Jones, L. (2014). Aaron Hernandez's behavior more "gangster" than serial killer. USA Today Sports. Retrieved from www.usatoday.com/story/sports/nfl/2014/05/15/aaron-hernandez-murders-serial-killer-model/9123941/

Key, J. (2018). Police: Mill Creek deaths not the work of a serial killer. Cincinnati.com. Retrieved from www.cincinnati.com/story/news/2018/07/20/police-bodies-mill-creek-not-victims-serial-killer/803415002/

Kiger, K. (1990). The darker figure of crime: The serial murder enigma. In S. Egger (Ed.), Serial Murder: An Elusive Phenomenon (pp. 35–52). Praeger.

Kolker, R. (2017). Serial killers should fear this algorithm. Bloomberg Businessweek. Retrieved from: www.bloomberg.com/news/features/2017-02-08/serial-killers-should-fear-this-algorithm

Kraemer, G., Lord, W., & Heilbrun, K. (2004). Comparing single and serial homicide offenses. *Behavioral Sciences & the Law*. 22(3):325–343.

Kryt, J. (2017). Murderous vacations: Serial killers stalking the Panama Highlands. Daily Beast. Retrieved from www.thedailybeast.com/murderous-vacations-serial-killers-stalking-the-panama-highlands

Lester, D., & White, J. (2014). A study of African American serial killers. *Journal of Ethnicity in Criminal Justice*. 12(4):308–316.

Mariani, S. M. (2020). Profiling serial killers using multiple supervised machine learning approaches. Unpublished thesis.

McKnight, Z. (2014). Bosma case: Why three murder cases don't necessarily mean a serial killer. The Hamilton Spectator. Retrieved from www.thespec.com/news/2014/04/11/bosma-case-why-three-murder-cases-don-t-necessarily-mean-a-serial-killer.html

Moon, J. (2019). Three Bear Brook murder victims identified; citizen sleuth, genetic genealogy provide key clues. NHPR.org. Retrieved from www.nhpr.org/post/three-bear-brook-murder-victims-identified-citizen-sleuth-genetic-genealogy-provide-key-clues#stream/0

Morton, R., Tillman, J., & Gaines, S. (2014). Serial Murder: Pathways for Investigations. Federal Bureau of Investigation, US Department of Justice.

Oakley, B. (2019). 1978:Year of the Serial Killer. Twelvetrees.

Pedota, C., & Maag, C. (2021). To catfish a killer: How a serial murderer was outsmarted and stopped. USA Today. Retrieved from www.usatoday.com/videos/news/2021/03/03/catfish-serial-killer-how-khalil-wheeler-weaver-stopped/4494482001/

QlikTech. (2011). QlikView used to track down alleged serial killer in Sweden. Qlik.com. Retrieved from www.businesswire.com/news/home/20110215006668/en/QlikView-Used-To-Track-Down-Alleged-Serial-Killer-in-Sweden

Robinson, S. (2018). A serial killer stalking Tacoma's homeless? Authorities say they're not aware of it. The News Tribune. Retrieved from www.thenewstribune.com/news/local/crime/article216632145.html

Sarteschi, C. (2016). Mass and serial murder in America. Springer.

Sasko, C. (2018). Philly police: No, there's no serial killer on the loose. Philadelphia.com. Retrieved from www.phillymag.com/news/2018/07/20/serial-killer-philadelphia/

Saunt, R. (2021). Senior coroner is suspended over her suggestion a serial killer murdered at least five elderly couples – after deaths were recorded as murder-suicides. DailyMail.com. Retrieved from www.dailymail.co.uk/news/article-9656759/Senior-coroner-suspended-suggestion-serial-killer-murdered-elderly-couples.html

Schug, R. (2021). Personality disorder traits, Rorschach performance, and neuropsychological functioning in the case of a serial killer: The importance of a multilevel approach in the assessment of personalities associated with extreme and repetitive violence. *Journal of Personality Assessment*. 1–13.

Shanafelt, R., & Pino, N. (2013). Evil and the common life: Towards a wider perspective on serial killing and atrocities. In R. Atkinson and S. Winlow (Eds.), New Directions in Crime and Deviancy (pp. 252–273). Routledge.

Shanafelt, R., & Pino, N. (2014). Rethinking Serial Murder, Spree Killing, and Atrocities: Beyond the Usual Distinctions. Routledge.

Sweeney, A., Williams-Harris, D., & Nickeas, P. (2018). While investigating 2 deaths, police try to quell rumors on social media that have roiled West side. Chicago Tribune. Retrieved from www.chicagotribune.com/news/local/breaking/ct-met-women-found-dead-20180614-story.html

Thomas, R. (2017). Walker PD debunks rumors of serial killer after woman found dead under bridge. WAFB 9. Retrieved from www.wafb.com/story/34381094/walker-pd-debunks-rumors-of-serial-killer-after-woman-found-dead-under-bridge/

Wallace, D. (2021). Portland police debunk social media post falsely claiming serial killer at large, 19 female bodies found. Fox News. Retrieved from www.foxnews.com/us/portland-police-debunk-social-media-post-serial-killer-19-female-bodies-found

Warren, J., Dietz, P., & Hazelwood, R. (2013). The collectors: Serial sexual offenders who preserve evidence of their crimes. *Aggression and Violent Behavior*. 18(6):666–672.

Watson, S. (2021). Mayor, Buffalo police debunk false rumor of serial killer. The Buffalo News. Retrieved from https://buffalonews.com/news/local/mayor-buffalo-police-debunk-false-rumor-of-serial-killer/article_ee0a3c6c-7abf-11eb-aac0-1361390852fa.html

Whiffen, G. (2017). No indication St. Anthony missing-person cases linked: Expert. The Telegram. Retrieved from www.saltwire.com/newfoundland-labrador/news/no-indication-st-anthony-missing-person-cases-linked-expert-27581/

Yaksic, E. (2019). Serial murder. In E. McLaughlin & J. Muncie (Eds.), The SAGE Dictionary of Criminology (4th ed., pp. 476–479). SAGE.

Yaksic, E., Allely, C., De Silva, R., Smith-Inglis, M., Konikoff, D., Ryan, K., Gordon, D., Denisov, E. & Keatley, D. (2019). Detecting a decline in serial homicide: Have we banished the devil from the details? *Cogent Social Sciences*. 5(1):1–23.

Yaksic, E. (2020). Evaluating the use of data-based offender profiling by researchers, practitioners and investigative journalists to address unresolved serial homicides. *Journal of Criminal Psychology*. 10(2):123–144.

Yaksic, E. (2022). Serial Murder. Encyclopedia of Forensic Sciences. Forthcoming.

INDEX

Note: Page numbers in *italic* denote figures, page numbers in **bold** denote tables.

CPSIA information can be obtained
at www.ICGtesting.com
Printed in the USA
LVHW021601131122
733014LV00006B/202

9 780367 672706